URBAN ENVIRONMENT AND SPATIAL SCIENCE

URBAN ENVIRONMENT AND SPATIAL SCIENCE

Edited by

Dr Mohd Akhter Ali

Assistant professor, Department of Geography,
Osmania University, Hyderabad, India.

Dr. Kabir Mohan Sethy

Professor, Post Graduate Department of Geography
Utkal University, Bhubaneswar, Odisha, India

Dr Muzafar Wani

Assistant professor, Department of Geography,
Government Degree College Pulwama, Kashmir, India

M.Kamraju

Student, Osmania
University, Hyderabad, India

Ane Books Pvt. Ltd.

New Delhi ♦ Chennai

Urban Environment and Spatial Science

Editors: Dr. Mohd Akhter Ali,Prof.Kabir Mohan Sethy,
Dr.Muzzafar Ahmad Wani and Mr.M.Kamraju

First Edition 2021

Price: ₹ 1495.00

Pages: xxxiv + 232 (Hb)

Size : (6.25" × 9.5")

Paper Quality (GSM) : 80

Published by

Ane Books Pvt. Ltd.

4821, Parwana Bhawan, 1st Floor, 24 Ansari Road, Darya Ganj,
New Delhi - 110 002, Tel.: +91(011) 23276843-44, Fax: +91(011) 23276863
e-mail: kapoor@anebooks.com, Website: www.anebooks.com

Branch Office

- Avantika Niwas, 1st Floor, 19
Doraiswamy Road, T. Nagar,
Chennai - 600 017,
Tel.: +91(044) 28141554, 28141209
e-mail: anebookschennai@gmail.com, rathinam@anebooks.com

ISBN : 978-93-90658-28-2

Printed at : Replika Press Pvt. Ltd.

DEDICATION

To Our Beloved

Professor Shah Manzoor Alam

Former. Vice- Chancellor, Kashmir University (1984-1987)

Consultant to the World Bank, Washington

Chairman, Indian School of Excellence

Founder Chairman of MEDNET

Founder Member of Indian National Cartographic Association

Professor Emeritus of the University Grants Commission

Visiting Professor in Universities of Australia and New Zealand.

Founder & Ex Director, Centre of Area Studies, Osmania University

Dean Faculty of Social Sciences, Osmania University

Former Head, Department of Geography, Osmania University

PREFACE

Urbanisation has been a global phenomenon. It is not confined to metropolis only. Cities are continuously expanding. The process of urbanisation, though associated with increase in employment opportunities, better living standard, increased level of income, increased production, investment and consumption and availability of social and economic infrastructure, has led to deterioration in the quality of these infrastructures and lowering of the quality of life in many metropolitan cities as well as in the medium and small towns of India.

It is a well known fact that the growth and development of a town is unsustainable without a proper social and economic base. Moreover, if the benefits of the growth and development do not percolate to the common people, the widening gap between the rich and the poor and between the developed and the undeveloped area has a dangerous potentiality of serious social conflicts and tensions.

The study of urbanisation, therefore, is assuming increasing importance all over the world and especially in the developing countries where the urban population is growing rapidly. In India also, urbanisation has tremendously increased during last two decades. Obviously, it has become a matter of attention for civil administrators, demographers and social scientists. An understanding of the causes and consequences of urbanisation and its relationship with economic growth and social change is essential for economic planning and policy making.

Spatial Science has grown multifold globally and Indian contribution to its growth over the years has been very significant. In addition, GIS/GPS allow to integrate the spatial and non spatial data to oversee planning, management and decision making process.

We hope the discussion emerge out of the above papers will further strength and offer newer initiatives in undertaking research and application in Urban and Spatial Science.

We express our sincere thanks to all the authors who have submitted their valuable contribution of papers, share their knowledge, experience and perception. Finally, we thank our Publishers Ane Books Pvt. Ltd., Delhi for publishing this edited book.

9/04/2021 New Delhi

Dr. Mohd Akhter Ali
Prof Kabir Mohan Sethy
Dr. Muzzafar Ahmad wani
Mr. M.Kamraju

Foreword

Dr Prithvish Nag
Former Vice Chancellor
-MGKVP, Varanasi & UPRTOU, Allahabad
-SSVV, Varanasi & DDU Gorakhpur University
Former Surveyor General of India
Former Director, NATMO.

254E, NSC Bose Road
Kolkata 7000047

6th March 2021

I am delighted to write the Foreword of the book entitled '*Urban Environment and Spatial Science*' which attempts to understand the processes of urbanization in the context of development. Both have intrinsic association, sometimes complementary to each other and *vice-versa*. The degree of urbanization is a considered as a good indicator of development in any region. However, the process of urbanization is an outcome of demographic expansion resulting out of natural increase as well as rural-urban migration due to the increasing pressure of population on land in rural areas. Moreover, development is a multi-dimensional dynamic process that encompasses within its realm the demographic changes, qualitative and quantitative, reflected in a society as well as in economy. The process of urbanization is associated with increase in employment opportunities, better living standard, increased level of income and production, investment and consumption, availability of social and economic infrastructure and the like. In several instances, it has led to the deterioration in the quality of these infrastructures and thereby lowering of the quality of life in many metropolitan cities as well as in the medium and small towns of India.

The volume of this nature is very important as India is becoming more and more urbanized. During the last census, some small states and union territories have recorded more than fifty per cent population as urban. In the forthcoming census (2021), several other states will cross this line. Urban India will have its spatial implications in terms of sustainability, environment and management. Some of these issues have been dealt here. They may not be exhaustive but they do indicate the writings on the wall.

This book highlights various features of urban populations - their growth, density and emerging patterns within urban areas. It also focuses on issues related to land use, urban stress, microclimatic conditions, as well as environmental and social problems. Further, this volume deals with the sustainable city, management policies, urban ecological footprints and some case studies of specific balanced development strategies.

I would like to extent good wishes to the editors of the book, Dr. Mohd Akhter Ali, Prof Kabir Mohan Sethy, Dr. Muzafar Ahmad Wani and Mr. M. Kamraju. This book should be very helpful to under graduate and post graduate students, researchers and civil service aspirants.

Dr Prithvish Nag

ACKNOWLEDGEMENTS

Our book ***'Urban Environment and Spatial Science'*** is all set for publication. We would take this occasion to express gratitude all those distinguished academicians and bureaucrats who took time of their hectic schedule and guided, boosted and enlightened us with their precious opinions and suggestions. Below is the list of academicians and bureaucrats we would like to acknowledge and thank.

1. Hon'ble Sri Justice G.Chandraiah, Chairperson
   Telangana State Human Rights commission
2. Honble Justice Dr. G. Yethirajulu (Rtd)
   Judge, AP High Court
3. Dr. Y.V.N.Krishna Murthy
   Sr. Professor and Registrar, IIST, Thiruvanathapuram
4. Honble Justice T. Rajani (Rtd)
   Judge, AP High Court
5. Dr. Swarna Subba Rao (Rtd)
   Former, Surveyor General of India, SOI
6. Major General Ramesh Chandra Padhi (Rtd)
   Former, Addl. Surveyor General of India, SOI
7. Dr. Nagaraja Ravoori (Rtd)
   Dy. Director, NRSC/ISRO
8. Dr. Shahab fazal
   Professor, Dept.Geography,Alighar Muslim University
9. Dr. Atiquir Rahman
   Professor, Dept.Geography,Jamia Millia Islamia
10. Dr. Shamim Ahmad Shah
    Professor, Dept.Geography, University of Kashmir
11. Prof. K Purushotam Reddy (Rtd)
    Environmentalist

12. C.L.N. Gandhi (Rtd)
    Addl.Transport Commissioner, AP
13. E.N Sirajuddin M Horaginamani
    Environmentalist, Bijapur
14. ER. Mohd Abdul Kabeer
    Dy. General Manager, HMWS&SB
15. Dr. Syeda Azeem Unnisa
    Asst. Prof., Department of Environment science, OU
16. Dr. Saleha Jamal
    Assot. Prof, Department of Geography, AMU
17. Prof. B.Laxmaiah (Rtd)
    Senior ICSSR Fellow
18. Prof. A.V Shashikala
    Senior ICSSR Fellow

CONTRIBUTORS

1. **Shaik Riyaz Basha** is a Ph.D Research (JRF-DST INSPIRE) Fellow, Department of Geography, Osmania University, Hyderabad. He Completed his Bachelors in Computer Science at Chilakaluripet, A.P. and masters in Geography, Department of Geography, Sri Venkateswara university, Tirupathi, Andhra Pradesh.

2. **Dr. B Laxmaiah** is a Senior ICSSR Fellow and Retired Professor, Department of Geography Osmania University. He obtained his Bachelor, Masters and Ph.D degrees from Osmania University. He has 31 years of experience in Teaching. He also served as a Principal in University College of sciences, Saifabad, OU.

3. **Kangagiri SN Prasad**, born in Nalagonda, Telangana State is a Research Scholar and an academician. He has worked with Centre for Economic and Social Studies (CESS) and International Crops Research Institute For The Semi-Arid Tropics (ICRISAT) for a period of 22 years. As an educationist, he is the co-founder of Ananda Jyothi Group of Educational Institutes. His keen desire to impart metamorphic ideals has moulded lives of thousands of students in India and abroad spanning three decades.

4. **Dr Muzafar Wani**, is presently working as Assistant professor at the Department of Geography, Government Degree College Pulwama, Kashmir. He has received his Masters in geography in 2009 and Ph.D. Degree in geography from university of Kashmir, India in 2017 . He is actively engaged with teaching and research activities . In the 2013 he has qualified UGC NET. He has also done advanced three months training course in GIS and RS from NRSC(ISRO) Hyderabad, India. His research interests are GIS &RS, urban geography, solid waste management, health and tourism Geography. He has published about twenty research papers in reputed international journals. He is also author of two books.

5. **Prof. Dr. Shamim Ahmad Shah**, is head, department of geography and disaster management university of Kashmir. He is also dean, school of earth and environmental sciences university of Kashmir India. He is actively engaged in research and teaching

related activities. He has published about 45 research papers in reputed international journals. He has successfully completed is a UGC major research project entitled sustainable environmental planning for trans Himalayas: An insight study on solid waste management on Leh, Ladakh. His interests are tourism geography, agriculture geography and environmental planning.

6. **Insha Mohideen** has done her masters in Geography from university of Kashmir and is currently pursuing B. ed from the same.

7. **Dr. Tanweer Ahmad Malik** is a lecturer at the Department of Geography, Government Degree College Pulwama, Kashmir. He has received his M.sc degree from Kashmir university India in 2007 and his ph.D Degree from Barkatullah Vishwavidyalaya Bhopal India 2014 . His research interests are urban environmental issues, health and environment and social Geography. He has also published 8 research papers in reputed international journals.

8. **Mrs Binita Tripathy** is a Post Graduate in Geography from Department of Geography, Utkal University in 1985 and completed her M.phil degree from the same Department in I986.She has carried out her Post Graduate Diploma in Remote Sensing for Urban Studies from Indian Institute of Remote Sensing, Department of Space in 1991. She has been working as a Scientist at Odisha Space Applications Centre (ORSAC) , Department of Science & Technology, Govt of Odisha for the last 32 years .Mrs Tripathy has undergone several professional courses in Digital Image Processing, GIS, Urban Planning, Disaster Management High Resolution Satellite Image Processing,etc from National Institutes like Department of Space, Delhi School of Planning ,Indian Institute of Technology, Kharagpur & Mumbai, etc.

9. **Dr. Kabir Mohan Sethy** is presently holding the post of Professor at Post Graduate Department of Geography of Utkal University, Bhubaneswa, Odisha. After completion of his Post Graduation and M.Phil in Geography from Utkal University ,Dr Sethy has achieved his Ph.D degree for the topic "Settlement Pattern and Service Center Analysis for Rural Development - Planning of

Compound Delta of Orissa Coastal Plain" .His areas of specialisation are Regional Planning, Economic Geography, Remote Sensing & GIS, Climate Change & Natural Hazards. So far 65 M.Phil students and 30 P.G Diploma students in Utkal University have completed their dissertations under the guidance of Professor Sethy.

10. **Dr. P. Mishra** is presently holding the post of Scientist at Odisha Space Applications Centre (ORSAC), Bhubaneswar, Odisha. After completion of his Post Graduation in Applied Geography from Ravenshaw College, Dr Mishra has achieved his Ph.D degree for the topic "Geoinformatics for Planning Sustainable Watershed Development in Orissa" from Utkal University .He has completed his Post Graduate Diploma in Remote Sensing from Indian Institute of Remote Sensing, Department of Space. His areas of specialisation are Remote Sensing based Natural Resources Management, Web GIS, GPS based vehicle tracking, Mobile Applications, etc.

11. **Dr. Syeda Azeem Unnisa** is currently working as Assistant Professor, Department of Environmental Science, Osmania University, Hyderabad, Telangana State, India. She is Ph.D., M.Sc., in Environmental Science and Technology from Jawaharlal Nehru Technological University Hyderabad. She is having 18 years of experience in teaching and research at Post Graduate level in the specialized area of water, wastewater, solid waste management and biodiversity. She has published 82 research papers in international and national journals

12. **Mr. Vattikoti Praveen** is pursuing his Ph.D in Environmental Science from Osmania University. He is working on Mushroom cultivation with various waste produced from agriculture sector. He has published research articles in national journal and attended conferences, seminars and training in environment and agriculture.

13. **Mr.Akhtar Rasool** is currently Ph.D. Student. His research areas are Nanomaterials and biological applications. During his Ph.D. work, he did an Internship (Asia Fellow) at Kaohsiung Medical University, Taiwan. He has published many peer-reviewed papers in reputed Journals, 3 Books. He is focusing on scientific development and scientific innovations with recent research practices

14. **Ms. Panda** is a Research Scholar continuing her research on studying coastal erosion issues using Geoinformatics in Odisha at Dept. of Civil Engineering, FET (ITER), Siksha O Anusandhan Deemed to be University, Bhubaneswar. She is also working as a GIS Expert in Forest Dept., Govt. of Odisha

15. **Prof. Manas Das** is presently engaged as Professor and HOD of Dept. of Civil Engineering, FET (ITER), Siksha O Anusandhan Deemed to be University, Bhubaneswar. He holds an experience of more than 26 years in Teaching and Research and more than 25 research publications including One Edited Book on Global Warming. His research interests include Geotechnical engineering, Structural Engineering, Water Resources and Geoinformatics applications.

16. **Dr. Nihar Ranjan Das** is a Consultant in The World Bank. He is also Secretary of Indian Meterological Society, Bhubaneswar Ch. He leads the research and consultancy team of Foundation for Environmental & Social Research. Also he is involved as a Visiting Professor in Dept. of Civil Engineering, FET (ITER), Siksha O Anusandhan Deemed to be University, Bhubaneswar. He holds around 25 research publications and books to his credit. His research and consultancy interests include Convergence areas of Environment, Natural Resources (Land & Water), Climate and Geospatial Technology Applications.

17. **Dr Mohd Akhter Ali** is currently working as Assistant professor in the Department of Geography, Osmania University, Hyderabad, India. He obtained his Bachelor, Master and Ph.D. degrees from Osmania University. He specializes in Environmental Geography, Urban and Regional Geography, Cartography, Rural Development, GIS and Remote Sensing.

18. **M.Kamraju** is Urban Researcher and student. He has obtained his Bachelor degree from Gauhati University in Geography Honours and Post Graduation from Osmania University. He has worked in two major projects by ICSSR and Telangana Biodiversity department. He has two years of teaching experience to Under Graduate students.

19. **P. Manisha** has completed her Masters in Geography from Osmania University Hyderabad. She had worked as surveyor in ICSSR Major Project in 2017.She did her Masters Project work from Indian Institute of Surveying and Mapping (IISM) Uppal, Hyderabad in Photogrammetry Department. She has 2 years of teaching experience to secondary students. She have attended many National and International Conferences and presented papers.

20. **Miss. Sanja Devi** has completed her Masters in Geography from Osmania University Hyderabad. She have attended 5 National and 2 International Conferences and presented papers there. She has 5 years of teaching experience to Degree and Intermediate students.

21. **Mr Bharath Raj H** has completed his M.Tech from JNTUH. He has executed his M.Tech dissertation in Department of Environmental Science, Osmania University on Formulation of Bioplastic and Extraction of Phytochemcials from Medicinal Plants. He has attended conferences and seminars in the area of Ethno botany.
22. **Mr. Aaron Jasper Molgeri** has completed his M.Sc in Department of Environmental Science, Osmania University. He has worked on heavy metal contamination in fruits and vegetables as his M.Sc dissertation. He has published research articles in national journal and attended conferences and seminars in environmental science.
23. **Mr. Fidel Rahmati** is an Assistant Professor at the Geography Department, Parwan University, Parwan Province-Afghanistan. He is currently Ph.D. Research Scholar at the Geography Department, Osmania University, Hyderabad, Telangana State-India.
23. **Dr. Mohd. Husamuddin**, Office Supridentent, UCE,Osmania University
24. **Dr. Sameer Fayaz** , (M.Sc, Ph.D, UGC-NET Geography), Contractual Lecturer, Department of Geography, GDC for Women Pulwama, Kashmir-192301, Email: bhatsameer3384@gmail.com
25. **Dr. G.M Rather**, Sr. Assistant professor, Department of Geography, University of Kashmir-190006,Email: gmrather@rediffmail.com
26. **Prof. M.Sultan Bhat**, Former Dean and Head, Department of Geography, University of Kashmir-190006, Email: msbhatgeog@yahoo.com
27. **Dr. MD. Sarfaraz Asgher** Department of Geography, University of Jammu, Jammu Persued M.A, Ph.D from Aligarh Muslim University, Aligarh Specialization in Environment Planning and Management,

Watershed, Hydrology and wetlands Teaching Experience 17 years Published 02 books and 39 research papers in National and International journals, Attended about 50 National and International Conferences, Supervised 05 P.hd and reviewer of research manuscript of selected SCI Journals.

28. **Dr. B. Kiran Kumar**, Assistant Professor; Department of Botany, O.U., has obtained his M.Sc., and Ph.D., from Osmania University. He had 13 years of undergraduate and postgraduate teaching experience and 16 years of research experience and his area of specialization of Molecular Genetics and Plant Biotechnology. He worked as DBT-Post Doctoral Fellow at National Research Centre on Plant Biotechnology, Indian Agricultural Research Institute (IARI) New Delhi on Genetic Engineering and Gene Pyramiding in Bt-brinjal.

29. **Ms. Shakuntala Pratihary** has done her M. Phil in Analytical and Applied Economics and currently pursuing her doctoral studies in the Post Graduate Department of Geography- Utkal University, Bhubaneswar, Odisha on the topic "Climate change and its impact on human capabilities: A comparative study of two Panchayats: Gupti of Kendrapara and Bhaliadal of Mayurbhanj districts of Odisha". She is a climate researcher and a writer. Besides her academic work, she writes about the struggle of climate survivors and women issues in the vernacular language and has got four books to her credit.

30. **Sraddha Giri** a research scholar at Post graduate Department of Geography, Utkal University. She has completed her Graduation from Ravenshaw University in the year2016, Post -graduation from Utkal University in the year 2018 and M.Phil 2020 with specialisation Regional Planning at P.G.Level and qualified NET in the year 2020 and completed NRSA course in RS and GIS.

31. **Sthitapragyan Panigrahia** research scholar at Post graduate Department of Geography, Utkal University. She has completed her Graduation From Ravenshaw University in the year 2017 Post -graduation from Utkal University in the year2019 and M.Phil 2021 with specialisation Regional Planning at P.G Level and NRSATraining Course in the field of GIS and Remote Sensing in the year 2020.

About The Editors

Dr Mohd Akhter Ali is currently working as Assistant professor in the Department of Geography, Osmania University, Hyderabad, India. He obtained his Bachelor, Master and Ph.D. degrees from Osmania University. He specializes in Environmental Geography, Urban and Regional Geography, Cartography, Rural Development, GIS and Remote Sensing. He is editor of many reputed journals in India. He has about eighteen years of teaching experience to under graduate and Post graduate students.

Dr. MAA is the life members of many academic organizations like NAGI, INCA, ISC, IGU, DGSI, etc. Dr Mohd Akhter Ali has a credit of getting three books and more than eighty research journals of National and international repute. Presently Six research scholars are perusing research under his supervision.

Dr. Kabir Mohan Sethy is presently holding the post of Professor at Post Graduate Department of Geography of Utkal University, Bhubaneswa, Odisha. After completion of his Post Graduation and M.Phil in Geography from Utkal University ,Dr Sethy has achieved his Ph.D degree for the topic "Settlement Pattern and Service Center Analysis for Rural Development - Planning of Compound Delta of Orissa Coastal Plain" .His areas of specialisation are Regional Planning, Economic Geography, Remote Sensing & GIS, Climate Change & Natural Hazards. So far 65 M.Phil students and 30 P.G Diploma students in Utkal University have completed their dissertations under the guidance of Professor Sethy.

Dr Muzafar Wani is presently working as Assistant professor at the Department of Geography, Government Degree College Pulwama, Kashmir. He has received his Masters in geography in 2009 and Ph.D. Degree in geography from university of Kashmir, India in 2017 . He is actively engaged with teaching and research activities . In the 2013 he has qualified UGC NET. He has also done advanced three months training course in GIS and RS from NRSC(ISRO) Hyderabad, India. His research interests are GIS &RS, urban geography, solid waste management, health and tourism Geography. He has published about twenty research papers in reputed international journals. He is also author of two books.

M.Kamraju is Urban Researcher and student. He has obtained his Bachelor degree from Gauhati University in Geography Honors and Post Graduation from Osmania University. He has worked in two major projects by ICSSR and Telangana Biodiversity department. Mr. M.K Raju has two years of teaching experience to Under Graduate students. He has also guided 120 undergraduate students (B.A Geography) for their final year project work in various fields (Agriculture, Urban, Economic, and GIS&RS.ect.) Besides that has done three months Internship from Indian Institute of Surveying and Mapping (IISM) Hyderabad, India in 2017.He has qualified UGC NET and APSET examination.

He is the life members of many academic organizations like NAGI, INCA, DERO, Agriculture and Food e-Newsletter, etc. Mr. M.Kamraju has also contributed chapters for eight edited books and more than fifty research journals of National and international standards.

View Point of Academician and Bureaucrats

1. **Hon'ble Sri Justice G. Chandraiah**

Born on 10.05.1954 in a farmer family in Timmapur Village, Jannaram Mandal of Manchirial District of Telangana State. Pursued LLB and LLM (Torts and Crimes) from Osmania University College of Law by boarding in the University's Hostel (E Room Nos. 45 and 20 respectively). Studied MA (Politics) from Osmania University. On 06.11.1980 enrolled as an Advocate on the rolls of Bar Counsel of Andhra Pradesh. Joined in the chamber of late Sri I.Venkatanarayana (who later became Judge of High Court and President of State Consumer Dispute Redressal Tribunal, thereafter practiced in Supreme Court of India) and Sri Syed Shah Mohammed Quadri (who retired as Hon'ble Judge of Supreme Court of India) respectively. Functioned as Administrative Judge of several districts.Functioned as Chairmen of Several Administrative Committees in the High Court. Functioned as 1st Chairperson of Telangana State Legal Services Authority.

Urbanization is a complex spatial process that converts rural land uses to urban uses, and causes various impacts on ecosystem structures, function, dynamics, and the livelihoods of human beings. It is expected that by 2030, there will be 2 billion new urban residents. Urbanization brings challenge; especially in the developing countries in terms of improving the urban environment and the living condition. Urbanization leads to the emergence of commercial and industrial activities within the area but the historic city areas, having failed to keep pace with the requirements of the modern economy, start to deteriorate.

Urbanisation is described as one of the most destructive forces affecting stream health and watersheds. Urbanizing these watersheds, replacing the vegetation with impervious services, reduces the infiltration area where groundwater can occur. Thus, resulting in a greater amount of water arriving at a stream more quickly, rising the frequency of more severe flooding. This runoff creates another problem, water pollution. As storm water flows over surfaces, it picks up potential pollutants that include pesticides, fertilizers, bacteria (from human and animal waste), metals, petroleum (leaking vehicles), and sediments. This water can be detrimental to animals, plants, and humans.

There is a strong correlation link between increasing urbanisation and declining biodiversity. The increasing population is a catalyst for the expansion of urban areas, which in turn increases the demand for natural resources, for example fossil fuels and timber. This inevitably results in the destruction of habitats. In the United Kingdom there is an increasing human population density, and it was found that within the surrounding urbanized areas, 35% of scarce plant species had become extinct as a direct result in the increase of urban development.

Urbanisation encourages innovation, green schemes (recycling bins), and new green technology which will be the long term future for environmentally friendly cities. Lastly, urbanized living has a higher standard of living, it provides people with better education, food, housing, and health care. Continued urban growth will generate revenue that can be invested in infrastructure projects aimed at reducing traffic congestion and improving public health.

Contrary to popular belief, urbanisation can be a source for positive impacts on the environment, although it relies on urbanisation being managed properly. Higher productivity is a factor of urbanisation, due to its positive externalities and economies of scale.Therefore, the same output can be produced using fewer resources because of urban clustering. Other sectors also benefit environmentally, such as the service sector, a more urban environment is key due to its concentration of clients in a relatively small geographical area, and services are less pollutant than manufacturing; resulting in a positive effect on the environment. Thus, urbanisation can reduce the urban footprint.

2. **Hon'ble Justice Dr. G. Yethirajulu**

Honble Dr. Justice Gurugubelli Yethirajulu was born on 1.7.1947 at Fareedpeta Village, Etcherla Mandal, Srikakulam District of Andhra Pradesh, India. He had High School education at Kinthali Village. Obtained B.Sc degree from Government Arts College Srikakulam. A Gold Medalist and a first class Law Graduate from Andhra University Law College, Visakhapatnam, M.A. in Public Administration from Andhra University.Appointed as a District and Sessions Judge by direct recruitment from the Bar and his first appointment was as IInd Addl. District & Sessions Judge, Cuddapah. Elevated to the Bench of A.P.High Court as an Additional Judge on 13.12.2001.

People are migrating to cities for livelihood. They are assured of some work in the cities, where as the availability of work in villages is seasonal and labour are paid lesser wages than in cities. Due to rapid migration of rural population to cities, the housing has become a big problem. Therefore they are raising huts nearby work places which is resulting in converting in to slums resulting in environmental hazards. The Industrial pollution, medical waste, vehicular emissions, human waste and other effluents are polluting the rivers, tanks and other water bodies resulting in causing various diseases. It is also causing air pollution affecting the health of the people. It is essential to create awareness among the people mostly urban population to co-operate in protecting the environment, so that the people can lead life free from environmental hazards. The Governments should also take effective steps to control the pollution by allocating sufficient funds and taking effective steps to save the environment

3. **Hon'ble Smt. Justice T. Rajani**

Practiced Law in Guntur from 1981 till getting selection as District Judge in August, 2002. After 4½ months of training at Judicial Academy, posted as II Additional District Judge in Karimnagar and later worked as I Additional District Judge, Karimnagar; Judge Mahila Court, Hyderabad; Economic Offences Court, Hyderabad; District Judge, Medak and Metropolitan Sessions Judge, Hyderabad. Elevated to High Court on 17.01.2017.

We understand environment as the surroundings or the conditions in which a person or animal or plants live or operate. But we have travelled to a stage where the word environment has subdivisions. Urban environment has now different meaning. It is no longer the environment which exists in other areas. The civic sense of a person is directly proportionate to the quality of the environment. Civic sense means social ethics. The level of personal awareness and the level of responsibility are reflected by the civic sense that a person displays. Uniformity in civic sense is norm of a harmonious society. It also means respect for the fellow beings which comes from the understanding of his own needs. Cultural foundation is also required for a person to have civic sense.

But the society is driven to a state where, the individuals are forced to sustain themselves by adopting selfish methods and means. The basic human norm is survival of the fittest. Only when a person makes himself fit for survival, can he think of improving his society. So long as he has a threat for his easy survival, he continues in his endeavor to live and be fit for living. It is from the times of an individual

Struggle that the society has grown to form institutions and bodies to take care to make the society congenial for the survival of each human being, irrespective of its fitness. So long as those bodies or institutions fulfill the purpose for which they are established, there would not be any need for any single person to strive for his existence and prosperity.

It is the failure of those institutions that has demarcated environment as urban and rural. Most of the cities in our country are now facing the dangerous consequences of the polluted urban environment. Due to rural areas not being able to self sustain, migration to urban areas is on the rise day by day. This resulted in space constraint. Unauthorized occupations are the results. It is of common experience to citizens of cities that even a simple rain floods the cities, blocks the roads and damages the structures. For example Hyderabad. Recent rains have given a frightening experience to the people there. Rain water seeped and flowed into the houses, calling for an honest thought and plan of action to manage and correct the situation. Even the drainages suffer from encroachments. For a person who is inclined to correct the situation, the question would be where to start.

We have poor town and city planning's. Spatial science would be of great help for the concerned institutions which are inclined to change the urban scenario. Geographical information system, for short, GIS, would help in planning smart urban development, to efficiently accommodate more in less. Urbanisation can be taken to new scales by GIS in urban planning. A combination of spatial analysis and GIS would help in exploring unique combination of space and time. Spatial analysis of urbanisation would help in improving the understanding of urbanisation and to achieve urban sustainability. Spatial patterns of ecosystem need to be understood, to take up urban planning that can enhance ecosystem services. It helps to manage urban green spaces, which is an eternal need.

4. Dr. Swarna Subba Rao

Former, Surveyor General, Survey of India

Dr. Swarna Subba Rao is a Surveying and Geo-Spatial professional who has 34 years of experience encompassing all disciplines of geospatial technology in developing geospatial strategies for Survey of India and other related ministries within the Government of India. He has excellent board management skills substantiated with experience in client management, business analysis, project management, strategic consulting studies, design, development and management of surveying and GIS databases, review spatial data framework policies, develop spatial analyses techniques and technology including Survey applications development for major government partners in India. He has led several Multi-Million Dollar National Mapping projects for the Government of India. As Surveyor General of India, Dr Rao has led several delegations to Pakistan, Myanmar, Bhutan, and Nepal for talks on International Boundary between India and neighboring countries successfully.

I am happy to provide my view point on this compilation of Edited Book on 'URBAN ENVIRONMENT AND SPATIAL SCIENCE' which will be covering geospatial technology and it's applications. It is no secret that geospatial technology plays an increasingly critical role in not only how we understand our world, but how we interact with the environment around us. With great GIS technology, however, comes great responsibility. However, modern geospatial technology includes a vast range of tools, software applications and systems used for analyzing spatial information. For example, although historic use of geospatial techniques focused on understanding Earth, NASA uses mapping applications to better understand our solar system and beyond. The evolution and changing dynamics of emerging technologies are playing a vital role in addressing and solving quests across various industries. And geospatial technology systems are one of the prominent pillars of these emerging technologies.

While there are many different factors at play in the changing technology-driven world, interconnectivity has been one of the most dominant trends of the last several years, particularly with the increase in smarter, location-aware technologies for both consumers and businesses. This is increasingly true of geospatial software and other technology, which can now be found in smartphones, warehouses, in sensors, household appliances and countless other areas.Through the miniaturization of sensors, geospatial technology opens a new perspective of data collection. The miniature versions of existing systems from drones to mini satellites integrated with sensors are discovering data from places where the human eye is impossible to reach.

Geospatial technology systems hold the future of how data is visualized or represented as industries become more and more relevant to this technology. As 80% of the data is utilized to optimize, industrial functions are extracted using geospatial technology. The digitalization and automation of industries that are solving quest and driving growth also rely on the same data extracted using geospatial systems. Hence gradually It will be an integral part of every technology opting up-gradation.

5. **Major General Ramesh Chandra Padhi**

Major General Ramesh Chandra Padhi is the former Addl Surveyor General of India and currently working as Professor emeritus with number of universities.

He holds graduate degree in civil engineering from NIT Rourkela, MBA in disaster management from GGSIP University Delhi , post graduate degrees in Survey engineering, Photogrammetry & Remote sensing from IISM Hyderabad and pursued specialized short training programs in Geospatial technology in many top institutions.

He has served in the the Indian army corps of Engineers and have received many military decorations & in Survey of India under Dept of Science & Technology on key appointments during his service with the Government of India of about 36 years. Post retirement from government service, he is currently associated with the technology related industries, universities,DRDO in mentoring, teaching & reserch work.

His areas of professional interests are Geospatial technology and it's applications,Drones, AI, public policy advocacy etc.

He is a fellow of several professional bodies.

Urban greening policies are important for revitalizing communities, reducing financial burdens of healthcare and increasing quality of life. Most policies focus on community benefits, and reducing negative effects of urban development, such as surface runoff and the urban heat island effect. Historically, access to green space has favored wealthier, and more privileged communities, thus recent focus in urban greening has increasingly focused on environmental justice concerns, and community engagement in the greening process. In particular, in cities with economic decline, such as the Rust Belt in the United States, urban greening has broad community revitalization impacts.

The benefits that urban open space provides to citizens can be broken into four basic forms; recreation, ecology, aesthetic value, and positive health impacts. Psychological benefits gained by visitors to urban green spaces increased with their biodiversity, indicating that 'green' alone is not sufficient; the quality of that green is important as well.

Urban areas tend to have higher temperatures than their surrounding undeveloped areas because of Urban Heat Islands, UHIs. Urban heat islands are areas with man-made infrastructure that contribute to the increased temperatures. The average temperature during the day in cities can be 18-27 degrees Fahrenheit higher than in the surrounding rural regions. This is an example of one type of UHI, surface heat islands. Surface heat islands encompass the area from the ground to the top of the tree-line. It is usually higher during the day when direct sunlight reaches urban structures (often with darker materials than natural areas) including the main contributor, pavement. The other type of UHI, atmospheric heat islands, are from above the tree-line to the level in the atmosphere where the urban area no longer has an effect. This type of heat island has increased heat at night due to the release of heat from infrastructure that built up throughout the day.

Green spaces within urban areas can help reduce these increased temperatures through shading and evapotranspiration. Shading comes from the taller plants, such as trees, planted in green spaces that can contribute to lowering the surface heat island effect. The shade provides protection from the sun for vulnerable populations, such as children, during periods of increased temperature, during the summer months or during a heat wave. Tree cover prevents some solar radiation from reaching thc ground with its leaves and branches. This reduces the effect of surface urban heat islands. Open spaces that include any type of vegetation help offset the high temperatures through the natural process of evapotranspiration. Evapotranspiration releases water into the air therefore dissipating heat. There are many elements of an urban open space that can contribute to the mitigation of urban heat islands including the type of open space (park or nature reserve), type of plant species, and the density of vegetation. Green spaces contribute to the reduction of local heat, decreasing the overall effect of UHIs. The larger the distribution of green spaces, the bigger the area of heat reduction. Green spaces that are clustered together will have an additive heat reduction resulting in a greater decrease in temperature in the local area compared to surrounding areas.

6. **Dr. Nagaraja Ravoori**

Dr. Nagaraja received his Ph.D. in Remote Sensing & GIS from Osmania University, Andhra Pradesh. As Dy. Direcor, NRSC/ISRO responsible for executing Satellite based National projects in the area of natural resource inventory, monitoring in the country. He has been responsible for the design and execution of various National projects like National Wasteland Mission, National Land use Mission, Large Scale Digital Database and Web-based Information System. He is the Project Director of Space Based Information Support for Decentralized Planning (SIS-DP) for generation of High Resolution Ortho-Image base and large scale natural resources database of the country for developmental planning, implementation and monitoring.

Since the seventies, many countries experiencing a rapid urbanization rate and becoming developed countries. Urbanization contributes many advantages in terms of economics, but if uncontrolled, would produce negative consequences to the physical, social and natural environment. With the advancement of Geo-information Technology (GIT), which considerably influenced the dynamic nature of urban and regional planning, incorporation of GIT becomes imperative for better and improved decision-making in urban planning and management. It offers a solution to the urban problems and decision-making, which is more reliant to the realtime spatial modeling. The development plans provide the development framework and guidelines which need to be continually updated according to the present situation of development. The integration of Geographical Information System (GIS) has provided a tool which can contribute to much clearer understanding of real planning problems as well as prescriptive planning scenarios to enhance the quality of urban planning and management.

After the Kyoto Protocol took effect, energy reducing environmentally friendly building and urban planning has gradually changed from voluntary to mandatory. The consideration of energy in urban planning is a global trend due to the revision of energy-related laws/regulations and urban planning and development laws/regulations. However, a system incorporating urban planning and energy planning is still dichotomized. The environmentally friendly city planning needs to facilitate the integration of 'urban planning' and 'energy planning' into a unified 'urban/local energy planning' system, elaborate on a systematic process, and support technology for each process.

India's fast growing economy, increasing population and the aspiration of the people in rural (68.8% of total population) and urban areas (31.2% of total population) are placing increasing demands on diversified resources and hence varied developmental challenges. Towards this, the planning strategy needs calibration and customization as per the local needs to form a bottom-up model. This involves developing credible plans at local level that are progressively aggregated at the higher levels. In addition, the bottom-up approach assists in priority action for enhanced programme implementation, measures for the inclusion of disadvantaged groups into the development process, measurable delivery in desired time frame and finally the good governance.

High resolution satellite images provide valuable information about the land-use/ land-cover (present and past), existing infrastructure, terrain characteristics etc. Space-based information & geospatial analysis tools also support many applications e.g., Urban and regional planning, Route alignment for road, rail, oil/ gas pipeline, Site suitability analysis for hydroelectric project, new township, Facility & Utility planning for identification of landfill sites, schools, hospitals, etc. and also for Environmental impact assessment.

This edited book on Urban Environment and Spatial Science covers many topics on GIS at strategic planning and management . Example of the use of GIS for variety of topics such as urban sprawl, city pollution, geopolitical issues, climate change, green space are discussed in this book. This book will also highlight on how GIS is applied for urban management purposes with focus on development control. GIS notably provide a strong platform to decision maker in its role as the main component in Planning Support System (PSS) and Decision Support System (DSS). This book will help graduate, post graduate students and research scholars who are pursuing research in spatial planning, Decision Support System , impact analysis etc.,.

7. **Dr. Shahab Fazal**

Shahab Fazal is Professor of Geography. He obtained his graduation and post graduation from Rajasthan University. He completed his Ph.D. from Aligarh Muslim University. Prof. Fazal started his teaching career in 1994 as Lecturer at Aligarh Muslim University. His research interests are in Land use, Land transformation issues in urban fringe, Remote Sensing and GIS. He has published fourteen books and more than seventy research articles in various national and international journals.

Urbanization is one of the most evident global land use land cover change. Rapid urbanization have promoted the economic and social transformations, at the same time demographic growth stimulates structural change through multiplier effects including behavioral changes which attracts immigrants. India, a developing country, also experienced rapid increases in urban population and this growth is impacting all spheres of life. Cities have become the centre of all the activities, they are expanding in size, land use is changing quickly, constantly intensifying urban lands and large-scale land transformation is taking place leading to the loss of natural vegetation, open spaces and wetlands due to substantial increases in urban land value and thus these areas have acquired centre stage. Understanding the cause and effect relationship in urban systems and addressing questions regarding changes in the spatio-temporal patterns of urban form are of paramount importance in urban studies and the volume by Dr. Akhter Ali and his colleagues in this context is a valuable contribution. The volume highlights features of Urban Populations, their rates and patterns, movements and contribution of natural change to patterns of population density within urban areas. It also focuses on Land-Use issues, urban stress, where Microclimates, Environmental and social problems are highlighted. It also deals with The Sustainable City, where Sustainable city management strategies, Urban ecological footprint and Case-studies of specific sustainable strategies.

8. **Prof. Shamim Ahmad Shah**

Prof. Dr. Shamim ahmad shah, is head, department of geography and disaster management university of Kashmir. He is also dean, school of earth and environmental sciences university of Kashmir India. He is actively engaged in research and teaching related activities. He has published about 45 research papers in reputed international journals. He has successfully completed is a UGC major research project entitled sustainable environmental planning for trans Himalayas: An insight study on solid waste management on Leh, Ladakh. His interests are tourism geography, agriculture geography and environmental planning.

Remote sensing technique has emerged as an effective tool for systematic survey, analysis, and better management of natural resources (land, soil, water, forests, mountains) along with the monitoring of desertification, flood, drought, and landform change. It provides a vast scope to explore, identify, and analyze the natural resources of undeveloped regions. It documents the dynamic changes in physical processes and resulting landforms, usually by satellite images. This paper provides a general overview of remote sensing. While this technique has been used on beaches, valleys, and other landforms, the main concern of this paper is its role in geography.

Despite advances in geographical studies, the methods of traditional geography have become insufficient to apprehend its reality and complexity, considering technological and scientific changes that have happened in the last 30 years. However, this does not mean that these changes are not useful for geographic research. This has become evident now that Geographical Information Systems (GIS) are developing spatial studies to appeal to such technologies as remote sensing and computer sciences.

As humans, we are intimately familiar with remote sensing in that we rely on visual perception to provide us with much of the information about our surroundings. As sensors, however, our eyes are greatly limited by sensitivity to only the visible range of electromagnetic energy, viewing perspectives dictated by the location of our bodies, and the inability to form a lasting record of what we view. Because of these limitations, humans have continuously sought to develop the technological means to increase our ability to record the physical properties of our environment.

Beginning with the early use of aerial photography, remote sensing has been recognized as a valuable tool for viewing, analyzing, characterizing, and making decisions about our environment. In the past few decades, remote sensing technology has advanced on three fronts: from predominantly military uses to a variety of environmental analysis applications that relate to land, ocean, and atmosphere issues; from analogue photographic systems to sensors that convert energy from many parts of the electromagnetic spectrum to electronic signals; and from aircraft to satellite platforms.

Remote sensing data has proven to be an important tool in geography. Multi-temporal satellite data help to delineate the various change of the earth surface. Remote sensing has progressively expended applications in various fields such as urban-regional planning, utilities planning, health planning, geomorphology, and resource planning. Because of its varied applications and ability to allow users to collect, interpret, and manipulate data over dangerous areas, remote sensing has become a useful tool for all geographers, regardless of their concentration.

9. **Prof. K. Purushotham Reddy**

Professor K. Purushotham Reddy, widely known as Man of the Environment and Masses in the state of Andhra Pradesh championed for causes of planet and people and his mission continues and inspires millions across the nations. He is a revered personality in the country and outside for his remarkable contributions for Environmental security, Social Development, Academic and Political enlightenment of the society. Professor's long public life and activism spans across areas such as Environmental Policies, Public Policies on Sustainable Development, Restoration of damaged Eco-systems, Conservation of Natural Resources, Sustainable Agriculture,

Water Resources, Academic and youth empowerment, Panchayat Raj and Rural Development, Urban Studies, Gandhian Studies.

An environment is made-up of the circumstances, objects or conditions by which a human, animal, plant or object is surrounded. The term environment' generally refers to the natural world as perceived by humans. The quality of the environment in which people live, work, and play influences to no small degree the quality of life itself. The environment can be satisfying and attractive and provide scope for individual development or it can be poisonous, irritating, and stunting.

Urbanization refers to the movement of the population from rural areas to urban areas. It is essentially the gradual increase in the proportion of people living in urban areas. Furthermore, urbanization is quite a popular trend in the contemporary world. Moreover, people mostly undertake urbanization due to more work opportunities and a better standard of living.

First of all, political causes play a big role in urbanization. Many people get forced to leave rural areas for urban areas due to political unrest. Therefore, many families go to urban areas in search of food, shelter, and employment.

Another important cause of urbanization is an economic cause. Furthermore, poverty is a widespread phenomenon in rural areas. Moreover, farmers are finding it very hard to earn enough money and make a living. Consequently, rural people move to urban areas in search of better job opportunities.

Education is a strong cause of urbanization. Urban areas offer opportunities for seeking high-quality education. Moreover, urbanization offers opportunities for studying at universities and technical colleges. Such handsome education opportunities attract many young people in rural areas to move to urban areas.

Environmental degradation also plays a part in contributing to urbanization. Deforestation destroys the natural habitat of many farming families. Furthermore, mining and industrial expansion also harm the natural habitat of farming families. Urbanization has a huge impact on the environment. The large-scale urban constructions change the original natural environment, and cause great changes for the original ecological environment.

The social cause is another notable reason for urbanization. Many young rural people migrate to urban areas in order to seek a better lifestyle. Moreover, many young people want to escape the conservative culture of rural areas. Most noteworthy, urban areas offer a more easy-going liberal lifestyle. Furthermore, cities have clubs to attract youth.

To sum it up, urbanization is a process which is on a continuous rise. Furthermore, urbanization ensures the transformation of rural culture into urban culture. Moreover, the government must be vigilant to the rapidly increasing urbanization. A fully urbanized world looks like the ultimate destiny of our world.

10. **C L N Gandhi**

Born on 15th May 1953 in Guntur, Perused M.Sc and B.L. He was Recruited by APPSC and Joined in the Forest Department as Forest Range Officer in 1976. He was recruited as RTO by APPSC under Group-I Service and joined in April Worked as RTO at Warangal, Guntur, West Godavari, East Godavari, Nellore and Hyderabad.He was Promoted as Additional Transport Commissioner 2008. In 2011 Enrolled as Advocate and is practicing in the High Court and also attending to Consultancy service.

Urbanization refers to general increase in population and the amount of industrialization of a settlement. It symbolizes the movement of people from rural to urban areas. Urbanization happens because of the increase in the extent and density of urban areas. Due to uncontrolled urbanization in India, environmental degradation has been occurring very rapidly and causing many problems like land insecurity, worsening water quality, excessive air pollution, noise and the problems of waste disposal.

Although India is one of the less urbanized countries of the world with only 27.78 percent of population living in towns, India is facing a serious crisis of urban growth at present time whereas urbanization has been an instrument of economic, social and political progress, it has led to serious socio-economic problems. Urbanization is a process that leads to the growth of cities due to industrialization and economic development.

Failure of governance in today's cities has resulted in the growth of informal settlements and slums that constitute unhealthy living and working environment. Serious attention should be given to the need for improving urban strategies, which promote efficiency in resource use. Urgent attention should be given to reduce the generation of solid waste at the sources through mandatory standards and regulation fee and tax incentives, and education and voluntary compliance. In case adequate steps are not taken to prevent pollution and to improve the quality of life by providing more social amenities, the life of the urban dwellers of India may become more miserable this may be the cause of health hazards and worst devastation. So this is the responsibility of government take necessary steps to prevent the environment by taking plausible solutions and also the planners should also concentrate on these views while planning and protect the environment. Although it is impossible to restrict urbanization it has to be ensured that urbanization proceeds in the right path causing minimum impact on environment.

11. **En. Sirajuddin M Horaginamani**

Environmentalist and President, Deccan Environmental Research Organisation Bijapur, Karnataka. Ex-Principal of SAH Degree College Gulbarga, Karnataka, He has bagged two gold medals in M.Sc Environmental Science from Kuvempu University Shiamoga, Karnataka, he has published many papers in National and International reputed journals. He has been actively organizing many National and International workshop and seminars from the last 10 years. He is the recipient of many awards like, Best Academician Award, Best Environmentalist Award, and Best Ecologist Award.

As we all know Human beings have become an increasingly powerful environmental force over the last 10,000 years. With the advent of agriculture 8,000 years ago, we began to change the land. And with the industrial revolution, we began to affect our atmosphere. The recent increase in the world's population has magnified the effects of our agricultural and economic activities. But the growth in world population has masked what may be an even more important human-environmental interaction: While the world's population is doubling, the world's urban population is tripling. Within the next few years, more than half the world's population will be living in urban areas.

Urban populations interact with their environment. Urban people change their environment through their consumption of food, energy, water, and land. And in turn, the polluted urban environment affects the health and quality of life of the urban population.

Urbanization also affects the broader regional environments. Regions downwind from large industrial complexes also see increases in the amount of precipitation, air pollution, and the number of days with thunderstorms. Urban areas affect not only the weather patterns, but also the runoff patterns for water. Urban areas generally generate more rain, but they reduce the infiltration of water and lower the water tables. This means that runoff occurs more rapidly with greater peak flows. Flood volumes increase, as do floods and water pollution downstream.

Many of the effects of urban areas on the environment are not necessarily linear. Bigger urban areas do not always create more environmental problems. And small urban areas can cause large problems. Much of what determines the extent of the environmental impacts is how the urban populations behave — their consumption and living patterns — not just how large they are.

12. **Er. Mohd Abdul Kabeer**

Dy. General Manager (Engg.) at HMWSSB (Hyderabad Metropolitan Water Supply & Sewerage Board), Experienced Deputy General Manager with a demonstrated history of working in the government administration industry. Skilled in ArcGIS, Spatial Analysis, Geomatics, ArcGIS Server, and ESRI. Strong operations professional with a BE NIIT focused in Civil & IT from Dazzling High School.

Urbanization is one of the most significant trends of the 21st century, affecting global economic development, energy consumption, natural resource use, and human well-being. Globally, 3.6 billion people live in urban areas. The next few decades will be the most rapid period of urban growth in human history, with 2.6 billion additional urban dwellers expected by 2050. All these new urban dwellers will need water, but surprisingly little is known globally about where large cities obtain their water or the implication of this infrastructure for the global hydrologic cycle

Hence urban growth is increasing the demand for freshwater resources, yet surprisingly the water sources of the world's large cities have never been globally assessed, hampering efforts to assess the distribution and causes of urban water stress. Achieving water security is one of the major global challenges in the age of climate change, urbanization, population increase and incapacitated institutions.

UWM is commonly seen as a strategy for achieving the goals of Water Sensitive Urban Design. IUWM seeks to change the impact of urban development on the natural water cycle, based on the premise that by managing the urban water cycle as a whole; a more efficient use of resources can be achieved providing not only economic benefits but also improved social and environmental outcomes. One approach is to establish an inner, urban, water cycle loop through the implementation of reuse strategies. Developing this urban water cycle loop requires an understanding both of the natural, pre-development, water balance and the post-development water balance. Accounting for flows in the pre- and post-development systems is an important step toward limiting urban impacts on the natural water cycle

13. Addressing Challenges of Urban and Regional Issues using Geo-Spatial Science

Dr. Atiqur Rahman (Professor)

Department of Geography, Faculty of Natural Sciences

Jamia Millia Islamia

Rapid urbanization in the world is quite alarming, especially in developing countries like India (Kumar et al., 2007). Urbanization is a process whereby productive agricultural lands, forests, surface water bodies and groundwater are reducing at at a fast rate (Pathan et al., 1991). It is mainly due to higher population growth rate and uncontrolled and unchecked growth of urban areas of all sizes resulting in several problems like air, water and noise pollutions, loss of biodiversity(Maktav and Erber, 2005), reduction of fertile land and many more. About 31% of India's population currently urbanized and contribute about 70-75% of India's GDP which was merely about 45% in 1990. At the same time the urban areas contributing to more than 70 percent of the total energy demand and a corresponding proportion of the world's carbon dioxide emissions, it is evident that when aggregated globally, local processes within urban areas will have the potential impact on the whole Earth system (Seto and Satterthwaite, 2010).

Rapid, haphazard urban growth and accompanying population pressures results in large scale changes like change in land use/land cover; loss of productive agricultural land and open green spaces; loss of surface water bodies; depletion of ground water; deterioration of infrastructure facilities; micro climate change; air, water, and noise pollution; and an increase in public health hazards (Rahman, 2007). Unplanned urbanization leads to serious problems with infrastructure development and may have unforeseen consequences. Effective infrastructure planning and development require spatial and socio-economic data for different time periods. In fact, humans are increasingly being recognized as a dominant force in global environmental change (Moran, 2001). Changes in land use are likely the most ancient of all human-induced environmental impacts, and the first to obtain a magnitude to warrant the title "global." The land-cover change, especially the conversion of forested areas into other uses, has been identified as a contributing factor to global climate change, accounting for 33% of the increase in atmospheric CO2 since 1850. It is very important to address such issues effectively; up-to-date and accurate data is much needed at regular intervals of time.

The social, economic, political and physical ramifications of urbanization continue to challenge scientists worldwide. Concentrating human activities to dense urban forms has many advantages including community building, employment opportunities, and the protection of outlying areas. The disadvantages are equally pervasive such as rapid disease spread, urban poverty, racial conflict, urban climate change, and pollution (Elizabeth et al., 2008).

In such situations remote sensing data provides excellent possibilities for mapping, monitoring, measuring, and managing various features of the urban environment. The use and availability of satellite data started with the launch of Landsat-1 of 77 meter spatial resolution data by NASA and later with the launch of IRS-1C and -1D satellites, the availability of high spatial resolution data of 5.8 meter, 23.5m LISS-III data to IKONOS, 1 meter spatial resolution, it is now possible to explore the potential of remote sensing data, either singularly or in combination, in different urban areas. Over the years, satellite remote sensing data have been used for assessing urban environmental conditions. Data is used for urban land-use and land-cover mapping, land-use dynamics, urban landscape design, and urban base map preparation. Remote sensing and GIS are repeatedly proving to be very valuable in urban studies, and particularly in the fields of urban management and planning (Shekhar, 2004).

Spatial data for different time periods can be obtained through remote sensing and, along with population data, would help identify patterns and trends in urban growth. GIS which is a very important spatial too widely used by people across the disciplines helps to integrate spatial and statistical data, and generate various theme-based maps for not only to address the urban and regional planning but the most important is to address various social and economic problems and challenges which is being faced today especially in the post-Covid-19.

References

1. Elizabeth A. W., Nelson D., Rahman A., Stefanov W L., & Roy S S. (2008). 'Expert System Classification of Urban Land Use/Cover for Delhi, India', International Journal of Remote Sensing, Taylor & Francis Publisher, Volume 29, Issue 15, London, UK pp. 4405- 4427.
2. Rahman A. (2007). 'Application of remote sensing and GIS technique for urban environmental management and sustainable development of Delhi, India', In Applied Remote Sensing for Urban Planning, Governance and Sustainability, (eds.) Netzband M. & Stefnow W. L., Redman, C L., Springer-Verlag Publishes, Berlin, Germany. pp.165-197. ISBN No. 978-3-642-06493-7
3. Shekhar S (2004) Urban sprawl assessment entropy approach. GIS Development 8 (5)

4. http://www.gisdevelopment.net/magazine/years/2004/may/urban.asp
5. Moran, E. F. 2001. Progress in the last ten tears in the study of land use/cover change and the outlook for the next decade. In A. Diekman et al. (eds.). Human dimensions of global change. Cambridge, MA.: MIT Press
6. Pathan, S.K., Shukla, V.K., PateL, R.G. and Mehta, K.S., 1991, Urban land use mapping—a case study of Ahmedabad city and its environs. Journal of Indian Society of Remote Sensing, 19, pp. 95–112.
7. Maktav, D. and Erber, F.S., 2005, Analysis of urban growth using multi-temporal satellite data in Istanbul, Turkey. International Journal of Remote Sensing, 26, pp. 797–810
8. Seto K C and Satterthwaite D (2010). Interactions between urbanization and global environmental change, Current Opinion in Environmental Sustainability, Volume 2, Issue 3, Pages 127-128.

CONTENTS

Urban Environment and Spatial Science
Dr Mohd Akhter Ali, Dr. Kabir Mohan Sethy, Dr Muzafar Wani and M.Kamraju
Ane Books Pvt. Ltd. 2021, , ISBN : 978-93-90658-28-2, P.P. : 1 – 7

1

Geospatial Technology and Applications in Urban and Regional Planning

Dr. Y.V.N. Krishna Murthy,
Sr. Professor and Registrar
Indian Institute of Space Science and Technology (IIST), Thiruvananthapuram

Introduction

The twentieth century has witnessed rapid industrialisation and urbanisation of the world's population. The global proportion of urban population has increased from a mere 13% in 1900 to 29% in 1950 and has reached 55% by 2020 as a result of higher population growth and migration, and which is anticipated to grow into 68% by 2050. About 4.1 billion people live in urban areas and as the world continues to urbanise, around 62% of the 8.6 billion global population, i.e., about 5.3 billion is expected to live in cities by 2030 (Revision of World Urbanisation Prospects, 2018). The developed nations also differ from developing nations with regard to number of megacities. In the year 1900, Europe and Northern America had 69 of the world's 100 largest cities; by 2020 this had shrunk to 17. By 2020, Asia alone has 58 of the world's 100 largest cities, compared to 22 in 1900 (https://www.iied.org/worlds-100-largest-cities-1800-2020-beyond). Such demographic trend in the developing countries would mean a greater stress on the natural resources, environment and infrastructure and quality of life, both within and outside the urban areas. Further, as the urban areas are considered as drivers of economic, social, political and cultural change, they are also viewed as a phenomenon with mainly negative consequences as far as quality of life is concerned. The developmental initiatives must address the enormous challenges and make the

Corresponding Author: Y.V.N. Krishna Murthy

best of opportunities brought by growing urbanisation to provide sustainable solutions to urban problems in the 21st century.

Urbanisation Scenario in India

Urbanisation phenomenon is no exception to India; in fact some Indian cities are among the fastest growing cities in the world. The migration of people from villages to towns and cities continues unabated. The rapid urban growth has resulted in increasing the share of India's urban population from 159 million (23%) in 1981 to 217 million (26%) in 1991, to 286 million (28%) in 2001 and 377 million (31.2%) in 2011 (Census of India, 2011). Thus, post-independence, while the population of India has grown three times, the urban population has grown five times. The total number of urban settlements have increased from 4029 (1981) to 4689 (1991), 5161 (2001) to 7935 (2011). The 7935 towns and cities house 377 million of the urban population (Census of India, 2011). The average population density/sq.km of the country is 382 persons/sq. km (https://www.niti.gov.in/niti/content/population-density-sq-km), whereas the urban population density is at 1260 persons/sq.km within an area of 26 million hectares or 0.6% of country's geographical area in 2006. The urban population in the country is expected to rise further around 600 million (40%) by 2030 (MoHUA, 2020). Thus, we are likely to face a scenario where a large number of people would have to live in smaller geographical areas. Further, urban India contributes to over 65% of the National GDP.

Geospatial Technology Driven Urban and Regional Planning

The need of the hour is to generate digital database of every sector of economy, demography and maps of natural as well as man-made resources at two levels i.e., at national or state level for making policies and programmes and at local body level for implementation of policies and programmes. Land use/ land cover (LULC) maps, urban growth and land use changes are the primary indicators for analysis of the socio-economic changes in the society. The conversion of land records into a digital mode has facilitated in enhanced revenue generation, transparency in land-administration and taxation.

Each government has a unique set of circumstances that result in different management responses to improve community services. An important factor in improving the delivery of customer service is through the investment in Geographical Information System (GIS) which is now widely recognized as efficient tool for various town-planning schemes. The access to reliable and up-to-date information reduces the uncertainty in planning and management through identifying the appropriate parameters, modeling and analyzing different scenarios and solutions, spatially. The value of information and the effectiveness of planning process and decision making are closely related to the quality and completeness of the information, and results in better process of good governance both for operational and enhanced services.

Some Aspects of Geospatial Technology

The modern technology of remote sensing which includes both aerial as well as satellite based systems, allow collection of a wide range of physical data that is timely, temporal, quantitative and with the aid of GIS facilitates in analysis with speed and on repetitive basis, and together with GIS helps us the data spatially, offering possibilities of generating various options (modelling), thereby optimizing the whole planning process. Generally, the remote sensing data products have following applications: mapping, monitoring, modelling and management of resources. Therefore, it is essential to know more in detail about the characteristics and capabilities of the remote sensing data products available to the various users, especially to the urban and regional planners (Krishna Murthy et al., 1991; Sreenivasan and Krishna Murthy, 2018).

Geospatial technology majorly encompass Surveying, Remote Sensing (RS), Photogrammetry, Geographical Information System (GIS) and Global Navigation Satellite System (GNSS), Location based services (LBS), Internet of Things (IoT) and are widely used to visualise, measure and analyse the earth's resources.

Remote Sensing forms the primary data source in Geospatial information. The objects on the earth's surface reflect, emit or backscatter varying amount of electromagnetic energy (EMR) in different wavelengths depending on their physical and chemical properties. The estimation of these energy through terrestrial/ airborne/ space-borne sensors forms the basis for understanding the characteristics of earth's surface features through remote sensing. Remote Sensing data obtained in optical, thermal or microwave spectral region have utilities in studying urban and regional areas. Thermal remote sensing is based on premise that there is a strong relationship between the amount of radiant flux radiated and the temperatures of an object. These systems are capable to sense the changes in land surface temperature (LST) associated with built-up changes in an urban set-up. Microwave remote sensing has the advantage of all-weather capability, unlike the satellite images acquired in optical region of electromagnetic radiation. Microwave remote sensing data acquired with multi-temporal and multi-frequency SAR data is useful in estimation of stand density, area delineation, species separation, tree height estimation, detection of plant stress, etc. in urban areas. Light Detection and Ranging (LiDAR) technique is a remote sensing method that uses light in the form of a pulsed laser to quantify distances. LiDAR data is quite useful in measurements of building heights which are helpful to build the 3D city models of urban areas. The photogrammetry methods are also useful to understand the 3D characteristics of urban areas. Using control points, the stereo pair of an optical band is triangulated to obtain the epipolar images for three-dimensional visualisation of urban surfaces or a Digital Elevation Model (DEM) can be created to visualise or analyse the urban built-forms. Unmanned Aerial Vehicle (UAV) remote sensing has great potential for 3D mapping in a complex cityscape due to their capability to capture images at low altitudes.

Application Potential of Geospatial Technology in Urban and Regional Planning

Broadly, the utilisation of Geospatial technology in urban and regional planning can be put under following categories: a) Inclusive Planning (mapping of informal settlements, vulnerability analysis, etc.), b) Urban Governance (Property Taxation, Municipal GIS, monitoring of urban encroachments, demographic studies, urban cadastral studies, etc.), c) Urban Environment (urban landscape, urban green spaces, solid waste disposal management and sites selection, urban heat island, urban pollution, micro-climate, solar potential, Health GIS, etc.), d) Regional Planning (Regional Plans and boundaries, sustainable development, socio-economic disparity, etc.), e) Heritage Conservation (applications of Close Range photogrammetry and Terrestrial Laser Scanner, analysis and mapping of heritage zones, etc.), f) Urban design (3D city visualisation using LiDAR, regeneration and redevelopment analysis, rainwater harvesting, etc.), g) Urban utility (surface/ subsurface utility mapping, transportation, hydro-geomorphological mapping, etc.), h) Urban Hazard (hazard mapping/analysis, micro-seismic studies, urban fires, urban flood, etc.), i) Site suitability and catchment area analysis, j) Modelling Urban Growth, etc.

Some Major applications of Geospatial Technology in Urban & Regional Planning accomplished in India are(1) Urban sprawl Dynamics and land use of major Urban agglomeration up to small towns and cities, (2) Mapping of Major slums in the country and defining appropriate planning and implementation, (3) Generation of Municipal level Information systems, (4) Solid waste management, (5) Disaster resilient urban planning (earthquakes, floods, fire etc.,) Geospatial Technology Utilisation in Development Schemes of GoI

National Urban Information System (NUIS)

Under National Urban Information System (NUIS), Ministry of Urban Development (MoUD), Govt. of India in 2006 has generated urban geospatial database at 1:10, 000 scale for 152 towns using high resolution satellite data. The NUIS Design and Standards Document prepared covers geospatial database of both primary themes (12 numbers) and attribute layers (4 numbers) at 1:10, 000 scale (NUIS, 2008). The Primary Layers generated in this scheme were as follows: (*a*) Urban land use/cover, (*b*) Physiography (outside core area, (*c*) Geomorphology (outside core area), (*d*) Geological Structures (outside core area), (*e*) Lithology (outside core area), (*f*) Soils (outside core area), (*g*) Drainage, (*h*) Surface Water bodies, (*i*) Road, (*j*) Rail, (*k*) Canal and (*l*) Transportation Nodes. Similarly, the incorporated layers are: (*a*) Administrative boundaries, (*b*) Forest boundary, (*c*) Settlement & village locations/names and (*d*) City/town boundaries. The above data sets are made available on Bhuvan, geoportal of NRSC / ISRO for use in Urban and Regional planning by the town planners. Appropriate training was provided to the planners and administrators for effective use of data in planning process and implementation.

Atal Mission for Rejuvenation and Urban Transformation (AMRUT)

Govt. of India has launched Atal Mission for Rejuvenation and Urban Transformation (AMRUT) programme with an aim to improve the quality of life for urban dwellers. The programme also has a mandate to enable GIS based Master Plan formulation for 500 cities/ towns in India under its Sub-scheme by the urban local bodies. High resolution satellite data especially from Cartosat series satellites is being used for the generation of urban geospatial database at 1:4, 000 scale, formulation of GIS-based Master Plan and appropriate capacity building at various levels using Bhuvan geoportal. The initial study carried out by the town planners on such platform and process is for Khammam town in the state of Telangana and extensively used as a case study for capacity building of the planners across the country.

Capacity building under AMRUT and enhancing the Planning Curricula

The urban planners are invariably exposed to spatial planning, mostly through conventional techniques and methods. It is therefore imperative to enhance the Geospatial component in their curricula such that urban planners are equipped with technological tools and concepts for handling the spatial aspects in their profession. A study was conducted by Kumar et al. (2014) to evaluate the existing model syllabi of All India Council for Technical Education (AICTE) for urban planning curricula at Bachelor and Master level and syllabi at 10+2 level (https://www.int-arch-photogramm-remote-sens-spatial-inf-sci.net/XL-8/1253/2014/isprsarchives-XL-8-1253-2014.pdf). The assessment of syllabi revealed uneven distribution of geospatial contents across semesters in planning curricula at Bachelor and Master Level. Therefore, suggestions were made to seamlessly integrate the Geospatial contents in a structured manner. It was also emphasized that students should be encouraged to use the Geospatial technologies in their studio exercises instead of conventional methods.

An Authoring Group constituted by Space Technology Application (STA) cell under MoHUA, Govt. of India prepared course contents for "Capacity Building under AMRUT Sub-scheme and Enhancing Geospatial Contents in UG and PG Courses of Planning in India", and finalised it in consultation with some leading Institutions specialised in the field of Geospatial technology and its applications in urban planning. The Authoring Group recommended three-tier training programmes under AMRUT Sub-scheme i.e., i) Training Course for Decision Makers (duration: 3 days), ii) Training Course for Middle Level Officials (duration: 2 weeks), and iii) Training Course for Junior (Operator) Level Officials (duration: 4 Weeks). For these courses, contents were recommended day-wise with theory, demonstration and practical. Field visit/ field based practical sessions were also included for better exposure of geospatial technology to the course participants.

Mobile App 'Sankalan'

Indian Institute of Remote Sensing (IIRS), ISRO along with Town & Country Planning Organisation (TCPO), MoHUA, GoI have jointly developed the course contents for country-wide training and capacity building under AMRUT Sub-scheme. During the training programmes conducted at IIRS, a need was felt for a Mobile App for collection and linkage of ground data with spatial layers. Hence, '*Sankalan*' Mobile App was developed by IIRS and TCPO based on AMRUT Geo-data standards. Its web-based dashboard provides software tools and utilities to generate various spatial and non-spatial data products as a map or a report. *Sankalan* is compatible to Mobile Phones with features viz., Android OS 1.6 or newer, GNSS/GPS Receiver and Camera. *Sankalan* is available for download from IIRS website (https://amrut.iirs.gov.in/).

Smart Cities

The Geospatial data sets generated using high resolution satellite data have become an effective base for integrating the data from IoT and employing efficient big data analytics tools to provide real time scenarios and solutions for the planners and the citizens. This has opened up an enormous opportunity for entrepreneurs as start-ups to provide operations services and products with less investment and recurring financial benefits.

Conclusions

Geospatial technology encompassing Remote Sensing (RS), Photogrammetry, Geographical Information System (GIS) and Global Navigation Satellite System (GNSS), Location based services (LBS), Internet of Things (IoT) etc are now indispensable tools for urban planners in effective planning and implementation with people participation and acceptance.

The capital city of Chhattisgarh has been identified using geospatial technologies, accepted by the elected representatives and evolved into an ideal smart city. State of Telangana has effectively used the high resolution data available on Bhuvan in enhancing the tax collection for all the towns and cities/towns through training the concerned officials without any other investments. Most of the state governments are employing the geospatial technologies innovatively and effectively based on the requirements. The greatest opportunity is for the entrepreneurs to offer real time services and products as per the need, as start-up employing big data analytics, AI and machine learning techniques, that are cost effective, mutually beneficial, transparent and the respective state governments should encourage such mechanisms.

Urban Environment and Spatial Science
Dr Mohd Akhter Ali, Dr. Kabir Mohan Sethy, Dr Muzafar Wani and M.Kamraju
Ane Books Pvt. Ltd. 2021, ISBN : 978-93-90658-28-2, P.P. : 9 – 18

2

An Overview of Urban Development

M.Kamraju
Student Osmania University
Hyderabad, Telangana

Abstract

In the present day all the countries are into a rat race for urban growth as every country is thinking in an economic way. Over the past hundred years earth's population has grown rapidly, and our economies have become more mechanized, moreover as a result lot of people have left primary activities and moved into cities. Urban development studies the various concepts involved in the process of urbanization like patterns of urbanization, components and consequences of urbanization. Urban development has been the subject of discussion among the academicians and researchers ever since evolution of cities. Throughout the world urbanization has been considered as an important index for socio-economic development. Nevertheless urban development has pro's, but in the long run it has many cons. So, in this paper an effort has been made to assess the constrains of urban development on environment. We have mostly relied on primary data secondary data for the review of this paper. The outcome of this research will be helpful for academicians and researchers for their future studies in the related themes.

Keywords: mechanized, urbanization, urban development, environment, academicians

Introduction

The term 'Urbanisation' implies the movement of people to urban areas. The concept of urbanisation in economic aspects relates to the movement of people from agricultural activities to non-agricultural activities. The growth of

Corresponding Author: M.Kamraju

urbanisation in ancient times was related to the process of civilization and is known as 'a cultural process'. Later on, in medieval- times the urbanisation as a result of a political process, because of the establishment and' downfall of kingdoms and dynasties. Lastly, in modem times, the urbanisation is mostly associated with industrialization and economic development and it is called an economic process. An Urban Area is a region which is having all the amenities, infrastructure, Density of Human Structure (Ali et al., 2020, p. 14).

Globally, 55% of the population today lives in urban areas. The number of people living in cities will rise by 1.5 times to 6 billion by 2045, adding an additional 2 billion urban residents. With more than 80 % of global GDP generated in cities, if managed well by increasing productivity, allowing innovation and new ideas to emerge ("Urban development," n.d.), urbanisation can contribute to sustainable growth.

Urbanization is closely linked to modernization, industrialization, and therefore the sociological process of rationalization. Urbanization can describe a selected condition at a group time, i.e. the proportion of total population or area in cities or towns, or the term can describe the rise of this proportion over time.

So the term urbanization can represent the extent of urban development relative to overall population, or it can represent the speed at which the urban proportion is increasing. Urbanization is not merely a modern phenomenon, but a rapid and historic transformation of human social roots on a global scale, whereby predominantly rural culture is being rapidly replaced by predominantly urban culture.

The last major change in settlement patterns was the accumulation of hunter-gatherers into villages many thousand years ago.

Village culture is characterized by common bloodlines, intimate relationships, and communal behavior whereas urban culture is characterized by distant bloodlines, unfamiliar relations, and competitive behavior. This unprecedented movement of people is forecast to continue and intensify in the next few decades, mushrooming cities to sizes incomprehensible only a century ago.

Indeed, today, in Asia the urban agglomerations of Dhaka, Karachi, Mumbai, Delhi, Manila, Seoul and Beijing are each already home to over 20 million people, while the Pearl River Delta, Shanghai-Suzhou and Tokyo are forecast to approach or exceed 40 million people each within the coming decade. Outside Asia, Mexico City, Sao Paulo, New York City, Lagos and Cairo are fast approaching being, or are already, home to over 20 million people (ScienceDaily: Your source for the latest research news, n.d.).

Urbanization can contribute to sustainable growth with more than 80 percent of global GDP generated in cities if it is well managed by increasing productivity, enabling innovation and new ideas to emerge ("Urban development," n.d.).

The speed and scale of urbanisation, however, poses challenges, including meeting the accelerated demand for affordable housing, well-connected transportation systems and other infrastructure, basic services, and jobs, especially for the nearly 1 billion urban poor living in informal settlements ("Urban development," n.d.). Conflicts are on the rise, leading to 60% of people being forcibly displaced.

Once a town is constructed, its physical form and patterns of land use can be locked in for generations, leading to unsustainable sprawl. The increase in urban land consumption surpasses population growth by as much as 50 percent, which is expected in the three decades to add 1.2 million km2 of new urban built-up area to the world ("Urban development," n.d.). This sprawl puts pressure on land and natural resources, leading to undesirable consequences.

In tackling climate change, cities are playing an increasingly important role because their exposure to climate and disaster risk increases as they grow. In coastal areas, nearly half a billion urban residents live, increasing their vulnerability to storm surges and sea level rise. There are 100 million individuals in the 136 biggest coastal cities, or 20 percent of their population, and $4.7 trillion in assets exposed to coastal floods. In developing countries, around 90 percent of urban expansion is near-hazard-prone areas and constructed through informal and unplanned settlements ("Urban development," n.d.).

In combating epidemics, cities are also at the forefront. With the COVID-19 pandemic, cities across the world are currently being tested to the extreme. It affects not only public health, but the economy and the social fabric as well. COVID-19 lays bare how well cities are planned and managed and the effect this has on the health crisis, social crisis, and economic crisis at the same time. For cities on the frontline, rich and poor alike, COVID-19 is a huge challenge. Due to their economic structure, their preparedness for such a crisis("Urban development," n.d.) , particularly the state of their public health and service delivery systems, and the extent to which the health and livelihoods of their population are vulnerable, the measures taken to control the spread of the virus have massive implications for cities.

History of Urbanisation

Urbanization's history is also the history of civilization. Urbanisation has always been a part of ancient culture, from Mesopotamia to the Indus Valley and China, from Egypt to Greece and Meso-America. But all around the world, it was not uniform. Localized growth was witnessed by different ages (Ali et al., 2020, p. 16).

Among scholars, there are many disagreements about exactly where, when, how, and why the first cities began. They are likely to have started independently over a range of times and for somewhat different reasons in different parts of the world. The ancient towns were mainly found in the area between the Persian Gulf and the Mediterranean, if the Periodization of world history is taken into account. The first towns were primarily the seats of political power. Urbanization became the product of the concentration of power, whether it was the city states of Greece, the walled city of Babylon or the ornate towns of Egypt. Administration emanated from these early cities together with religious control and military authority. Commerce and trade became more significant with the second phase of urban development (Ali et al., 2020, p. 16-17).

Table 2.1: Basic Characteristics of Preindustrial city*

Size	*Maximum of 250000 inhabitants*
Geographical significance	Local(centre of trade for imminent locality)
Physical structure	Dense,compace structure enclosed in rampants
Functional structure	Mixed-house has a housing function and a production function.
Social structure	The prestige of social strata decreased from centre to the outskirts.
Economic structure	Centre of agriculture, crafts and trade
Political function	Independence of gentry(citizens were serfs)

****Source:*** (Ali et al., 2020, p.30).

During the late eighteenth century, a watershed in the history of urbanisation was achieved. The nature of urbanisation itself underwent a major shift with the Industrial Revolution that transformed the very concept of a city. It was a real breakthrough as an enormous productivity growth was brought about by the implementation of inanimate energy and machinery in the newly established industries (Ali et al., 2020, p. 16-17).

Urban process in India

Urbanization is an important part of economic growth and, as the economy grows, the per capita income and demand for non-farm products in the economy are growing. These goods are not heavily dependent on land and make more use of other factors of production, especially labour and capital ("Growth of Urbanisation in India," n.d.). As urban settlements enjoy agglomeration economies in manufacturing services and infrastructure provision, they are cheaper if produced in the urban sector of the economy. Economic growth affects the rate of urbanisation, whereas urbanisation affects the rate at which the economy is growing (P., Nelavigi. 2007).

In its wake, urbanisation presents a number of challenges, such as rapid population growth in urban settlements, which in most literature on this subject are cited as the greatest challenges. These are the consequences of death-exceeding births, rural population migration to urban centres, as well as the classification of rural settlements as cities. There are other challenges, apart from growing populations,

Many of these inadequacies, rather than population growth, are the result of effective and faulty urban management. In most towns in India, these issues are visible.

Characteristics of Urbanisation

The level of urbanisation is considered to be an economic development index. There is a strong positive correlation between the two processes. The level of economic development measured by per capita income is related to urbanisation. Urbanisation also increases when per capita income increases, but not as much. Economic growth is leading to a shift in demand and thus a reallocation of land resources ("Growth of Urbanisation in India," n.d.).

Until recently, cities in developed countries were based on industry, but they were dominated by services in the past industrial age, and yet no one considers them over-urbanized. Not only is an urban settlement characterised by the relative importance of production and services, but, more importantly, by a high population density ("Growth of Urbanisation in India," n.d.). When produced on a large scale, a lot of production is cheaper

In addition, inputs are readily available to external economies, especially skilled labour, information and repair services, from which each producer profits when it is one of many clustered in one location. People like living in the vicinity of their place of work ("Growth of Urbanisation in India," n.d.). Economies of scale and the cost of transport cause production and people to concentrate in a particular location. The large-scale manufacturing market extends well beyond the borders of the city where it is located, to the rest of the country, and sometimes even abroad. Industrialization contributes to urbanisation, but the former does not necessarily lead to the latter. Thus, it is better for a wage labourer to migrate to larger cities than to smaller ones, where he is more likely to be fully employed. All these variables boost the population density in the cities (P., Nelavigi. 2007).

Table 2.2: Total population and urban population from 1901 - 2011*

Census Year	*Total Population (Million)*	*Urban population (million)*	*Percentage of urban population to total population*
1901	238.3	25.8	10.83
1911	252.1	25.9	10.27
1921	251.3	28.1	11.18
1931	278.9	33.5	12.01
1941	318.6	44.2	13.87
1951	361	62.4	17.29
1961	439.2	78.9	17.96
1971	548.1	109.1	19.91
1981	683.3	159.4	23.33
1991	846.3	217.6	25.71
2001	1027.1	285.4	27.78
2011	1210.2	377.1	31.16

Source: *Census of India census 1901 – 2011*

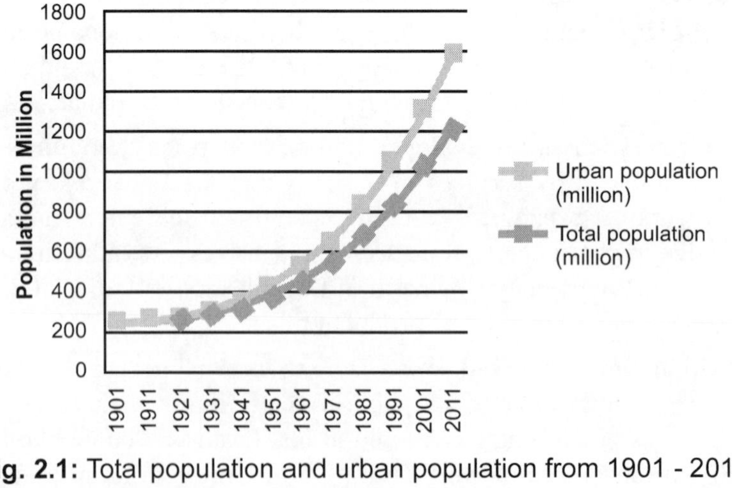

Fig. 2.1: Total population and urban population from 1901 - 2011*

Source: Census of India census 1901 – 2011

Table 2.2 shows the total population and urban population from 1901 to 2011 census years. The population has increased from 238.3 million in 1901 to 1210.1 million in 2011. The size of the countries urban population is increased from 11 percent in 1901 to 31 percent in 2011 ("Growth of Urbanisation in India," n.d.).From this, it has been observed that there is more than tenfold increase in the countries urban population and the countries level of urbanization has increased by only about 2 1/2 times during past 100 years. From table it is observed that during first half century 1901 to 1951, the growth rate of urbanization has been very slow but after 1951 it starts increasing very sharply ("Growth of Urbanisation in India," n.d.).

Table 2.3: Tempo of urbanisation 1901 - 2001*

Year	*Tempo of Urban*	*Tempo of population Rural*
1901-1911	-0.5309	0.06149
1911-1921	0.8489	-0.0997
1921-1931	0.7161	-0.0916
1931-1941	1.4398	-0.2139
1941-1951	2.204	-0.4063
1951-1961	0.3801	-0.0825
1961-1971	1.03	-0.0329
1971-1981	1.5854	-0.644
1981-1991	0.9713	-0.3153
1991-2001	0.7743	-0.2815
2001-2011	1.1481	-0.4793

****Source:*** Census of India census

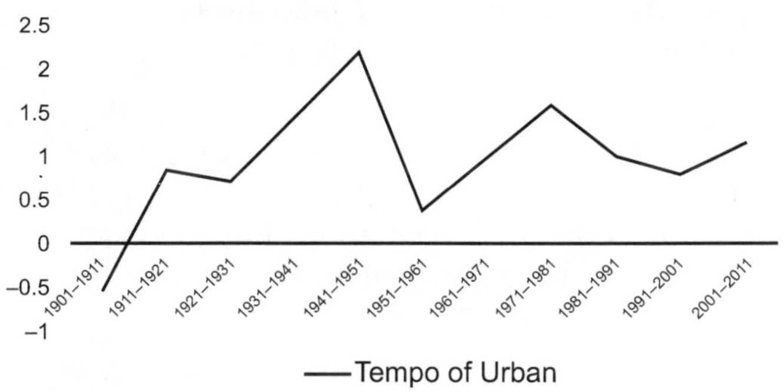

Fig. 2.2: Tempo of Urbanisation 1901-2011

Table 2.3 Shows tempo of urbanisation refers to speed of urbanisation is measured as change registered in the level or degree of urbanisation over the years, from table it is clear that tempo of urbanisation is not uniform over the years, it shows a fluctuating trend over the years 1901-1981 and declining trend during 1981 – 1991 and 1991- 2001 ("Growth of Urbanisation in India," n.d.).

Development of Urbanisation

The growth of the urban population in our country, when compared to other means of development, is almost similar to that of other modern developments , particularly after independence. It was noted that around 10 % of the population lived in urban areas at the beginning of the 20th century, especially in smaller cities, with less than 20,000 people out of 26 million urban people (Davis & Notestein, 1951,).

Urban growth has shown increasing trends during the 19th century except due to accidental decline, especially from 1901 to 1911 due to epidemics such as plague and other population outbreaks in many cities were temporarily evacuated and millions of urbanites died. The growth rate of the urban population was quite slow during the latter period until 1941.

That is because of the national spread of the independence movement against British rule and the effect of economic depression, the increase in urban population, not more than 1 percent, affected the overall development of urbanisation in India. In the period between 1901-1941, the size of the urban population increased from 25.9 million to 44.1 million, adding approximately 18 million people.

During the decade 1941-1951, the enormous increase in the size and percentage of urban population accounted for and the percentage of urban population increased to 18.3 percent. This increased the urban population volume due to massive population displacement at the time of the partition of the country in 1947.

Large numbers of Pakistani displaced people have settled in large cities in India. In addition , job creation opportunities are being generated in the urban, government and service sectors. The opening of a large number of schools and colleges and other educational institutions in cities has increased the level of security and increased self-confidence and freedom to live anywhere in India (Amitabh Kundu, 2000)

The exponential growth rate was recorded as 2.34 in the period from 1951 to 1961. The population growth rate was slow. In the urban population, the percentage gain is only about 0.07, which was less than the 0.34 percent gain during the decade of 1941-1951. This decrease is due to the reorganisation of state borders during 1956, as well as the adoption of a new definition of rural, urban area classification.

The census report from 1981 to 2001 shows that the rate of urban population growth was slow, with an average annual exponential growth rate of 3.9 and 2.73 per annum between 1981 to 1991 and 1991 to 2001. In 1961-2001, however, the percentage increase in the urban population stood at 17.97 to 27.78.

It shows almost uniformity with respect to urban population growth. The average growth rate of the urban population rose to 3.38 percent during the period from 2001 to 2011, which is about 92 million urban population added, due to globalisation, attracted more employment opportunities and improvement in both technical and professional education, as well as more security of life and safety (Ali et al., 2020,).

CONCLUSION

For more than a century and a half, social reformers, city planners, public health officials and social scientists have been concerned about life in cities and, by extension, in cities and more modern urban forms. Millions of words have been written on the subject and, until recently, they have focused overwhelmingly on public health concerns, the social conditions of the poor and proposals to improve them. These traditional issues have been complemented over the last thirty years by a genuine explosion of new studies exploring wider environmental perspectives, including urban nature, the impact of cities and towns on the wider environment and the sustainability of modern urban life.

There may be many attributes in normal times that cities strive to compete and excel at the global level, including livability, competitiveness, and sustainability, but a city must function well for its citizens in any given day, and especially in a time of crisis. Intensive policy coordination and investment choices are required to build "working" cities that are inclusive, healthy, resilient, and sustainable. There is an important role for national and local governments to play in taking action now, shaping the future of their development and creating opportunities for all.

References

1. *Ali, M. A., Kamraju, M., & Wani, M.* (2020). *Urbanisation and Urban Systems (01st ed.). Rajesh Publisher.* p.14.
2. *Amitabh Kundu.* (2000, March 1). *Urban poverty in India: Issues and perspectives in development*- SAGE Journals. Retrieved June 9, 2020, from https://journals.sagepub.com/doi/abs/10.1177/004908570003000202

3. *Davis, K., & Notestein, F. W. (1951). The population of India and Pakistan, by Kingsley Davis*. [Foreword by Frank W. Notestein.].
4. *Kamraju, M.et.al (2018). Changing Pattern of Urban Growth in Hyderabad City: A Study. Jai Maa Saraswati Gyanadayani*, 3, 483-503.
5. *Kishan, A. B., Ali, M. A., & Kamraju, M. (2019). Impact of Urban Growth on Land Use-Land Cover in Hyderabad City.*
6. (n.d.). *Science Daily*: Your source for the latest research news. Retrieved June 6, 2020, from https://www.sciencedaily.com/terms/urbanization
7. *P., Nelavigi. (2007). Impact of Migration on Urbanization in India a Statistical Analysis.* Retrieved August 25, 2020, from https://shodhganga.inflibnet.ac.in/handle/10603/161997.
8. *Urban development.* (n.d.). World Bank. Retrieved June 7, 2020, from https://www.worldbank.org/en/topic/urbandevelopment
9. *Vani, M., & Kamraju, M. (2016). Impact of Urbanisation on Lakes: A Case Study of Hyderabad. Journal of Urban and Regional Studies* VOL, 5(1).
10. *Venkatesh, K., & Kamraju, M. (2018). Urban Sprawl and Sustainable Development in Hyderabad:* A Geoinformatic Approach. International Journal of Creative Research Thoughts (IJCRT), 6, 1285-294.

Urban Environment and Spatial Science
Dr Mohd Akhter Ali, Dr. Kabir Mohan Sethy, Dr Muzafar Wani and M.Kamraju
Ane Books Pvt. Ltd. 2021, , ISBN : 978-93-90658-28-2, P.P. : 19 – 38

3

Urbanization-The Future of Cities: An unrealistic growth causing Societal Pandemic

Kanagiri SN Prasad, Dr. Mohd Akhter Ali
[1]*Research Scholar, Centre for Economic and Social Studies*
[2]*Assistant professor. Department of Geography, Osmania University*

ABSTRACT

The present paper addresses the issues of unbalanced and biased growth of major cities and its impact on certain, critical factors that we would never imagine nor foresee. Especially in such crucial times with the pandemic spreading like wildfire in major urban pockets. The reason being, densely populated areas, the upsurge of slums, and the improper disposal of waste, associated with urbanization. The major working/labor section in urban areas is entirely reliant on the migratory workers. As they work for lesser wages with minimum needs. The major issues of the migrant workers were never thought of and addressed. Their contribution in the development of cities, building huge glass towers to roads is praiseworthy. They being the unsung heroes of urbanization, corrective steps must be taken to contain and provide basic amenities for the continuous growth upholding ethical values. For our future generation, we need to nurture the eco-friendly environment to sustain them in the long run. The steady concentration of wealth and recourses contained around selective few cities needs to be addressed effectively. This paper tries to address such issues to some extent and may be given an insight by the eminent scholars, sociologists and policymakers. The covid pandemic has given us time to ponder and unearth the roots of urbanization and human values.

Corresponding Author: Kanagiri SN Prasad

Urbanization in India

The population residing in urban areas in India, according to the 1901 census, was 11.4%. This count increased to 28.53% according to 2001 census, and crossed 30% as per 2011 census, standing at 31.16%. In 2017, the number increased to 34%, according to The World Bank.

Source: Population of Cities in India (2020)

India is the 7th largest country in the world by area, and a country this large has a population to match. When breaking down the numbers, it shows that India has many large cities that contribute to its massive population. The country has a total of 39 cities that each has a population exceeding one million residents. Of these cities, two have a population that exceeds 10 million- **Mumbai and Delhi.** While these megacities contribute millions to the population, the country also has smaller but still very densely populated cities, including 388 that have a population exceeding 100,000, and a whopping 2,483 cities with a population of over 10,000. When looking at these numbers, it isn't hard to see why India is the second- most populous country, falling only to China.

Even though it has larger cities than many countries, this developing country still has a very large rural population that contributes to its total number. While cities continue to develop and expand, the rural population hasn't witnessed a significant decrease through the decades like other countries. 67% of the population is situated in rural areas, while 33% make up the population in the larger cities. While this has decreased from 1960s 82% rural population, it isn't as significant of a change as some countries, which have far more residents who have moved from rural areas to pursue greater opportunities found within cities. However, because India is still a developing country, these numbers are expected to continue to decline in the future.

The Gravity of Districts/Small Towns

Small towns are an important but often neglected element of rural landscape and food supply system. They perform several essential functions, from market nodes for food producers and processors to providers of services, goods and non-agro based employment to their population and that of their surrounding rural region. They are also home to about half the world's urban population and are projected to absorb much of its growth in the next few decades. Such is their importance that they no longer be ignored by policies concerning poverty reduction, food and nutrition security.

With regards to regional planning policies, small towns can contribute to regional and rural development in **five main ways**:

1. By acting as centres of demand/markets for agricultural produce from the rural region, either for local consumers or as links to national and export markets. Access to markets is a prerequisite to increase rural agricultural income, and the proximity of local small and intermediate centres to production areas is assumed to be a key factor.
2. By acting as center's for the production, distribution of goods and services to their rural region. Such concentration is assumed to reduce costs and improve access to a variety of services, both public and private and for both rural households and enterprises. Hence, services include agricultural extension, health and education (and access to other government services), as well as banking, post, services of professionals such as lawyers and accountants, lower-order services such as bars and restaurants, and wholesale and retail sales of manufactured goods from within and outside the region.
3. By becoming centres for the growth and consolidation of rural non-farm activities and employment, through the development of small and medium-sized enterprises or the relocation of branches of large private or parasitic enterprises.
4. By attracting rural migrants from the surrounding region through demand for non-farm labor, and thereby decreasing pressure on larger urban centres.
5. By managing natural resources in ways that respond to the needs of growing rural and urban population with special attention to protecting natural habitat.

A recent study by Urmila Chatterjee, Rinku Murgai and Martin Rama from the World Bank suggest that small towns have contributed significantly in generating non-farm employment as compared to large cities. Another study by John Gibson, Gaurav Datt, Rinku Murgai and Martin Ravalli on also highlights the importance of small towns in rural poverty alleviation compared to large cities.[2]

But it is the approach to urbanization which continues to remain fixated with large metropolitan cities that have rendered these small towns **Trishankus**, a term used by Jairam Ramesh, the cabinet minister in the previous government. The absence of an administrative structure suited to urban governance eludes them since they are counted as rural in the administrative scheme of the government. The 'neither here, nor there' status of these census towns and small towns raises important questions of sustainability of these as drivers of growth[3].

WHAT MIGHT BE THE PULL FACTORS?

Push and pull factors in geography, refer to the causes of migration among people from one place or native place to others. The reasons can be social, economic, environmental or political. People migrate from a place because of unsustainable conditions such as insecurity or unemployment - these are referred to as **push factors** as they drive people towards better life factors. The factors which attract people to live in a particular environment can include security, employment, political stability and climate. They are referred to as **pull factors**.

The pull factor that attracts the youth and unemployed is the learning of IT skills and preparation for the competitive examinations. Vocational coaching and skill-based courses are the best when compared to towns. It also attracts unskilled workers from villages in search of alternative employment, mainly in construction and its allied fields. As the population increases, the need for transport also increases considerably, even though metro rail and other public transport are available in the cities. The need for cabs, autos and other means has become another important source of income and decent employment to a certain extent.

We can witness many auto and cab drivers from rural background work for their livelihood, as their native villages do not guarantee proper employment or provide options to try and test their skills. It is not only the case of Hyderabad, but similar to all metropolitan cities. As the migrants desire a steady income, they can earn via varied job opportunities and support their families. Most of the construction workers hail from the neighboring states and villages. We can witness security guards employed, hail from other states and cities earning their livelihood with dignity.

Cities are, after all, not just densely populated areas within the confines of an arbitrary administrative boundary. They are an agglomeration of firms and workers. Urbanism Alain Bertaud refers to cities as labor markets. Hence, the actual limits of cities may at times go beyond administrative limits.

So, why aren't we even taking the first step of recognizing more of India as urban? Losing access to centrally sponsored schemes that are targeted at rural areas, like the Mahatma Gandhi National Rural Employment Guarantee Scheme or Pradhan Mantri Gram SadakYojana, is one of the main reasons why rural political leaders, as well as rural residents, resist conversion from RLBs to ULBs. Anecdotal evidence and qualitative research also throw light on other reasons for resisting conversion—the fear among residents that they may have to pay higher taxes, say, or fear among local politicians that they may lose power and access[4].

The reality of the Cities in a pandemic:

Most of the cities have a deserted look and the migratory people shifting from cities to their native towns and villages. We witness fear and insecurity among them, staying back in cities, high cost of living and minimal job offers. The labor section is the worst hit by the pandemic as major projects, either private or govt. aided have come to standstill. The concentration of covid cases is too high in 10 states across India and in major 10- 12 cities. The density of population and the slums associated can certainly be the cause for the spread of the pandemic and create panic in the minds of the commoners.

The Pandemic that Shook the Urban Workforce-IMPACT:

India added a record 14,000+ new Covid-19 cases, with high surges in Delhi, Maharashtra and Uttar Pradesh, among other states. Maharashtra and Delhi recorded their biggest single-day jumps, with 3,752 and 2,877 fresh infections, respectively. The surge came on a day when the number of people who have recovered from the disease crossed the 200,000 mark. With 14,052 cases, India's Covid-19 caseload stood at over 381,000 lakh, with active cases rising to more than 164,000, as per data from state governments. The previous high for the national case count was set just a day earlier when 13,219 cases were reported.

Apart from Maharashtra and Delhi, Uttar Pradesh reported its biggest surge in infections, with 630 new cases reported on Thursday. The states of Andhra Pradesh (every day nearly 10,000 new cases) and Telangana (2000 cases) also recorded their highest single-day numbers so far.

Table 3.1

Urban Agglomeration	*CFR*	*Cases/ million*	*Deaths/ million*	*Growth rate (14 days)*	
				Deaths	*Cases*
Ahmedabad	7.6	2,083	157	2.3	1.7
Kolkata	5.4	599	32	2.7	4.1
Bengaluru	5.2	69	4	9.7	5.0
Mumbai	4.8	3,869	187	6.2	2.8
Pure	4.7	1,865	87	3.6	3.2
Delhi	4.0	2,332	94	8.5	5.0
Surat	4.0	371	15	2.6	2.9
Chennai	1.3	3,496	46	8.0	5.1
Hyderabad	0.6	407	3	0.0	5.7
Total (9 cities)	4.2	1,899	79	55	3.7

According to research by the *Times Intelligence Group*, **Ahmadabad** has the highest case fatality rate and **Mumbai** the highest number of cases and deaths per million among the country›s nine largest megalopolises. However, the growth of cases and deaths over the last fortnight has been sharpest in Bangalore, Chennai and Delhi. Worryingly, the case fatality rate (CFR) — the number of deaths for every 100 positive cases — has worsened over this period in six of the nine cities *(see graphic)*. The jump in CFR in Delhi, Mumbai and Chennai, to a significant extent, is because of the addition of hundreds of earlier deaths following data reconciliation exercises.

The Major Role of Migrants in Cities

We need to understand clearly that, we cannot build cities and infrastructure without the migrant labourers as the native or local workforce will not be enough to cope with the needs of the city. Invariably, we need them yet; we do ignore them, once our work or project is completed. We gaze at the skyscrapers with great pride and accomplishment, but yet the lives of the people who labored and toiled to raise such huge structures, still face the plight of survival.

We have witnessed a phenomenal migration, since the past four months of lockdown. Maybe, because of the improper and untimely delayed policies of the governments, we are shocked to hear that hundreds of labors died on their journey back home to their villages. Its heart rendering to eyewitness people die of hunger and thirst on the highways. The journey of the migrants began as the cities, they toiled and labored for, suddenly rendered them homeless, cutting their supplies with no income. They gazed at the cities, the leaders desperately and expected a little support in tough times, but none came to their rescue.

Fatigued by their long journey on foot, 16 migrant workers returning home to Madhya Pradesh from Maharashtra where they worked in a steel factory fell asleep on the railway tracks and were crushed to death by a goods train on Friday, May 8, 2020.

In another incident, five migrant workers died when the truck that carried them and many others from Hyderabad, Telangana, to their villages in Uttar Pradesh, overturned on the night of Saturday, May 9.2020.

We need to appreciate the noble gesture of kindness shown by Mr.Sonu Sood (Bollywood Actor) and team Sending **migrant** workers to their homes. But the manner in which, he assures them in tweets and messages, that they are definitely going home is truly heartening. What **Sonu and his team** did for the **migrant** workers is what India is known to stand for -harmony, equality, peace, and brotherhood. For migrant workers, he is God incarnate by not only saving their lives but also helping them reach their destination with dignity, pride and comfort. The best act is that he never asked for any funds as he bore the entire expenses amounting to crores.

Need to Redefine The Labour Laws

The recent dilution of the labor laws in three states to push forth economic recovery has been initiated. The cumulative picture is of a blatant disjunction between the reality of the worker-migrant and the policy adopted to tackle the crisis of 'the labor question.'

Declining labor standards exhibit this trend in a fairly long-term framework. A 2015 research paper in *Seminar*, pointed out that in the organized manufacturing sector, the share of profits has tripled from 20-60% of net value- added, whereas the labor share has fallen by exact same proportion since the 1980s. Almost at the same time scale (1980s-2012), as Prabhu Mohapatra points out, 'contract labor' (through the subcontracting system) in the manufacturing sector has risen from 7-35%.

Perception

The recent decoding in labor laws has led to a crucial shift in the way the plight of the worker-migrants has been understood in the foreground of COVID-19 induced lockdown. Until now, for much of the mainstream media and to a larger extent, the middle-class, the worker-migrant was a figure of aberration. The group that did not follow the strictures laid out for the lockdown, were questioned and even ridiculed as irresponsible, opportunistic and insensible. Their divided social and household locations – sharing a tenement in the city and having a 'home' in the village, which is an outcome of the nature of the labor market – was downplayed to create an image of their reckless behavior[5].

Rights Amidst Shady Grooves

In 1952, when India's Supreme Court upheld the rights of citizens to assemble peacefully, it said the Constitution had assigned the responsibility of guarding against violations of fundamental rights, the way a sentinel protects, Sixty eight years later, the sentinel seems to be letting its guard down.

Across India, lakhs of migrant workers, their livelihoods devastated by the nationwide lockdown to slow the spread of Covid-19, are walking hundreds of kilometers in an attempt to get back to their home villages. Approximately 120 of them have died in accidents along the way. While the Centre mounted a massive mission titled "Vande Bharat" to bring back Indians stranded overseas, it has not shown the same zeal in trying to get poor workers to reach their homes. Instead, the Centre has put the blame on the state for the chaos.

In the post-Emergency era, the Supreme Court developed the idea of public interest litigation (PIL) into a diverse and potent jurisdiction. The court became activist, intervening in issues that involved the public good. Since then, many Indians have looked up to the Supreme Court not only to check state excesses when it violates rights but also as a powerful institution that will nudge the government to do the right thing. Environment protection, for example, owes a great debt to the jurisprudence of public interest litigation.

The court has used PILs so much over the decades that it had even led to criticism that it was transgressing constitutional boundaries and involving itself into policymaking. So it has come as no surprise that several activists and lawyers have approached the Supreme Court over the last few weeks, urging it to help the migrant workers.

They expected the court to act as the sentinel of the rights of the workers. But it has fared poorly, accepting the government's submissions almost mechanically, not doing much to alleviate the sufferings of the workers. If the Supreme Court was looking for models for how it could have acted, some were right under its nose. Last week, two High Courts, through orders that were marked by empathy and concern, held up a mirror to the Supreme Court.

Migrant Crisis: SC Lays Out Interim Guidelines

Almost 64 days after the central government imposed lockdown, with just four hours' notice, a nationwide lockdown for the first time and afterwards thrice extending it, albeit, with more relaxations each time, the Supreme Court on Thursday issued interim directives to ensure proper repatriation of India's internal migrants. A bench of Justices Ashok Bhushan, SK Kaul and MR Shah said:

- No fare either by train or bus will be charged from migrant workers. Railways to share fare.
- All migrants who are stranded shall be provided food by the concerned state at places publicized and notified to them so that they can make both ends meet. While they wait for their turn to board trains or buses, they can survive this way.
- The Originating state should provide food and water and thereafter, food to be provided by the Railways. Receiving state shall give transport, food and water from stations to their villages.
- States shall speed up registration of migrant workers and build help desks near places where they are stranded. Complete information needs to be publicized so that migrants are aware of this.

- Whenever a migrant is found walking on the road they will be taken to the camps at the earliest and provided with facilities.

Justice Bhushan also observed that "there needs to be a time in a place which the migrant worker has to wait within which he will be transported and also be provided food and facilities in the interim," reports the Bar and Bench. The court then called for a "uniform policy" on the matter to avoid confusion between the states, centre and the railways.

"But... it is a sad situation that some lawyers and retired judges are trying to run down the institution," the bench observed. The SC took Suo Moto cognizance of the migrant crisis after several retired judges and senior advocates wrote to Chief Justice SA Bob decriticizing the court for its "deference" to the executive even "in the face of an unfolding human disaster". On Thursday, in the audience were Kapil Sibal, P Chidambaram and Indira Jaising, who were among the signatories of the letter[6].

Did We Contain the Pandemic Crisis

In the second tranche of COVID-19 relief package announcement, Finance Minister Nirmala Sitharaman announced the steps taken by the government for migrants and farmers during the lockdown, including free ration for stranded workers. Acknowledging the significance of the Mahatma Gandhi National Rural Employment Guarantee Scheme (MGNREGS) during the pandemic, she said it had helped provide jobs to returning workers in rural areas and advised States to continue the process in the monsoon season as well. Migrant workers, the urban poor and small farmers are the targeted beneficiaries of this announcements[7].

The National Sample Survey Office of the Ministry of Statistics and Programme Implementation had estimated that there were around 1,49,53,750 urban workers who had vulnerable jobs. These workers included helpers in a household enterprise and who did not receive a regular salary and casual labourers who received daily wages; besides this, the number considers only those in the bottom 50% of the wealth pyramid in 2017-18, based on their monthly per capita expenditure. This number extended to an estimated 2.5 crore people, if those who had salaried jobs but did not receive any paid leave and other benefits were included. Migrant workers numbered more than 81 lakh people among this segment.

Is it Time for an Urban Employment Guarantee Scheme?

Ashima Goyal, professor at the Indira Gandhi Institute of Development Research and a member of the Economic Advisory Council to the Prime

Minister, has suggested that India should consider an urban employment guarantee scheme, like the Mahatma Gandhi National Rural Employment Guarantee Act (MGNREGA), for urban poor to limit the damage caused by the pandemic. Goyal said the view was personal and not in her capacity as an advisor to the government[7].

The background

The coronavirus pandemic is projected to cause a contraction of the Indian economy this fiscal year. The World Bank said the Indian economy could shrink by 3.2% this fiscal, while the Organization of Economic Co-operation and Development (OECD) has projected 3.7% or less depending on two scenarios of the outbreak. An economic contraction (or even slower growth) causes higher unemployment.

A recent study by the King's College, London and the Australian National University said the pandemic could push global poverty above 1 billion people once again, and much of the impact is likely to be felt in emerging Asian economies of India, Bangladesh, Indonesia and the like. In India's case, the higher proportion of informal workers — who are not accorded the safety net of formal employment — makes it particularly vulnerable. The International Labour Organization (ILO) in April stated that the pandemic could push 400 million workers in India, deeper into poverty. Another cause of concern is the state of migrant workers, especially seasonal migrants — those who move between rural and urban India based on agricultural seasons. Since the lockdown, many of these workers have returned home, but the rural economy is not capable of absorbing such a large number of workers, even with the MGNREGA. An urban employment scheme could prevent further reverse-migration to rural India, say some experts.

A Roadmap

Researchers at the Azim Premji University and the Centre for Sustainable Employment last year said India could implement an urban employment scheme in around 4,000 smaller cities and towns, which is decentralized and overseen by the urban local bodies, but with the cost borne by the central and state government. A guaranteed wage of Rs 500 a day for 100 days for the urban poor in such towns could cost between 1.7% and 2.7% of GDP, the researchers said.

Vice President, Mr.M Venkaiah Naidu underlined the need for "proper" data on migrant workers to help authorities impart them with required skills and provide employment opportunities as the country exits the coronavirus-triggered lockdown. In a Facebook post on the novel coronavirus and ways to deal with it, he said, unfortunately, the poor, the daily wage earners, farmers, and small businesses have been severely affected by the events triggered by the pandemic.

The governments at the Centre and in the states have taken several measures to alleviate the suffering of the poor and the needy, especially migrant workers, he said. "The recent events underline the need for having proper data on the migrants in the country. Creating such data will help the governments to impart skills and create employment opportunities to them in their respective places".

At the same, there is a need to create awareness among the migrants on the facilities available for their welfare and upliftment, he opined. Over the past few weeks, lakhs of migrant workers have returned to their native states as the lockdown had rendered them jobless[8].

HYDERABAD, TELANGANA

The state government, in a decisive step, has come to the rescue of migrant labourers stuck in Telangana on account of the nationwide lockdown. Chief Minister, K. Chandrasekhar Rao, speaking to the media, said all their needs would be taken care of.

"We will provide them with shelter and 12-kg rice, in addition to Rs. 500 to each member of a family of a maximum of four. "The CM added that there are about 3.5 lakh migrant labourers in Telangana, who mostly hail from Jharkhand and Bihar. Reiterating that the government would not let the migrants starve, Mr CM said, they could approach any MLA, the Collector or the SP, if they meet with trouble[9].

DID THE GOVT. JUSTIFY THEIR PLIGHT

The labourers make up nearly one-fifth of India's workforce, building its cities and running its factories. Their anguish has been a constant backdrop of the country's coronavirus response since;Mr Modi announced a lockdown from March 25 with just four hours' notice, leaving many stranded with no cash and no support from local authorities.

Fig. 3.1

One policy misstep that may hurt the administration in places like Bihar was a plan to use special trains to ferry workers home cities to rural villages. It started only a month into the lockdown and has been mired in chaos and tragedy. Many people had no choice but to walk or cycle hundreds of kilometres, dragging luggage and carrying children on their shoulders. One desperate group travelled inside the cavity of a cement mixer. Hundreds perished on the way with starvation and casualties.

Migrant workers wait in a bus on the banks of the Yamuna while being transferred to a shelter in Delhi, on April 15.

"These migrants used to speak highly of Modi, but now they are very critical," said Shaibal Gupta, an economist and founder of the Asian Development Research Institute in Bihar, a non-profit organization that specializes in economics, politics and development. Their discontent at the "raw deal" they received from the government will have an impact. There has already been an outbreak of social unrest. In the city of Surat in PM Modi's home state of Gujarat, police subdued angry workers with tear gas in five separate clashes in April and May as citizens demanded that, the government arrange trains to help them return to villages.

"Most migrant labors decided to move when the lockdown was extended and some incidents were indeed tragic," said spokesman Shahnawaz Hussain. "But the government moved quickly and showed that it cared for them and was committed to their wellbeing," he said.

The main opposition party has, so far, failed to seize the political moment despite its harsh criticism of the government. Congress spokesman, Manish Tewari said the attitude of Modi's administration toward the workers was clear: "'You broke the lockdown, now go to hell.' Nothing else can explain their brutalization."

Unprotected by unions and politicians, migrants are often at the mercy of their employers for wages and benefits in industries such as textiles, garments and construction. They've struggled to access the $277 billion support package announced by Finance Minister Nirmala Sitharaman, which promised cheap credit to farmers, direct transfer of money to the poor and easier access to food security programs.

Kishen Kumar Sharma, 28, who's paralyzed from the waist down following an accident, was being treated in a Delhi hospital until the virus outbreak put the country's medical system on red alert. His treatment stopped, both his brothers lost their jobs and they were thrown out of their rented room and had to live on the streets for a week.

"Even animals are treated better," Mr Sharma said as he pushed his wheelchair along the highway trying to cover the 800 kilometers to his village in the northern state of Uttar Pradesh while his family members walked with him.

Let's Uphold the Truth

Action plan based on Facts

Decentralization

All state governments have to realize, that we have to focus on towns and villages and concentrate on decentralization. We have witnessed, Mr Jagan Mohan Reddy (CM Andhra Pradesh) idea of having their capital city seems to be a welcome sign as he had foresighted the situation much in advance. Other states should not allow their cities to spread further and restrict the activity. This act must be extended to the suburbs and towns. We need to understand the hard fact and develop satellite cities with much concentration on class 1 to class 4 towns. It will be too late if we don't understand the gravity of the situation and it is a caution call to all of us as to, what we need to do in the near future for the next generation.

Observations

When we take a close look at the date available to us on the spread of the COVID-19, it is restricted to major cities of our country. Nearly 70 to 80 percent cases are from the top 10 cities only due to the density of population. The cities are spread with blotches of slums and we have witnessed the case of the Dharavi slum in Mumbai. The covid count was the highest in India and second being Delhi, where the density of population is quite high. Delhi, being the capital of India, all preventive and precautionary measures taken by the state and central government agencies went futile.

Dharavi is a locality in Mumbai, Maharashtra, India, considered to be one of Asia's largest slums. Dharavi has an area of just over 2.1 square kilometres (0.81 sq miles); and a population of about 1,000,000. With a population density of over 277,136/km^2 (717,780/sq mi), Dharavi becomes one of the most densely populated areas in the world. India's slum population was about 104 million in 2017 or around 9 percent of the total projected national population of 1.28 billion that year. We can hardly imagine the steep rise in slum population based on the latest census.

This means, that the urban population will face escalating challenges as these slums will mostly proliferate in sleepy towns and in a semi-rural area, consequences of an accelerating rural to urban shift across the nation.

According to data provided in parliament, the states of Maharashtra, Uttar Pradesh, AP,Telangana and MP will host largest chunks of India's slum population, in times to come.

Permanent Means to Contain Migration Laborer's

The respective state governments and the agencies that hire the migration laborer's must provide certain basic accommodation as long as they work for a particular project.

1. They should be insured up to ten lakhs.
2. They need to have Aadhaar card and they can avail ration irrespective of their native place. One Unique rationing card should be issued so that it can be applied anywhere in India.
3. The management's should also look after their family welfare by insuring them or issuing family health card.
4. They should be provided with decent hygienic conditions i.e. neat toilets and bathrooms and not neglect their basic minimum needs.
5. In a situation of distress or a pandemic, the management and the government should stand by them and provide all necessary provisions and instill confidence among these migrant workers.

These are some of the critical observations and causative measures that we can ponder on, so that the working /wager segment of our society is benefited to build a better and stronger India. All the major projects of our state and nation are labored by the efforts of the toiling section of our society. Let's try to sense the pain and agony the migrant labors faced on their tiring journey back home, hungry, and empty-handed and with no hope.

Smart City-A Vision

A developed urban area that creates a sustainable economic base and better quality of life by excelling in multiple key areas i.e. economy, mobility, environment, people, living, and government. Excelling in these key areas can be done so by strong human capital, social capital, and/or ICT infrastructure.

The Smart City

The cities which are capable of handling the pandemic effectively and that can save the lives of its citizen, has the infrastructure to withstand any natural or unnatural calamity without panic can be considered as the smartest city.

Highlights of Mr.Venkaiah Naidu's Speech While Announcing the List of Smart Cities

1. Making cities smart will make them engines of economic growth besides giving decent life to the citizens.
2. 13 crore population across 98 cities which is 35% of the urban population will be covered under the Smart City Mission.

3. Central government proposes to give financial support to Mission to the extent of Rs 48,000 crores over 5 years.
4. State/UTs & urban local bodies have an important role to play in the implementation of Smart City Mission.

Five Elements of the Proposed Smart Cities Identified by the Urban Development Ministry

1. In terms of infrastructure, smart cities should have 24x7, availability of quality utility services like water and power.
2. A robust transport system that emphasizes on public transport is also a key element.
3. In social infrastructure, the cities should provide opportunities for jobs and livelihoods for its inhabitants.
4. Thc smart cities should also have proper facilities for entertainment and the safety and security of the people. State-of-the-art health and education facilities are also a must.
5. The smart cities should minimize waste by increasing energy efficiency and reducing water conservation. Proper recycling of waste materials must be done in such cities.

The government on Thursday (27-08-2015)released a list of 98 cities, including 24 state capitals, which are to be developed as smart cities….

List of Smart Cities Released by the Government

Port Blair, Vishakhapatnam, Tirupati, Kakinada, Pasig hat, Guwahati, Muzaffarpur, Bhagalpur, Biharsharif, Chandigarh, Raipur, Bilaspur, Diu, Silvassa, NDMC, Panaji, Gandhinagar, Ahmedabad, Surat, Vadodara, Rajkot, Dahod, Karnal, Faridabad, Dharamsala, Ranchi, Mangaluru, Belagavi, Shivamogga, Hubballi-Dharwad, Tumakuru, Davanegere, Kochi, Kavaratti, Bhopal, Indore, Jabalpur, Gwalior, Sagar, Satna, Ujjain, Navi Mumbai, Nasik, Thane, Greater Mumbai, Amaravati, Solapur, Nagpur, Kalyan-Dombivalli, Aurangabad, Pune, Imphal, Shillong, Aizawl, Kohima, Bhubaneswar, Rourkela, Oulgaret, Ludhiana, Jalandhar, Amritsar, Jaipur, Udaipur, Kota, Ajmer, Namchi, Tiruchirapalli, Tirunelveli, Dindigul, Thanjavur, Tiruppur, Salem, Vellore, Coimbatore, Madurai, Erode, Thoothukudi, Chennai, Greater Hyderabad, Greater warangal, Agartala, Moradabad, Aligarh, Shaharanpur, Bareilly, Jhansi, Kanpur, Allahabad, Lucknow, Varanasi, Ghaziabad, Agra, Rampur, Dehradun, New Town Kolkata, Bidhannagar, Durgapur, Haldia[10].

POPULATION LIVING IN SLUMS (% OF URBAN POPULATION) – INDIA

Definition:

Population living in slums is the proportion of the urban population living in slum household. A slum household is defined as a group of individuals living under the same roof lacking one or more of the following conditions: access to improved water, access to improved sanitation, sufficient living area, and durability of housing.

According to the estimate made by the Committee on **Slum** Statistics/ Census, the **slum population** constituted 75.26 million (26.31 **percent**) out of the 286 million urban **population** of the country in 2001. As per the estimates, the **slum population** of **India** is estimated to have reached 93.06 million in 2011and estimated 104 million by 2017.The United Nations report on **India's** urban **population** was projected at 33 crores in 2001, 45.4 crores in 2010, 59.1 crores in **2020** and 65.8 crores by 2025 against the projected **population** of 122 crores approximately.

THE METROPOLITAN COVID SCENARIO-A STUDY

In 2018, Mumbai was found to be home of the highest number of millionaires, followed by India's capital New Delhi, and the IT capital - Bangalore. This comes as no surprise since all three cities have the largest share of high net worth households along with a booming economic outlook. Overall, India had around 104 billionaires in 2019 and ranked fifth globally in terms of its ultra-net-worth individuals[11].

Hyderabad city has a population of over one crore with more than 450millionaires or the super-rich class. However, due tocovid-19, everyone is affected irrespective of income group, except for the small Kirana vendors, Milk vendors, Medical stores and fruits vendors as they can sustain by selling utilities. The rest of the private or the working class from varied sectors is severely affected, except for the state and central government employees'. It is a pathetic state of affairs as unemployment has hit the roof and most of the software companies had to terminate or lay down their employees.

The Problems faced by the employees working in private schools or in petty shops and street vendors do face arduous time to sustain during this crucial period. The state and the central governments are issuing free provisions to the white ration cardholders. But this pandemic has created havoc and added unbearing problems to the lives of the lower middle class. They are barely able to sustain their basic needs and stand helpless in agony.

The point we intend to state here is that, except the rich, i.e. 10 percent of the population of our city, they remain unaffected by the pandemic. But, nearly 90 percent need help and support from the Government. As some states are providing free ration twice a month, whatever measure taken by both the state and the central governments are merely satisfying a certain segment of the society. We believe that this act of support to sustain should be extended to all the needful in our society. This though may be hard to digest, but it's an open reality and the policies need to be revised.

Doctors–God Incarnate

Health Care

We need health care, free of cost and insurance of all the individuals should be taken care of, by the state and central governments. Earlier, we used to have Arogayasri, for the white ration card holders, not only in government hospitals but can also avail medical services in private hospitals. We need to extend the same to those who do not have white ration card, or be grant a concession on the medical billing of at least 50 percent from the government.

We need more doctors

The irony of our health care system is that we have only one doctor for every 1,445 Indians as per the country's current population estimate at 135 crores, which is way lower than the WHO's prescribed norm of one doctor for every 1,000 people, as stated on November-2019. The concerned government and key medical policymakers must ponder on this issue very seriously. As we have realized the importance of having sufficient medicos in govt. hospitals to fight this pandemic situation. There has to more number of medicos and policymakers must take a serious note of it. This is the need of the hour.

Preserve our Cities for the Future Generation:

We have never seen such a pandemic affecting more than 200 countries across the globe. The whole world is still fighting with this deadly virus and most of the countries are under lockdown. All national and international borders are sealed to protect the world and it is our duty as responsible citizens to collectively follow social distancing. We got to protect our world and we should give a healthy environment to our future generations such that they can breathe clean air, drink clean water and enjoy the beautiful bounteous gifts of Mother Nature.

We need to decentralize our activities and it is not advisable to concentrate on the expansion of existing metropolitan cities. We are encouraging the real-estate mafia to construct more flats as we need to understand the physical and resource capacity of the city. Can the city accommodate or will it cause disastrous damage to the existing city structure? We have witnessed, no city can withstand a 10 cms rainfall in India. The existing cities are designed for alimited population with all its natural resources.The existing drainage system needs to be upgraded to accommodate the growing populace. We need to justify the people by providing all basic amenities. On the health sector, we claim to have the world's best infrastructure and facilities, but we have witnessed from the day of lockdown, where we rate ourselves in healthcare? We don't have the basic health check equipment's and beds to accommodate patients in case of emergency. This is the plight in some of the best, so-called advanced Govt. hospitals with the latest technology.

We need the 108 and 104 services with well-equipped facilities as few state governments are proving in each and every Mandal. It is surprising to note that we barely have 92 vehicles for 108 services for a population of one crore in Hyderabad city, out of which only 42 vehicles are provided for the Covid emergency patients. In the entire Telangana state, we have not more than 400,on road ambulance vans, which are not sufficient. We have Primary Health Centres and Praja Hospitals, Basti Dawakanas recently inaugurated during covid times. Are they going to cater to the health needs of the people? People are scared of visiting government hospitals as we have failed in this aspect. The need of the hour is to instill faith and confidence in the heart of the common man.

Need to Develop Towns and Villages

A total of 2.7 million officials visited households in 7,935 *towns* and 600,000 *villages*, classifying the *population* according to gender, religion, education and occupation. We conclude that the majority of India, still lives in villages.

We need to develop villages and towns in a phased manner and restrict the growth of the major metropolitan cities from overcrowding and overpopulating. Due to the pandemic, most of the working class in the Metros and cities has moved to their hometowns and villages. And this sudden shift has created a serious imbalance with regards to human resource. The present urban population stands at35- 40 percent approximately i.e. still 60 percent of the people live in rural India.

In mid-2009 it was declared that the tipping point has been crossed: World urban population crossed the 50% mark for the first time in human history. Contrary to the general impression, the bulk of this urban population does not stay in big metros. Over 53% of the world's total urban population of 3.4 billion resides in towns with less than 5 lakh population. Of these, about 1.14 billion, or one third, stay in towns with less than 1 lakh population[12].

Gandhi's views on Village Development

We would say that, if the village perishes, India will perish too. India will be no more be India. Her own mission in the world will get lost. The revival of the village is possible, only, when it is no more exploited. Industrialization on a mass scale will necessarily lead to the passive or active exploitation of the villagers as the problem of competition and marketing comes in. Therefore, we have to concentrate on the village being self-contained, manufacturing mainly for use. Provided, this character of the village industry is maintained, there would be no objection to villagers using even the modern machines and tools that they can make and can afford to use. They should not be used as a means of exploitation by others.

The real India lies in the 7,00,000 villages. If Indian civilization is to make its full contribution to the building up of stable world order, it is this vast mass of humanity that has to be made to live again. We have to tackle the triple malady which holds our villages fast in its grip: (I) want of corporate sanitation; (ii) deficient diet; (iii) inertia . . . They [villagers] are not interested in their own welfare. They don't appreciate modern sanitary methods. They don't want to exert themselves beyond scratching their farms or doing such labor as they are used to. These difficulties are real and serious. But they must not baffle us.

We must have an unquenchable faith in our mission. We must be patient with the people. We are ourselves novices in village work. We have to deal with a chronic disease. Patience and perseverance, if we have them, can overcome mountains of difficulties. We are like nurses, who may not leave their patients because they are reported to have an incurable disease. Villages have suffered long from neglect by those who have had the benefit of education. They have chosen the city life. The village movement is an attempt to establish healthy contact with the villages by inducing those, who are fired up with the spirit of service to settle in them and find self-expression in the service of villagers.

Gaons (villages) isn't a bad place to live In fact, some of them are way better than any metro. And these exemplary examples prove just that. Only those, therefore, who have faith in themselves and in their mission will serve the villagers and influence their lives. ***-M.K Gandhi***

References

1. https://worldpopulationreview.com/countries/india-population/cities
2. https://pubs.iied.org/pdfs/10815IIED.pdf

3. https://www.livemint.com/Opinion/1duwvJZqyB5oZKVFFxm55H/Making-small-towns-a-priority-for- growth.htmlhttps://www.livemint.com/Opinion/1duwvJZqyB5oZKVFFxm55H/Making-small-towns-a-priority-for-growth.html
4. https://www.livemint.com/news/india/why-india-has-the-fastest-growing-cities-11580053066942.html
5. https://thewire.in/labour/migrant-worker-crisis-lockdown
6. Times of India
7. https://www.thehindu.com/news/national/coronavirus-package-will-migrant-workers-benefit-from-the-centres-measures/article31603590.ece
8. https://www.outlookindia.com/newsscroll/naidu-underlines-need-for-proper-data-on-migrant-workers/1857986
9. https://www.newindianexpress.com/states/telangana/2020/mar/30/migrant-labourers-in-telangana-will-be-looked-after-kcr-2123310.html
10. https://www.blogger.com/u/1/blog/post/edit/3610750404571258183/9176544870096665997
11. https://timesofindia.indiatimes.com/india/53-of-urban-population-lives-in-small-towns/articleshow/5729437.cms
12. Source: https://www.statista.com/statistics/652926/number-of-millionaires-by-city-india/

Urban Environment and Spatial Science
Dr Mohd Akhter Ali, Dr. Kabir Mohan Sethy, Dr Muzafar Wani and M.Kamraju
Ane Books Pvt. Ltd. 2021, ISBN : 978-93-90658-28-2, P.P. : 39 – 58

4

"Analysis of Urban Sprawl and Water Dynamics of Kalinganagar Industrial Region of Jajpur District of ODISHA"

Panigrahi. S, Giri. S, Sethy. K.M
[1]*Research Scholar, Department of Geography, Utkal University, Vanivihar, Bhubaneswar.*
[2]*Professor, Department of Geography, Utkal University, Vanivihar, Bhubaneswar.*

Abstract

Today urban sprawl is one of the contemporary issues of the cities all over the world. Rapid industrialization and over population leads to uncontrolled or uncoordinated growth spreads towards the zone of influence, the rural land and its periphery of an urban area. With this rapid urban expansion, the quality of environment is getting degraded which is a serious threat for the people living near and the surrounding areas. The present paper is an attempt to identify the physical driving factors of urban sprawl and analyze the rate of urban growth in Kalinganagar, Jajpur district. A detail comparative analysis of landsue of 2005 and 2020 has been done to find out the development and growth of Sprawl at Kalinganagar Urban Area Development Authority. Also a detailed quantitative analysis has been done to show the spatial changes in land use which is arising out of dynamic interaction between urban function and its impact on the health and environment quality. Development of Urban sprawl usually create a threat in water pollution in Industrial Regions. In study area an attempt has been made to find out the water dynamics through some of

Corresponding Author: Panigrahi. S

the statistical methods. The key findings shows the rapid growth of sprawl and environmental threats in this area.

Keywords: Change detection of land use, Sprawl, Environmental degradation, Kalinganagar.

Introduction

Change of human activities from primary to secondary and tertiary usually leads to the change of standards of living of human beings in the present time. Starting from the medieval period to the modern era, the development of the scientific knowhow has been changing the characteristics of the settlements/ habitation from rural to urban. The 21st century observes the rapid growth of industrialization which leads to the fast growth of urbanization. In India, due to the urban development, the rural migration to the urban areas for employment is very high as per the census data.

Decrease of interest in agriculture among the young population leads to the increase in migration from rural to urban. Odisha, one of the coastal states of India, is full of natural resources which attracts the industrial activity from the different corners of the country and outside of the country. Rapid industrialization leads to the fast growth of cities and towns and change in land use pattern. Urbanization is a process that leads to the growth of cities due to industrialization and economic development and that leads to urban specific changes in specialization, labour division, and human behaviors. Industrialization is the basic driving force of urbanization and urbanized cities are the important land for industrialization. Industrialization is the initiator of urbanization and urbanization is the inevitable result of industrialization .This leads to transformation of the social and economic pillar and human society into an industrial one. Urbanization typically begins when a factory or multiple factories are established within a region thus creating a high demand for factory labour and other business such as building manufactures, retailers and service providers.

In simple words, as population increases in an area or city it expands to accommodate the growth, this expansion is called as sprawl. "Sprawl in simple terms is the spreading out of the city over the rural and at the periphery of the urban area". Urban sprawl leads to urban growth.

Oxford English dictionary (2001) defines the word as "straggling expansion of an intermediate urban or industrial environment into an adjoining countryside; the area of this advancement.

There is a trend representing a shift from the old agricultural practices to non agricultural jobs creating a modernized society. Now the people from different region migrate towards the industrial areas as they have got the chance to work in various industrial sectors to stir the economic development. This process leads to the shift of surplus population from rural to urban areas along with the gradual growth of some industrialized urban centers. Due to the social and economic issues people from backward villages and nearby areas tend to move or get attracted towards the fringe areas in search of new jobs, as newly established industries and ancillary activities offer more job opportunities. There is an increase in the pace of change in land use pattern of the area as it leads to the changing landscape of human settlement with significant implication for living, environmental and developmental conditions in different parts of the nearby areas and changes in infrastructure and services.

With rapid urban growth in the Jajpur town urban land transformation has taken place in large scale from agricultural land, river banks etc for urban uses, which includes development of residential areas conversion of agricultural land to plotted land development acquired primarily for future residential requirements.

This transformation of land into industrial land use to residential housing was possible due to developed transport facilities easy communication availability of natural resources (land, water, minerals) and nearby urban centers (Khorda, Bhubneswar,Bhadrak,Cuttack,Paradeep). All these development are under the process of converting the primarily agricultural land which tends to indefinite type of growth and expansion. This undergoing rapid changes leads to the haphazard and uncontrollable growth towards the peripheral of urban centers called as the "sprawl" which is a significant contributor to land use pattern/ change.

There are many key driving force of urban sprawl such as:

Sprawl is considered as economically vital and not an environmental threat. Somehow uncontrolled momentum of urban sprawl and land use change raise many issues which might have both positive and negative impacts.

Positive impacts: rise in economic growth, region becomes highly urbanized, increase in living standard, improved connectivity.

Negative impacts: environmental degradation, human health hazards, loss in agricultural productivity.

Whenever activity grows there is urban growth which creates huge loss and negative impacts on the environment, which is found in both the developing and developed region. Basically sprawl in developed countries is usually 'a matter of preference' where as in developing countries it is a result of 'necessity'.

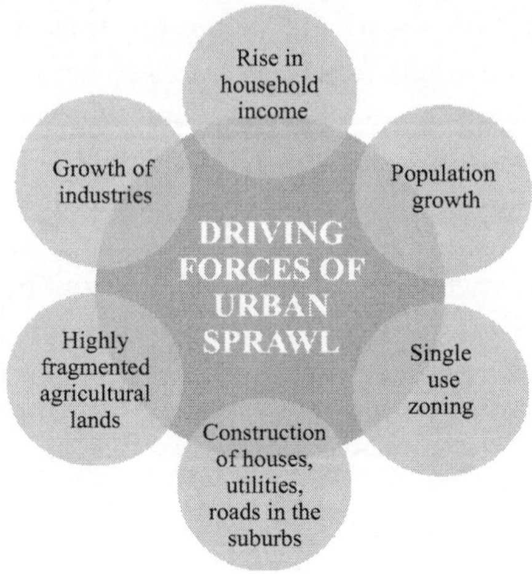

Fig. 4.1

So the consequences of urban sprawl growth may have both positive and negative impacts however negative impacts are generally more highlighted as this cause uncontrolled or uncoordinated growth.

AREA UNDER STUDY

1. **Location:** The location of Jajpur town is within the resource region of Odisha on one side lies the industrial belt of Rourkela on the other mineral belt of Tomka–Daitary–Sukinda. The agricultural belt of Keonjhar, Dhenkanal and Cuttack lies in the adjoining areas. Kalinganagar is one of the planned industrial towns located in Jajpur district of coastal odisha. The Kalinganagar development area is located between 85°57'29.67"E to 86°5'57.14"E longitudes and between 20°53'39.29"N to 21°03'57.35"N latitude.
2. **Physiography and climate:** The study area is surrounded by rugged topography, hills and forest in the north and plain agriculture lands in the south. The forest region of Sukinda is well endowed with mineral resources particularly iron ore. The north–west region is covered by laterite soil whereas the southern region is the coastal belt composed of alluvial soil.

   The district is characterized by humid sub–tropical monsoon climate. The maximum and minimum temperature is 38.6°C and 14.9°C respectively. The mean annual rainfall is 1506.8mm.

   The district is mainly drained by river Brahmani and Baitarani along with its tributaries. A number of streams and pond spreads over the study area which ultimately drains to the Brahmani River.

3. **Socio–economic profile:** as per the 2011 census the total population of Jajpur district is 1,827,192 of which male and female are 9, 26,034 and 9, 01,158 respectively. The population density is 630 persons per sq.km and means literacy rate is 80.13. The average work force participation rate is 30.2 which are lower as compared to the state's work participatory rate of 41.8.

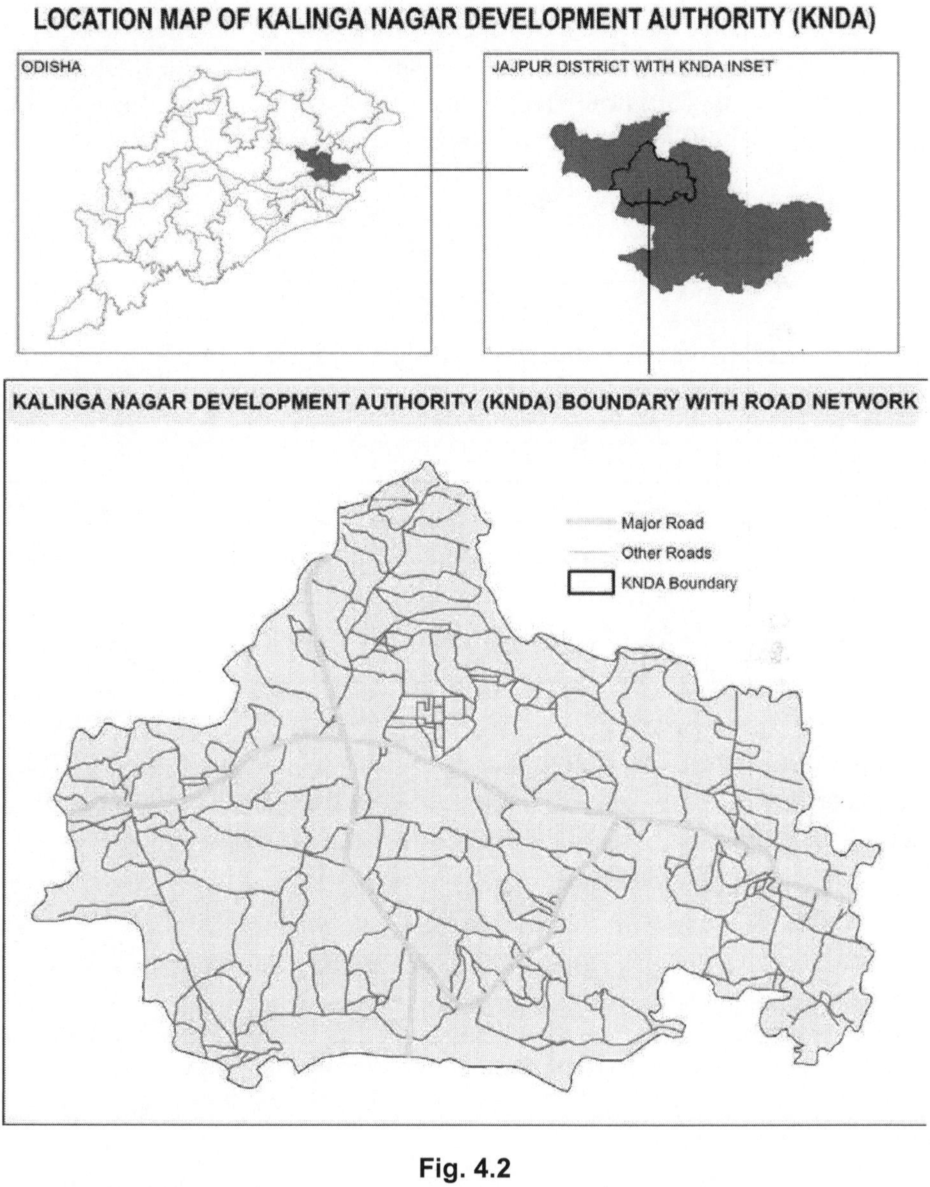

Fig. 4.2

4. **Connectivity:** The district is well connected with transport networks.

   Roadways: NH–53 connects the site to the sea port of Paradip in the east and industrial town of Angul in west. NH–215 connects the site to Keonjhar in the north.

   Railways: The Jajpur–Keonjhar railway station lying on the Kharagpur–Bhubaneswar railway line, connects the site with east coast railway network.

   Air and waterways: The closest airport is the Biju Patnaik International Airport at Bhubaneswar which connects it to all metro cities. Nearest port at the proximity to site is Paradip and Dharma port.

Classification of Study Area

Table 4.1

Sl. no.	*Criteria*	*Data*
1	Total area	458.78 sq.km
2	Total villages	161
3	Villages within municipality	20
4	Villages within industrial area	29
5	Total municipal area	81.92 sq.km
6	Total industrial area	70 sq.km
7	Left over rural land	306.86 sq.km
8	Total population	219919
9	Population density	4.79 person per ha

Objective of the Study

The objective of this paper is to give a better understanding of the concept "sprawl". The aim is to review the background information regarding urban sprawl, indicate the problems and suggest relevant solutions.

1. To assess the status of land use/land cover of Kalinganagar Development Authority from 2008–2020.
2. To analyse the socio–demographic aspects of the Kalinganagar development authority.
3. To study the impacts of urbanization on water bodies and water quality dynamics.

Review Of Literature

Dooddarasalah G. and Shivali (2007) have studied population growth and spatial expansion of Mysore city. The paper focused on analyzing the growth of population in Mysore city and find out the spatial expansion of city. Studies revealed that there is a decline in the growth rates of IT and other industries. The rate of physical expansion was not same in all decades. The spatial expansion of urban areas is followed by an increase in population and concentration of economic activities. Problems such as scarcity of space, housing infrastructure, loss of agricultural land emerged with the expansion of agricultural land.

Ramesh Kumar Gupta (2011) published a research study on change detection techniques for monitoring spatial urban growth of Jaipur city. He has focused on monitoring the land use/ land cover over 34 years. The result shows that the growth of population was 0.63 million in 1971 to 2.9 million in 2001. Population growth has major driving forces of land use change.

Singh, Abha Lakshmi (2008) have made an attempt to assess the effect of city expansion on the countryside, especially on loss of agricultural land and conversion of agriculture land into non–agriculture uses. The city population has increased 6 times. Cultivated l ands are utilized for residential purpose. The natural landscape at proximity is also destroyed.

Khandelwal, Shweta (2009) have studied about urban sprawl of Jaipur metropolitan area. They examined the causes behind rapid urbanization and its impact of land use patterns and suggest strategies for land use planning for future. It reveals that the process of rapid growth of industry and urbanization are based on changes such as rapid growth of population, secondary and tertiary economic activities and changes in land use patterns.

Rao P. Kesava (2016) examined in his paper urban sprawl of Vijayawada city, Andhra Pradesh that high rate of urban population growth is a major concern amongst the urban planners.

So there is an urgent need to adopt modern technology of remote sensing and GIS to analyze and model the whole planning process. It was found that Shannon's entropy analysis model was the most effective measure to identify sprawl of Vijayawada city.

Bhat Parvaiz. A (2017) examined on his paper "Urban sprawl and its impact on land use dynamics of Dehradun city", that urban sprawl has resulted in loss of productive agricultural lands, open green spaces and loss of surface water bodies. He attempted to monitor the land use pattern over a period of time (2004–2014) for change detection analysis and assess to urban sprawl using IRS–P6 data.

Skhukla Anugya and Jain Kamal (2018) on their paper "modeling urban growth trajectories and spatio–temporal pattern of Lucknow city, India" observed that Indian cities are in phase of rapid expansion. The unprecedented speed of expansion is a major challenge for urban planners. The spatio–

temporal analysis of expansion model integrated with driving factors is required for sustainable development of the city.

Problem of the Study

The fast growing population is creating a sprawl effect in the adjacent agricultural and vacant land of Jajpur district. It is one of the fastest growing towns in Odisha from which Kalinagnagar is growing at an alarming rate. The growth of the town is towards the peripheral areas. Major driving force behind the growth is the establishment of Tata steel industry which forms a major portion of the small ancillary industries in and around Kalinganagar region.

Thus the peripheral growth of the urban sprawl resulted into increased residential areas, transport facilities and connectivity improved. After the establishment of Tata steel at Kalinganagar the region showed tremendous rise in the built up area there was a change in the land use pattern area under agriculture, vegetation and vacant land reduced which resulted in the expansion of industrial and residential areas.

Thus the town/ region is experiencing haphazard growth and leads to increasing pressure on lands, loss in agricultural productivity and increasing urban infrastructural facilities.

Due to demographic changes and functions like trade and commerce open spaces, recreational areas, agriculture industries etc are encroaching upon the existing residential areas and other activity. As a result people prefer more to live in adjacent areas due to which the demand and land value is gradually getting higher. With the effect of urban sprawl as a result of settlement business and industrial areas are getting closed to natural and protected areas where countless natural resources are consumed causing serious threat to environment and heavy serious damage on eco system. Especially consumption of land and water which are non renewable resources is at alarming rate, leads to increased air and water pollution. Urban sprawl has direct and irreparable effects on natural areas resulting in worsening of water quality and problem of disposal of solid hazard waste. Such destruction of natural ecosystem around the Kalinganagar region makes the Jajpur town vulnerable towards the impact of climate change.

Database and Methodology

For the present study both qualitative and quantitative data has been used.The data has been collected from Primary and secondary sources. The analysis of Landuse and landcover has been made from the Toposheet and Sattelite Images (2005and 2020), *Source–Google Maps*.with the help of ARC GIS Version –10.

Some of the secondary data also we have used from the reports published by the different Industries of the Kalinganagar.(We acknowledge them)

The Water Samples has been collected from the different parts of the study area and being analyses with the help of 10 physico–chemical parameters following the procedures prescribed by APHA(2005) .To present the result some of the statistical methods has been adopted.

Abstract Information of Kalinga Nagar Development Authority (KNDA)

Total area of KNDA– 458 Km^2 as per the Comprehensive Development Plan–Vision 2030

Note: The KNDA boundary map has been generated from the CDP Report using GIS software. There will be minor changes in the boundary and it may not match exactly with the actual boundary map of KNDA. This boundary map is used only to address the objective of this research paper.

Landuse and Landcover of KNDA–2005

KNDA is highly dominated by agriculture. The result shows that out of the total geographical area, the agriculture covers 77.33% (354.1 Km^2) of land. The built up land during the year 2005 covers an area of 8.85% (40.5 Km^2). The forest area which is mostly the scrub forest covers (5.79%) which is 26.5 Km^2 area. The wasteland are those area with dense scrub and open scrub and it covers 4.12% (18.88 Km^2). The water body class covers 2.67% (12.22 Km^2) and 1.23%(5.65 Km^2) is covered by wetlands. Table 4.2 shows the details statistical information of landuse and landcover of year 2005.

Table 4.2: Landuse and lancover information–2005

Lucode	*Lulc Class*	*Area (Km^2)*	*% Covered*
1	Agriculture	354.182232	77.33%
2	Built–Up	40.528729	8.85%
3	Forest	26.528619	5.79%
4	Wasteland	18.884174	4.12%
5	Waterbodies	12.22373	2.67%
6	Wetland	5.653772	1.23%
TOTAL		458.00	100.00%

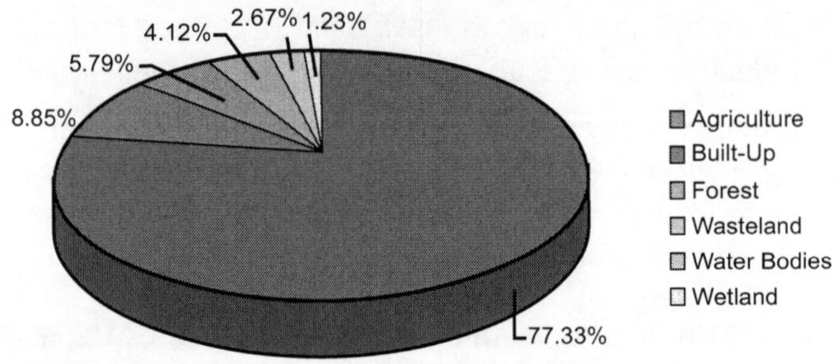

Fig. 4.3: Land use and Land cover information 2005

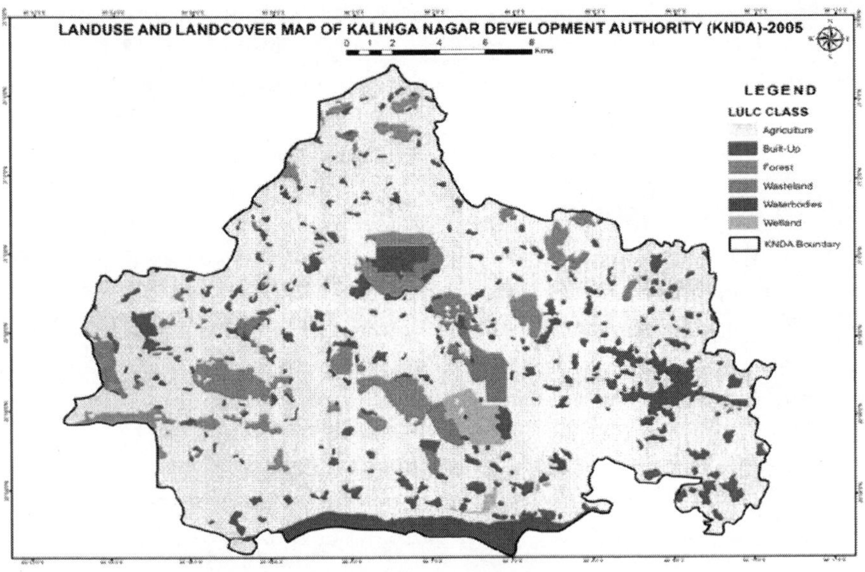

Fig. 4.4

Landuse and Landcover Of KNDA–2020

The landuse and landcover of KNDA during the year 2020 shows that out of the total geographical area, the agriculture covers 64.73% (296.4 Km^2) of land. The built up land covers an area of 16.44% (75.2 Km^2). The forest area covers 4.53% which is 20.7 Km^2 area. The wasteland with dense scrub and open scrub covers 10.95% (50.1 Km^2). The water body class covers 3% (13.7 Km^2) and 0.36% (1.6 Km^2) is covered by wetlands. Table 4.3 shows the details statistical information of landuse and landcover of year 2020.

Table 4.3: Landuse and lancover information –2020

Lucode	*Description*	*Area (Km²)*	*% Covered*
1	Agriculture	296.484907	64.73%
2	Built–Up	75.293151	16.44%
3	Forest	20.727611	4.53%
4	Wasteland	50.145295	10.95%
5	Waterbodies	13.723022	3.00%
6	Wetland	1.627272	0.36%
	TOTAL	458.00	100.00%

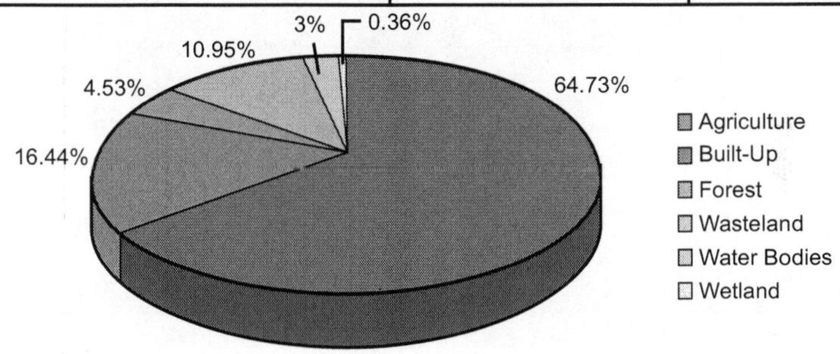

Fig. 4.5: Land use and Land cover information 2020

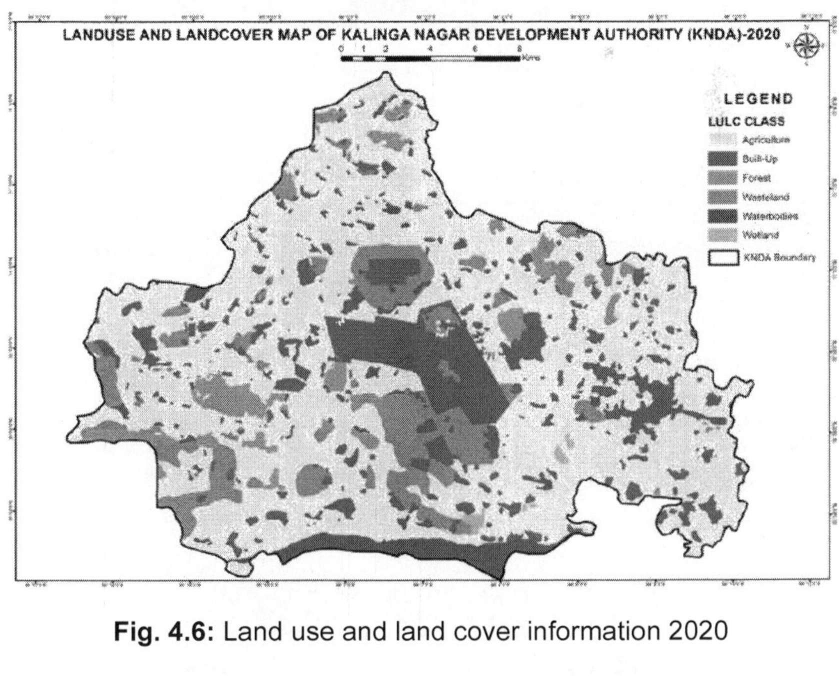

Fig. 4.6: Land use and land cover information 2020

Landuse and Landcover Change Detection Analysis

The change detection of landuse and landcover of KNDA has been carried out using the satellite image of the year 2005 and year 2020. The base year is considered as the year 2005 and it is compared with the 2020 year image. The change detection process is highly necessary in monitoring and managing the changes of natural resources. The major objective of change detection analysis of KNDA is to identify the major changes of LULC that has occurred during this 15 years.

In table 4.4 the details changes of the LULC is shown. It is observed that during this 15 years, there was a huge change in the wasteland. An increase of 166% shows that most of the land has been changed to wasteland. The agriculture area has decreased to 16%. The built–up has increased to 86% during these 15 years. The forest area shows that there is decrease in 22% over the years. The wetlands has decreased to 71% where as on the other hand the water bodies has increased to 12%.

Table 4.4: Landuse and landcover percentage of changes from 2005–2020

Lucode	*Lulc Class*	*2005*	*2020*	*% of Changes*	*Status*
1	Agriculture	354.2	296.5	16%	Decreased
2	Built–Up	40.5	75.3	86%	Increased
3	Forest	26.5	20.7	22%	Decreased
4	Wasteland	18.9	50.1	166%	Increased
5	Waterbodies	12.2	13.7	12%	Increased
6	Wetland	5.7	1.6	71%	Decreased
TOTAL			458.001258		

Detailed Landuse and Landcover Change Detection Analysis

In table 4, the detailed change analysis of KNDA is shown. The information shows that the agriculture land which has decreased 16% from the base year is converted to other landuse like built–up, wasteland, water bodies and wetland. There is an increase of 86% in the built–up class.

The information shows that some of the agricultural land, forest and wasteland has been converted to built–up. Decrease in the forest cover shows that during the years some of the pockets are converted to built–up and wasteland.

The major changes that has been noticed in this change detection is that there is an increase of wasteland during this 15 years. The major classes that have converted to wasteland are agricultural land, forest, water bodies and wetland. There is marginal increase of water bodies over the year. The wetland which has changed to wasteland also gives us the information that there are changes in the cover.

WATER DYNAMICS

Impacts of Urbanization on Water Near by Designated Surface Water

Kalinganagar is an industrial area where some large and medium scale industries are operating. In industrial operation several byproducts generated which negative impact on every component of environment including air, water, soil. Water is regarded as a very essential component for whole biosphere. The growth of population, acceleration of industrialization and mining activities exerts a severe pressure on our large but limited water resources.

Drinking water is a potential source of human exposure to toxic substances released by various human activities. Not only surface water is being used in potable water supply for both urban and rural society but also is being widely used for agricultural purpose, economic growth, environmental protection and maintaining ecological balance (Srinivas et al. 2015; Kumar et al. 2015). Its quality degradation is related to various types of disease (Singh et al. 2016). In this regard water quality assessment study has been conducted in eight surface water location to find out the impact of urban growth on surface water. For this purpose water quality index (WQI) using eq.1 (Bora and Goswami 2017), correlation study eq.2 (Kreyszig 2004) and regression study has been conducted.

WQI is calculated as given below:

$$\text{WQI} = \sum_{i=1}^{n} q_n w_n / \sum w_n \qquad \text{(eq. 1)}$$

Where, q_n = Quality rating of nth water quality parameter.

W_n = Unit weight of nth water quality parameter.

$$r = \frac{\sum_{i=1}^{n}(x_i - \bar{x})(y_i - \bar{y})}{\sqrt{\sum_{i=1}^{n}(x_i - \bar{x})^2}\sqrt{\sum_{i=1}^{n}(y_i - \bar{y})^2}} \qquad \text{(eq. 2)}$$

Where,

n = number of data points,

x = values of x–variable,

y = values of y–variable,

$\bar{x}$ = mean of all variables of x

$\bar{y}$ = mean of all variables of y

r = Pearson Correlation.

Table 4.5 : Eight sampling location for suface water sample collection

Sl. No.	*Location*	*Latitude & Longitude*
SW1	Bramhani River at Manoharour	20° 22' 53.68"N 85° 49' 32.07"E
SW2	Bramhani River at Chakua	20° 22' 49.41"N 85° 51' 44.26"E
SW3	Ganda Nadi at Nuagaon	20° 25' 38.51"N 85° 44' 15.74"E
SW4	Ganda Nadi at Marthapur	20° 24' 07.78"N 85° 49' 29.10"E
SW5	Pond at Chatrakana	20° 25' 18.44"N 85° 48' 50.47"E
SW6	Pond at Jagatpur	20° 26' 43.34"N 85° 45' 02.63"E
SW7	Bhalupada Nala at Dalagaon	20° 26' 58.87"N 85° 47' 23.62"E
SW8	Pond at Bada Pingala	20° 24' 13.58"N 85° 50' 55.76"E

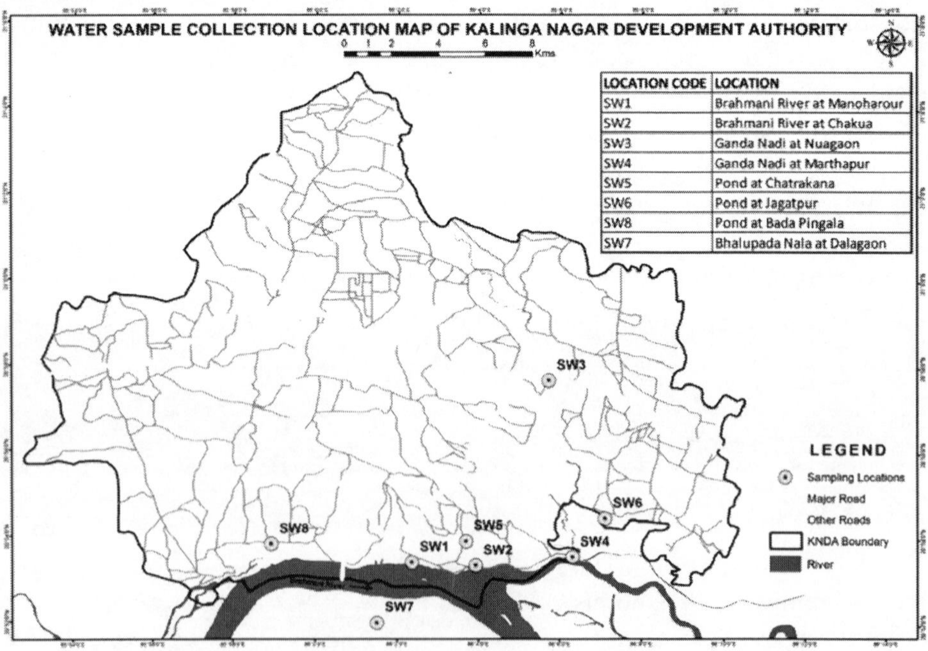

Fig. 4.7

Surface water Samples were collected from eight sampling stations of Kalinga Nagar industrial complex are presented in Table–4. Samples were collected in clean dry sterilized plastic bottles of (2L) in such a way that no bubbles were formed in the bottles. After collection the samples were analysed in the Lab for 10 physico–chemical parameters i.e. colour (Clr), pH, total disolved solid (TDS), iron (Fe), chlorine (Cl^-), sulphate ($SO4^{2-}$), nitrate(NO^{3-}), Fluoride (F^-), dissolved oxygen, biological oxygen demand (BOD) by following the procedures prescribed by APHA (2005) . Obtained result from laboratory analysis is presented in Table 4.6 and are used for statistical analysis including WQI calculation.

Table 4.6: Statistical summary of physicochemical parameters and its BIS 2012, 1998 standards for surface water samples

Parameter	*Colour*	*pH*	*TDS*	*Cl^-*	*SO_4^{2-}*	*NO_3^-*	*D.O*	*B. O. D*	*F^-*	*Fe*	*WQI*
Unit	Hazen		mg/l	mg/l	mg/l	mg/l	mg/l	mg/l	mg/l	mg/l	31.9
S W1	2	7.2	98	26	4.4	1.5	5.1	1.8	0.11	0.4	35
SW2	2	7.1	102	29	4.6	1.7	47	2	0.14	0.44	34
SW3	2	7	105	27	4.8	2.1	4.8	2.1	0.12	0.36	37
SW4	3	7.1	110	28	5.1	2.2	5.1	2.2	0.12	0.38	28
SW5	2	7.4	136	31	4.1	1.3	7.5	2	0.05	0.26	29.5
SW6	2	7.2	135	25	3.2	1.6	7.2	2.4	0.04	0.18	32
SW7	3	6.8	84	23	2.6	1.1	4.5	2.1	0.06	0.2	34
SW8	3	7.3	114	27	4..5	1.4	7.4	2.2	0.1	0.27	31.9
BIS 2012, BIS 1998*	5	6.5–8.5	500	250	200	45	6*	3*	1	200	

RESULT AND DISCUSSION FROM WATER QUALITY PARAMETER:

From experimental analysis shown in tale 4.3 it has seen that all water quality parameter are below BIS 2012 standard for surface water. The pH value shows the suitability of water for various purposes. The experimental water bodies recorded approximately neutral. The TDS value is ranging from 84 to 136 mg/L. Among all parameter high values of TDS water quality parameter has observed and was expected because of discharge of industrial waste water to near by surface water and and from anthropogenic activities. Result from WQI reflecting that the quality of water is fit for domestic and irrigation purpose as the WQI score lies bellow 50 mark (Table 4.7) and was rangin from 28 to 37 mark shown in figure 4.5. The quality of water from all eight locations are regarded as good as it lies between 25 to 50.

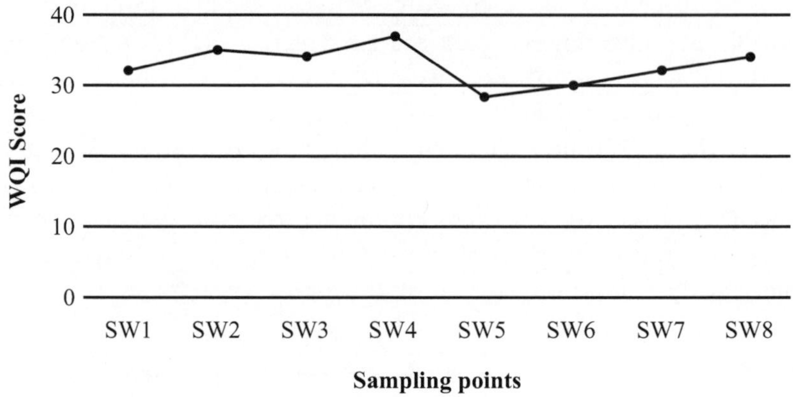

Fig. 4.8: Variation of WQI over eight sampling points

Table 4.7 : Water quality index score and its scaling

Index	*Reference*	*Range*	*Quality*
WQI	Bora and Goswami 2017	0–25	Excellent: Drinking, irrigation and industrial
		26– 50	Good : Drinking, irrigation and industrial
		51–75	Poor : Irrigation and industrial
		76–100	Very poor : Irrigation
		>100	Unfit for drinking: Proper treatment required before use

In the present study statistical tool correlation study clears that there exist more or less positive and negative correlation among all studied water quality parameter which shown in table 4.5. Strongly positively correlation exist between water quality parameters like pH with TDS and Cl^-(correlation co–efficient r = 0.783, 0.663 respectively), Cl^- with SO_4^{2-} (r = 0.654), SO_4^{2-} with NO_3^-, F^- and Fe(r = 0.726, 0.789, 0.806 respectively), NO_3^- with F^-(r=0.612) and F^- with Fe (r = 0.921).

Also it is cleared form correlation study that the water quality parameters like F^-, Fe, SO_4^{2-} and NO_3^- are mainly influencing the water quality as there exist strong correlation with WQI with correlation coefficient of r = 0.844, 0.637, 0.606, 0.645 respectively.

Another statistical tool regression study reveals that for water quality index prediction F^- water quality parameter is a good candidate (R^2= 0.7138). Next to it other parameter for WQI prediction are Fe, SO_4^{2-} and NO_3^-. The regression study for these water quality parameter are shown in Figure 4.9(*a–d*)

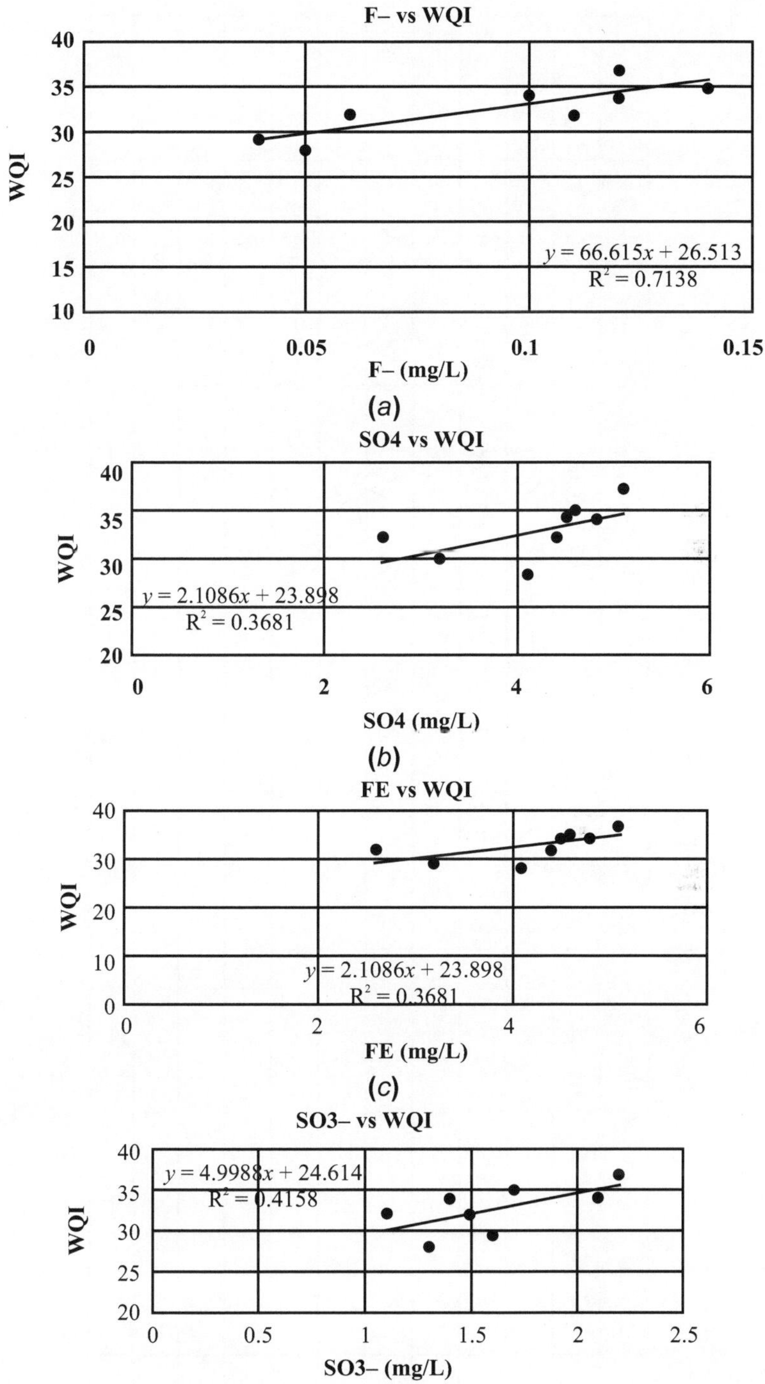

Fig. 4.9: *(a – d)* Regression study among WQI with water quality parameter F^-, Fe, SO_4^{2-} and NO_3^-

Table 4.8: Correlation study among water quality parameter and with WQI

	Colour	*pH*	*TDS*	*Cl^-*	*SO_4^{2-}*	*NO_3^-*	*D.O*	*B.O.D*	*F^-*	*Fe*	*WQI*
Colour	1	−0.317	−0.364	−0.338	−0.093	−0.1	−0.307	0.311	0.018	−0.239	0.082
pH		1	0.783	0.663	0.348	−0.089	−0.01	−0.04	−0.16	0.005	−0.384
TDS			1	0.504	0.064	0.047	−0.119	0.438	−0.487	−0.35	−0.528
Cl^-				1	0.654	0.261	0.366	−0.263	0.265	0.446	0.001
SO_4^{2-}					1	0.726	0.204	−0.257	0.789	0.806	0.606
NO_3^-						1	0.066	0.191	0.612	0.579	0.645
D.O							1	−0.197	0.474	0.502	0.275
B.O.D								1	−0.388	−0.591	0.022
F^-									1	0.921	0.844
Fe										1	0.637
WQI											1

Conclusion – From WQI study clears that the quality of water lies in good quality category and fit for domestic purpose. Correlation study clears that F^-, Fe, SO_4^{2-} and NO_3^- water quality parameter are strongly influence quality of surface water. Regression study depicts that F^- water quality parameter is best at predicting WQI.

Concluding Remarks

After the thorough study on landuse and landcover it is found that most of the land use changed from agriculture to Industrial use. And also it is resulted that there is an increase of waste land during this 15 years. The major classes that have converted to waste land are agricultural land, forest land water bodies and wetlands. In case of water dynamics after the correlation study there exist more or less positive and negative correlation among all quality parameters. Though a strong negative result has not been found but according to the Bora and Goswami reference the quality of water is only in good condition. If it is existing like this it may leads to the negative trend in future. So ,before it goes to the stage of worst the authority of industrial region should take optimum care to restore the quality of water for the future generation.

Bibliography

1. Alberti.M. (2005). The effects of Urban patterns on Ecosystem function. *International Regional Science Review* , 168–192.
2. APHA. (2005). Standard methods for the examination og water and waste water. *American Public Health Association, American water works Association and water environment Federartion, New York.*
3. BHATTA, B. (2010). Analysis of urban growth ans sprawl from remote sensing data. *Springer*, 1867–2434.
4. Bora, M. (2017). Water quality assesment in terms of water quality index(WQI): case study of the Kolong River, Assm, India. *Applied water science 7, Springer* , 3125–3135.
5. Dadras, M. (2014). Land use/ cover chnage detection and Urban sprawl analysis in Bardar Abbas city, Iran. *The scientific world Journal* , 1–12.
6. Erwin, K. (2011). *Advanced engineering and mathematics.* Singapore: John wiily and Sons(Asia) Pte. Ltd.
7. H.S.Sudhira, e. (2004). Urban sprawl:Metrics, Dynamics and Modelling using GIS . *International Journal of Applied Earth Observation and Geo Information* , 29–39.
8. Herlod, M. e. (2003). The spatio temporal form of urban growth : measurement,analysis and modelling. *Remote sensing and Environment* , 286–302.

9. Hisam, A. J. (2019). Urbanisation and Urban sprawl issues in City structure: a case study of the Sulayamaniah Iraqi Kurdistan region. *MDPI*, 1–21.
10. Karakayaci, Z. (2016). The concept of urban Sprawl and its causes. *The Journal of International Social Research*, 815–818.
11. Kiran, K. (2015). Urban sprawl:A case study of Lucknow city. *International Journal of Humanities and social science invention*, 11–20.
12. Padmasri.S et.al. (2012). Urban Sprawl and its Transformation over Landuse/ land cover using Geo– informatics: A case study on Madurai fringe area. *Journal of Industrial Engineering and Management Science*, 41–45.
13. Parvaiz A. Bhat et.al. (2017). Urban Sprawl its impact on land use/ land cover dynamics of Dehradun city, India. *International Journal of Sustainable built Environment*, 513–521.
14. Prashant K. (2015). Index–Based ground water vulnerability mapping models using hydrologicalsettings:A critical evaluation. *Environmental Impact Assesment review*, 38–49.
15. (2019). *Project Report for Proposed Kalinganagar National Investment Manufacturing Zones.* Bhubaneswar: Odisha Industrial Infrastructure Development Corporation.
16. Rao P.Kesava, e. (2016). Identification of urban Sprawl– a case study of Vijaywada city,Andhra Pradesh, India. *International association of Lowland Technology*, 60–64.
17. Singh.S et.al. (2016). Assessment of Pollution potential of leachate from the municipal solid waste disposal site and its impact on ground water quality,Varanasi environs, India. *Arabian Journal of Geoscience 9*, 1–12.
18. Srinivas, R. (2015). Ground water quality Assesment in some selected area of Rajasthan, India using Fuzzy Multi–criteriadecision making Tool. *Aquatic Procedia*, 1023–1030.
19. Supriyo, H. (2017). Issues related to Urban sprawl in South 24 Praganas with special reference to Diamond Harbour Municipality,West Bengal. *International Journal of Petroleum and Gas Engineering Research*, 21–31.
20. Toll, J. a. (1982). Detecting residential landuse development at the urban fringe. *Photogrammetric Engineering and Remote sensing*, 629–643.
21. Yar, S. A. (2017). Study of Urban Sprawl and its Social and Environmental Impacts on Urban society in Latifabad,Hyderabad,Pakistan. *Journal of Civil and Environmental Engineering*, 1–5.

Urban Environment and Spatial Science
Dr Mohd Akhter Ali, Dr. Kabir Mohan Sethy, Dr Muzafar Wani and M.Kamraju
Ane Books Pvt. Ltd. 2021, , ISBN : 978-93-90658-28-2, P.P. : 59 – 72

5

Spatiotemporal Analysis of Dog Bites in Srinagar City

Muzafar Ahmad Wani, Insha Mohideen,
Shamim Ahmad Shah, Tanweer Ahmad Malik
[1]Assistant professor, department of geography, Govt. Degree College Pulwama, Kashmir, muzafargeo@gmail.com 192301
[2]Student, department of geography and regional development university of Kashmir
[3]Head, department of geography and regional development and Dean, school of earth and environmental sciences, University of Kashmir, shamimcrocus@gmail.com
[4]Lecturer department of geography GDC Boys Pulwama Kashmir, email tanweer_geo@rediffmail.com

Abstract

Stray dogs are the most common animals found in the urban environmental condition all over the world. Uncontrolled growth of the dog population is associated with the rapid spread of rabies, more particularly in developed countries. The attack and the fear of being attacked by stray dogs have made human life miserable in the city, and the issue is emerging as a challenge to the administration and as well as the local population. The study aims at a Spatiotemporal analysis of stray dog-bites in Srinagar city, the summer capital of J&K, to make comperative analysis with other northern studies of india. We have identified that Srinagar city is one of the worst-hit cities as it has the highest stray dog and human population ratio among all northern cities of India. On average, every year about 5000 dog bite cases are reported in

Corresponding Author: Muzafar Ahmad Wani

the city making the life of its dweller's miserable. This results of this study are expected to help authorities, administrators, animal welfare department, NGOs and research students to carry out the research investigations in this field and also devise sustainable stratedies to tackle the menace.

Keywords: Dog, India, Cities, Menace, Bite.

Introduction

The dog has accompanied man all over the world since its domestication 15,000 years ago (Savolainen et al. 2002), and today it is one of the most abundant creatures on planet earth (Green and Gipson, 1994). Worldwide dog population are estimated at around 500 million, (Wandeler, et al., 1993). One of the direct effects of dogs on human health is in the form of rabies a zoonotic, viral disease. It is one of the oldest diseases known to humanity, and even at present, it is still a significant public health challenge. However, it is a vaccine-preventable disease, but once the symptoms develop, it becomes virtually 100% fatal. In up to 99% of cases, domestic dogs are responsible for rabies virus transmission to humans. It is spread to people and animals through bites or scratches, usually via saliva. It is found in all continents, except Antarctica, with over 95% of human deaths occurring in Asia and Africa (WHO, 2020). sadly, tragic to mention in theses continents, about 3 billion people are at risk rabies (WHO, 2020). It has been found that more than 59,000 people die of rabies annually, because, lack of access to proper health care facilities. That means about 1 person is dying of rabies after every 9 minutes (CDC, 2015). An estimated 45% of all deaths from rabies occur in South- East Asia, out of which about 36% of the world's deaths from rabies happen in India itself (Singh, V. 2018) as such dog menace has been referred a significant hazard in India (Markandyaa, *et al.*, 2008). Presently, an estimated 35 million stray dogs live in its urban landscape (WHO, 2020). In India, about 20,000 cases of rabies are registered annually (Singh, V. 2018).

Statement of the Problem and Significances of This Study

Every dog seems to be having his day in the Srinagar city, the summer capital of Jammu and Kashmir, where, as per official data, are about 48,000 stray dogs roaming the city, but unofficial estimates say the number is about 150,000 (Kakkar, *et, al.* 2012, lone el al 2014, IANS 2012, Kashmir observer 2018). If we compare this with the human population, putting the dog-human ratio at about 1:12. (Lone, *et al.* 2014). The total increase in cases of dog bites in the region is significantly higher as compared with other published reports in India (Umarigar *et al.* 2012). The dog bite incidents are assuming alarming proportions and herds of Stray dog can be seen roaming independently on streets, chasing cars, pulling down bicycle riders and often attacking pedestrians and school children. About 96% of the victims are attacked by stray dogs, and only 4% of cases by household pets (lone, *et al.* 2014). Among all the ten districts of Kashmir valley, Srinagar alone accounts for about 80% of the reported cases of a dog bite (Outlook Bureau, 2018, Pervize, A. 2019).

More than 13 persons died of rabies from 2010 to 2015(Outlook Bureau, 2018). The peripheral hospitals of Directorate of Health Services Kashmir receive around 25,000 cases of dog bites every year (Kashmir observer 2018). The situation is so worse; if the dog population is kept unchecked, it could trigger fear psychosis among people. The issue needs to be dealt with seriousness, or else the dog population would outnumber Srinagarities. (the Kashmir walla 2017). Despite lofty claims of Srinagar Municipal Corporation (SMC) of controlling the canine population in the summer capital, people in various areas fear to come out of their homes especially during morning and evening hours as a large number of dogs are on prowl (Yatto, I. 2018). People feel the need to carry sticks to ward off any attack while going into the market or workplace etc. during the day and dogs bark aggressively at nights gives an impression of being in a jungle (Zia, A. 2012). As a result, the locals of the city complain that they hardly get to sleep in peace due to continuous barking of the dogs during night hours. Children and older adults who are ill feel tortured by such irritation (Kashmir vision 2019). young School going children are comfortable among the primary victims of the Stray dogs, which as creating panic among parents, which in turn has affected the proper schooling of their wards (Lans English, 2015).

The increased rate of attacks of stray dogs has forced the people to stage the protests in the city (Ahmad M. 2012). Stray dogs in the city led to frequent road accidents as they obstruct the movement of pedestrians and vehicles, especially bike riders. Sometimes they become the cause of traffic jamming while they crossroad or fight on the road. Many school-going children have been bitten in these areas, making the others too scared to go out and play. Stray dogs bite people, chase them when they go to prayers early in the morning (Raafi, M. 2017). Some of the victims have died of rabies. Recently there have been so many reports of dogs mauling infants, attacking children and commuters affecting people of all walks of life (Mansoor, F. 2018). Dogs have not only affected the residents of Srinagar city but also the tourists. Many tourists have been bitten by dogs in the city, which make other tourists scared of visiting. (Hamdani, 2013). In March 2013, in less than a week of the deadly attack in the tourist hub of the Boulevard have wounded 40 people, including 11 tourists (Hamdani 2013). Looking at the gravity of the problem, the Jammu and Kashmir State Human Rights Commission has described dog attacks as "violation of human rights" (Malik O, 2016).

The leading cause of this aggravated dog menace is attributed to improper solid waste management (Wani and Shah 2014) and heaps of garbage become a source of food for the dogs. (yatto irfan, 2018). The city is the dirtiest city of India in terms of solid waste management and sanitation (Ministry of Urban Development2010). The aesthetic and psycho-sociological consequences of trauma caused by a dog bite repeatedly burden the quality of life of the affected persons and their families (Kakkar et al., 2012). Failure of Srinagar Municipal Corporation (SMC) to take adequate measures for controlling the fast-growing population of stray dogs is taking a heavy toll (Kashmir pen 2018). Managing a rabies exposure, where the average cost of rabies post-exposure prophylaxis (PEP) is currently estimated at an average of US $108 can be a catastrophic financial burden on affected families whose average daily income may be as low as US$ 1–2 per person (WHO, 2020). The situation is worse in the outskirts of the city where the municipal corporation is not active enough in checking the menace (Mir, I. 2018).

Authorities seem to be falling short of resources to deal with this issue effectively (Ahmed 2011). As per a report submitted by the SMC to the High Court, the corporation required 191 million US dollars for the construction of 1800 dog pounds to tame stray dogs of Srinagar city (Rukaya S. 2020). It seems quite impossible as a requirement of financial assistance is very huge. Although tall claims to control the menace by the Government authorities and Srinagar Municipal Corporation, the population of stray dogs in the city is only increasing in leaps and bounds. Over the period, dog invasion has become more and more apparent posing severe challenges to public health, aesthetic beauty, and environment as well.

Study Area

Srinagar city is located between 33^{0}53′49″- 34^{0}17′14″ N latitudes and 74^{0}36′16″- 75^{0}01′26″ E longitudes at an altitude of 5200 ft. absl. (Fig 1.1). The city has cradled along the banks of river Jhelum. The area of the city is about 278.1km2, with a population size of 1192792 souls (Census 2011). It has grown 12 times in terms of population and 23 times in terms of area between 1901 and 2011, thus being ranked as one of the 100 fastest-growing urban areas in the world (Pevaize A. 2018). The city is famous for its lakes, houseboats, gardens and shrines. Srinagar city has witnessed quick urbanization, but lack of commensurate investment in urban infrastructure and services has resulted in an overall deterioration of urban quality of life. Srinagar is the summer capital, and an important tourist place is adversely affected by the lack of several infrastructure facilities. The city once called Venice of East is presently facing a severe problem in the form of improper solid waste disposal (Wani A.

M and Shah A. S, 2014). One of the direct impacts of the improper solid waste management is in the form of the ever-increasing dog population and frequent incidence of dog bites which has deteriorated the quality of life in the city.

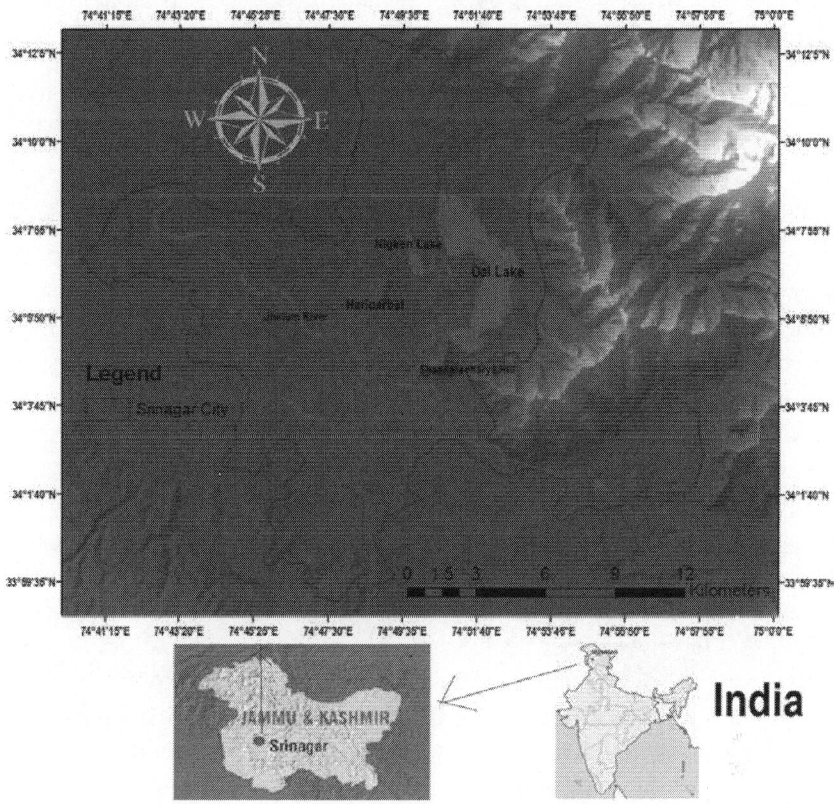

Fig. 5.1: Location Map of The Study Area*

Source: Generated from carto-DEM Satellite data and SOI Toposheets.

OBJECTIVES

The objectives of the present study are:

- To understand the trends in the dog bites of Srinagar city.
- To understand the spatiotemporal distribution of dog bite incidents in the Srinagar city.

DATABASE AND METHODOLOGY

In this study, we describe the distribution pattern of dog bites incidents in the city, using geographic information system (GIS) through Spatio-temporal and hot spot analysis. The information has been gathered using a variety of methods to understand situation, issues and opportunities regarding the present research work. For the present study ward map was obtained from Srinagar municipality committee (SMC) has been used as a base. The committee has divided the city into 68 municipal wards for the proper administration of the city. The maps were first scanned to convert them into digital format. Georeferencing was done with the survey of toposheets at 1:50,000 scale, bearing code number: J12, J16 and K13, to bring spatial character to data, i.e. latitude and Longitude systems, on WGS-84-UTM-43N.

Dog Population and Dog Bite Data

The terms stray dog, 'street dog' and 'free-living dog' all refer to 'domestic dogs or free-ranging urban dogs (Canis lupus familiaris) that are not owned by humans (Daniels, T. J. 1983, Pal, S. K. 2001). However, the term 'stray dog' denotes a Western understanding of dogs as 'out of place' if they are not human property (Srinivasan et al. 2019). For this purpose, both primary and secondary data were used. Secondary data about dog bite cases were obtained from various internet sources and Anti-Rabies Clinic (ARC) of Shri Maharaja Hari Singh (SMHS) Hospital, Government Medical College, Srinagar, run by the Department of Community Medicine. Primary data was obtained by making general observation in the fields through field surveys. To make a comparative analysis of the dog menace of Srinagar city with other major northern cities of India like Delhi, Amritsar, Dehradun, etc. has also been included in current research work, to draw meaningful inferences. The informant population of dogs in other northern cites India was generated through an intensive literature review process through the internet. Literature survey helped us in drawing some useful inferences through a comparative analysis of dog menace in other northern cities of India.

Results and Discussion

Spatio-Temporal Temporal Variation of Dog Bites in Srinagar City

Spatial refers to space, temporal refers to time therefore the spatiotemporal analysis is geographer's methodology is used to describe a process in a definite location and time. In order to accurately identify the spatiotemporal distribution pattern of rabies, it is necessary to use geography as base of understanding. Most of the previous rabies epidemiological investigations are based on aggregated areas which lacks in vital spatial patterns of disease distribution (Song M, *et al*. 2009). In order to understand the exact epidemiological features of disease via spatial temporal analysis provide a technical basis for the effective control of this dangerous disease and formulation of very sound policy related health issues. (Yu, G. *et al.* 2018). Geographical interpretation of relationships is very important aspect of holistic policy orientation but these relationships have frequently been ignored by evaluators (Smith, N. L. (1979). Dur this immense significance this is widely used in Methods for data analysis in geographical studies (Turner, M. G. (1990).

Table 5.1: Temporal Variation of Dog Bites in Srinagar City

Year	*Number of Dog Bites*
2008	3772
2009	4200
2010	3711
2011	7002
2012	5390
2013	6051
2014	4916
2015	5100
2016	5120
2017	5216
2018	4300

The trend analysis of patents of dog bite cases attending anti-rabies clinic located in SMHS hospital run by department of community medicine is shown in table and fig. 5.2. This number only includes patients treated at the state government-sponsored anti-rabies clinic in the Shri Maharaja Hari Singh (SMHS) However, actual figure is expected to be even more higher as the cases treated at periphery hospitals in various districts are not counted in it (Bhat, B. 2019). It is indicative of the fact that the city has been facing an alarming threat from the stray dog menace, so the situation is turning worse with every passing day. In 2008 about 3772 dog bite cases were treated and in 2018 the number of rabies patient of the city has gone up to 4300. the highest number of dog bites were recorded in the 2011 when 7002 cases were reported, and lowest number was reported in year 2010 when only 3711 were reported. However, it is pertinent to mention that on an average the city reported about 4797 cases of dog bites are reported from the city annually which highest in north Indian cities of India. Though the SMC has taken various like sheltering and sterilization of stray dogs, but unfortunately has failed curb the rate dog bite incidents significantly in the city. However, SMC claims that stray dog population has decreased from about 90,000 in 2011 to 50,000 in 2014 and to 22,000 at present. However, it seems very intriguing expression ss SMC has not specified how the number has gone down (Outlook Bureau 2018).

ASS aptly remarked by (Hussain, A. 2020) the abrogation of article 370 by in by Indian administration in the 2019 which was followed by prolonged curfew and the Covid-19 pandemic in 2020 has put halt to all efforts to aimed at control of stray dog population. the packs of stray dogs roaming freely is a common sight gives an impression that the city is a heaven for dogs.

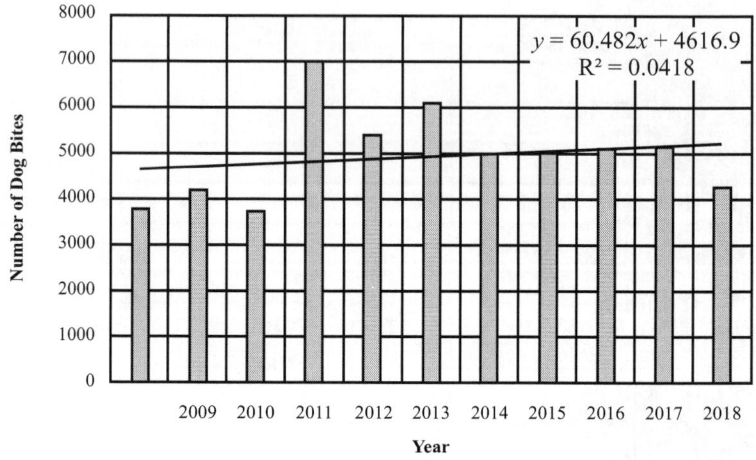

Fig. 5.2: Temporal Variation of Dog Bites in Srinagar City*

****Source:*** Anti-Rabies Clinic SMHS Hospital Srinagar

Table 5.2: Spatial Comparison of Dog Menace of Srinagar City other Cities of India*

Name of City	*Number of Stray Dogs*	*Population*	*Ratio*
Srinagar city	100000	1180570	1:11
Chandigarh	12900	961587	1:74
Shimla	2500	169578	1:67
Delhi	562000	16787941	1:29
Amritsar	25000	1132383	1:45
Jaipur	50000	3046163	1:60
Dehradun	34000	569578	1:16

****Source:*** Young Bites (2018) Gupta Vivek (2019) Dhillon S G (2020), Jaiswar KP (2020), Times of India (2018) Jha Prashant (2019), Census (2011).

The method of comparison is one of the frequently applied frequently applied methods to present geographic reality of the region in order to understand the problem under investigation very effectively (Robinson, J. 2006, Peck, J. 2015, Wilcke, H., & Budke, A. 2019). So, for the highest human population and stray dog ratio is observed in Srinagar city i.e. 1:11. The main reason behind this terrible ratio is improper waste management in city (Wani and shah 2014, Yatto, I. 2018, Yaqoob, M. 2020). On an average about one lakh poultry birds are killed in the city on basis, producing about 40000 kg of protein rich waste for stray dogs (The Tribune 2020). Another factor which induces the growth of stray dog population in city is the dietary habits of its dwellers who are accustomed of nonvegetarian food like mutton and beef and also generates waste in form high-protein offal for dogs (Kashmir post 2018). If this highly nutritious and energy-rich edible offal is not managed properly, each dog can have access to about 1 kg. of such an energy-rich diet. The breeding efficiency and lifespan of stray dogs can then increase, and the population can touch alarming levels, (FIAPO, 2017). The lifespan of dogs increases due to the availability of energy-rich diet. Moreover, the counter measures to control the menace which were adopted by Srinagar Municipal Corporation (SMC) like dog sterilization and killing of dogs has miserably failed (KNS, 2019) New Delhi the capital city of India which has human population about 1.7 crore has only one stray dog/29 persons. The other cities of India including Shimla, Amritsar, Jaipur and Dehradun have much higher human and stray dog ratio. Therefore, we can safely infer from the table that the dog menace in these cities less aggravated than Srinagar city. Chandigarh which is capital city of two states of India namely Punjab and Haryana, just only have 12900 stray dogs for a population of about 10 lakh. These statistical figures corroborate the common knowledge that Srinagar is the worst sufferer of the stray dog menace India (Rashid, A. 2020).

Conclusion and Suggestions

Spatiotemporal methodlogy has been has been widely applied in the public health and has immensely contributed to improving understanding of diseases occurrence through mapping disease area clusters, the detection of disease spread trends, the identification of the spatial and temporal distribution of diseases. In this study, we selected Srinagar city located in the heart of the Kashmir Himalayas, to analyse spatiotemporal analysis of dog bite occurance. our findings provided the basis for understanding the spatial-temporal patterns of dog bite incidence occurrence. It provided necessary information related to the trends of dog bite occurance and the potential risk factors associated with human rabies exposure. Every dog seems to have his day Srinagar city making the life of dwellers hell, despite the fact the city being called paradise on earth. The magnitude of dog menace can gauge from the fact the stray dog and human population is 1: 11 in the city, which highest in north India . Moreover, it has been found on an average of about 5000 dog bites are registered annually, which again explains the aggravation of the problem. It is pertinent to mention stray dog are most feature is most commonly seen urban feature in the city, and the menace has developed as full-grown disaster over the period. The menace of stray dogs in Srinagar city has become a cause of concern not only for the residents but also for the authorities who have so far failed to put a check on the growing population. Therefore, in the absence of accurate data on trends of dog bite occurrence at the locational basis, the results of this study can provide useful information to administrators, planners, practitioners, NGOs, and research scholars to bridge that gap. In light of this research work it is strongly suggested an in-depth investigation should be undertaken to explore the cultural and socioeconomic factors associated with increased risk of human rabies.

References

1. Ahmad, Mukhtar. (, 2012). In Srinagar, An Angry Protest With A Difference, Https://Www.Rediff.Com/News/Slide-Show/Slide-Show-1-In-Srinagar-An-Angry-Protest-With-A-Difference/20120218.Htm
2. Bhat Bisma. (2019).11000 Dog Bite Cases Recorded In Two Years: Canine Terror Gives Sleepless Nights To People, Km, Https://Www. Thekashmirmonitor.Net/11000-Dog-Bite-Cases-Recorded-In-Two-Yearscanine-Terror-Gives-Sleepless-Nights-To-People/
3. CDC. (2015). Every 9 Minutes, Someone In The World Dies Of Rabies, Centre For Disease Control And Prevention Cdc News Room, Https:// Www.Cdc.Gov/Media/Releases/2015/P0928-Rabies.Html
4. Census (2011) Population of Srinagar City", Www. Census 2011.Co. In. Org.Html
5. Dhillon S G. (2020). Free Parking, Zero Garbage Collection Fee: In Shimla, Adopting A Stray Dog Has Its Rewards, The Indian Express, Https://Indianexpress.Com/Article/Governance/Free-Parking-Zero-Garbage-Collection-Fee-In-Shimla-Adopting-A-Stray-Dog-Has-Its-Rewards-6306016/
6. FIAPO. (2017). Red-Tapeism' And Internal Conflict Add To J&K's Growing Stray Dog Menace, Federation Of Indian Animal Protection Organization, Http://Www.Fiapo.Org/Fiaporg/News/Red-Tapeism-And-Internal-Conflict-Add-To-Jks-Growing-Stray-Dog-Menace/
7. Wani A, M. and shah A S. (2014). Geospatial Based Approach For Enhancing Environment Sustainability Of Srinagar City - A Study On Solid Waste Disposal, International Journal Of U- And E- Service, Science And Technology Vol.7, No.3 Pp.289-302.

8. Green J.S and Gipson P.S. (1994). Feral Dogs. Prevention and Control of Wildlife Damage 1994. Cooperative Extension Division Institute of Agriculture and Natural Resources, University of Nebraska.
9. Gupta Vivek. (2019). 65% Rise In Chandigarh's Stray Dog Population In 7 Years, Hindustan Times, Https://Www.Hindustantimes.Com/Cities/65-Rise-In-Chandigarh-S-Stray-Dog-Population-In-7-Years/Story-Wbtsms1bgpvfdccfugzmal.Html
10. Hamdani (2013) 40 Wounded As Stray Dogs Go On Biting Spree Again, Greater Kashmir, Http://Epaper.Greaterkashmir.Com/Epaperpdf/2332013/2332013-Md-Hr-5.Pdf
11. IANS (2012) Hundred Dog Bites A Day and Counting In Srinagar, Sify News, Www.Sify.Com/News/Hundred-Dog-Bites-A-Day-And-Counting-In-Srinagar-News-National-Melmogeejecsi.Html
12. Jaiswar Kp (2020). Stray Dog Menace Plagues City, Rural Belt As Well,The Tribune, Https://Www.Tribuneindia.Com/News/Archive/Amritsar/Stray-Dog-Menace-Plagues-City-Rural-Belt-As-Well-365781
13. Jha Prashant (2019). Dogs On The Prowl: Dehradun's Rising Stray Menace, The Times Of India, Https://Timesofindia.Indiatimes.Com/City/Dehradun/Dogs-On-The-Prowl-Doons-Rising-Stray-Menace/Articleshow/70718099.Cms.
14. Kakkar M, Venkataramanan V, Krishnan S, Chauhan Rs, Abbas Ss. (2012) Moving from Rabies Research to Rabies Control: Lessons from India. Plos Neglected Tropical Diseases. Vol. 6(8): E1748.
15. Kashmir Vision. (2019). Sterilization Of Dogs Won't Help, Culling Will, Https://Kashmirvision.In/2019/08/02/Sterilization-Of-Dogs-Wont-Help-Culling-Will/
16. KNS, (2019). Stray Dogs Have A Free Run In Sgr City, 'Smc Action Plan In Tatters', Kashmir News Service, Http://Www.Knskashmir.Com/Stray-Dogs-Have-A-Free-Run-In-Sgr-City---Smc-Action-Plan-In-Tatters--36424
17. Lone, Bilquees, Salimkhan, Haq. (2014). Analysis Of Dog Bites In Kashmir: An Unprovoked Threat To Population, National Journal Of Community Medicine, Volume 5(1) Pp 66-68at: Https://Www.Researchgate.Net/Publication/321867070
18. Malik O. (2016). Stray Dogs Population Under Control: SMC, Rising Kashmir, Http://Www.Risingkashmir.In/News/Stray-Dogs-Population-Under-Control-Smc

19. Mansoor F. (2018). The Dog City, Greater Kashmir, Https://Www.Greaterkashmir.Com/News/Opinion/The-Dog-City/
20. Markandyaa, Anil; Taylor, Tim; Longo, Alberto; Murtyd, M.N.; Murtyd, S. And Dhavalad, K. (2008). 'Counting the Cost of Vulture Decline—An Appraisal of The Human Health and Other Benefits of Vultures in India'; *Ecological Economics* 67 (2), 15, Pp 194–204
21. Mir Ifran. (2018) Street Dog Population Out Of Control In Chanapora Srinagar, Fast Kashmir, Https://Fastkashmir.Com/2018/01/Street-Dog-Population-Out-Of-Control-In-Chanapora-Srinagar/
22. Outlook Bureau (2018) Srinagar: Govt Says Population Of Dogs Decreasing Even As Dog Bite Cases Go Up, Out Look The Fully Loadaed Magazine, Https://Www.Outlookindia.Com/Website/Story/In-Srinagar-Dog-Population-Goes-Down-Says-Jk-Govt-As-Dog-Bite-Cases-Increases-Fr/311678
23. Peck, J. (2015). Cities Beyond Compare. Reg. Stud.,49, 160–182.
24. Pervize Arthur (2019). Down To Earth, Dog Bites Decrease In Srinagar But The Fear Remains, Https://Www.Downtoearth.Org.In/News/Waste/Dog-Bites-Decrease-In-Srinagar-But-The-Fear-Remains-64981
25. Rashid Arif. (2020). Almost 70 Thousand Dog Bite Cases Treated At SMHS In Past Decade And Half, Kashmir Reader, Https://Kashmirreader.Com/2020/05/31/Almost-70-Thousand-Dog-Bite-Cases-Treated-At-Smhs-In-Past-Decade-And-Half/
26. Robinson, J. (2006). Ordinary Cities: Between Modernity and Development; Routledge: London, Uk.
27. Savolainen P., Zhang Y., Luo J., Lundeberg J.Andleitner T.(2002). Genetic Evidence For An East Asian Origin Of Domestic Dogs. Science .298.
28. Song M, Tang Q, Wang D-M, Mo Z-J, Guo S-H, Et Al. (2009) Epidemiological Investigations of Human Rabies in China. Bmc Infectious Diseases 9: 210–218.
29. The Kashmir Walla. (2017). Stray Dogs Continue Terror, Officially 48000 Dogs In Srinagar, Https://Thekashmirwalla.Com/2018/11/Stray-Dogs-Continue-Terror-Officially-48000-Dogs-In-Srinagar/
30. The Tribune. (2020). Stray Dog Deaths Due To Hunger Rise In Kashmir, Https://Www.Tribuneindia.Com/News/J-K/Stray-Dog-Deaths-Due-To-Hunger-Rise-In-Kashmir-13407
31. Time Times of India. (2018). Jaipur: 50,000 Street Dogs Lead To Survival Conflicts, Says Report, Https://Timesofindia.Indiatimes.

Com/City/Jaipur/50k-Street-Dogs-Lead-To-Survival-Conflicts-Report/Articleshow/71639804.Cms

32. Umarigar, P., Parmar, G., Patel, P., & Bansal, R. (2012). Profile of Animal Bite Cases attending Urban Health Centres in Surat City: A Cross-Sectional Study. National Journal, 3(4), 631–635.
33. Who, (2020) Rabies, World Health Ordanization, Https://Www.Who.Int/News-Room/Fact-Sheets/Detail/Rabies
34. Wilcke, H., & Budke, A. (2019). Comparison as A Method for Geography Education. *Education Sciences*, *9*(3), 225.
35. Yaqoob, M. (2020). No Let-Up In Canine Terror, Authorities In Slumber,Greater Kashmir, Https://Www.Greaterkashmir.Com/News/Srinagar/No-Let-Up-In-Canine-Terror-Authorities-In-Slumber/
36. Yatto Irfan. (2018).No Let Up In Dog Menace In Srinagar, People Annoyed, Rising Kashmir, Http://Www.Risingkashmir.Com/News/No-Let-Up-In-Dog-Menace-In-Srinagar-People-Annoyed--338502.Html
37. Young Bites. (2018). Stray Dog Menace in Jammu- A Threat Perception, Http://Www.Youngbites.Com/Newsdet.Aspx?Q=242992
38. Zia Ather. (2012). Of the Dog Days in Kashmir, The Mantle, Http://Www.Mantlethought.Org/Other/Dog-Days-Kashmir
39. Wandeler, A. I., Matter, H. C., Kappeler, A., & Budde, A. (1993). The ecology of dogs and canine rabies: a selective review. *Rev Sci Tech*, 12(1), 51-71.
40. Singh, Varsha. (2018). Are stray dogs a major problem in India? An estimated 35 million stray dogs live in India, Media India Group, https://mediaindia.eu/society/stray-dogs-a-major-problem-in-india/
41. Smith, N. L. (1979). Techniques for the analysis of geographic data in evaluation. *Evaluation and program planning*, 2(2), 119-126.
42. Turner, M. G. (1990). Spatial and temporal analysis of landscape patterns. *Landscape ecology*, 4(1), 21-30.
43. Yu, G., Yang, R., Wei, Y., Yu, D., Zhai, W., Cai, J., ... & Qin, J. (2018). Spatial, temporal, and spatiotemporal analysis of mumps in Guangxi Province, China, 2005–2016. *BMC infectious diseases*, 18(1), 360.
44. *Daniels, T.J. (1983). "The social organization of free-ranging urban dogs. I. Non-estrous social behaviour". Applied Animal Ethology. 10 (4): 341–363.*
45. Lans English, (2015). Stray dogs attack school children in Kashmir, One India,

46. Hussain, A. (2020). World Rabies Day: Srinagar reported 55,000 animal bite cases in past decade, the times of India., https://www.hindustantimes.com/cities/world-rabies-day-srinagar-reported-55-000-animal-bite-cases-in-past-decade/story-wqt6O2x3UVgQ5XRNH3JMmI.html
47. **Press Trust of Kashmir (2018). Dog menace continues in Srinagar, SMC unable to deliver,** https://www.presstrustofkashmir.com/2018/11/08/dog-menace-continues-in-srinagar-smc-unable-to-deliver-2/
48. Singh Varsha (2018) Are stray dogs a major problem in India?An estimated 35 million stray dogs live in India, media india group, https://mediaindia.eu/society/stray-dogs-a-major-problem-in-india/
49. Kashmir observer (2018) 48000 stary dogs roam city streets, https://kashmirobserver.net/2018/10/13/48000-stray-dogs-roam-city-streets/
50. Raafi, M. (2017) stary dogs on powl in Srinagar, Kashmir life, https://kashmirlife.net/stray-dogs-prowl-srinagar-132088/
51. Srinivasan, K., Kurz, T., Kuttuva, P., & Pearson, C. (2019). Reorienting rabies research and practice: Lessons from India. Palgrave Communications, 5(1), 1-11.

Urban Environment and Spatial Science
Dr Mohd Akhter Ali, Dr. Kabir Mohan Sethy, Dr Muzafar Wani and M.Kamraju
Ane Books Pvt. Ltd. 2021, , ISBN : 978-93-90658-28-2, P.P. : 73 – 82

6

Geoinformatics Aided Urban Land Bank Identification and Mapping- A Case Study of Berhampur Municipal Corporation of Ganjam District, Odisha State, India

Binita Tripathy, K.M.Sethy and P.Mishra
[1]*Scientist, Odisha Space Applications Centre, Bhubaneswar*
[2]*Professor, Department of Geography, Utkal University, Bhubaneswar*

Abstract

Identification of suitable sites for urban development in old and unplanned cities is one of the critical issues of urban planning. Creation of spatial database on Land Bank has become inevitable for various developmental initiatives in urban regions. The study illustrates the use of geoinformatics for identification and geodatabase generation on urban land bank in Berhampur Municipal Corporation of Ganjam district of Odisha state,India. For this purpose, High Resolution ortho rectified satellite images like World View, Cartosat-II and IRS P6 LISS IV along with georeferenced digital cadastral mosaic have been used through softwares like Autocad and Arc GIS 10.2.The Land Bank information thus generated under this study depicts the spatial location,extent and land

Corresponding Author: Binita Tripathy

use category of all types of vacant lands at plot level in Berhampur Municipal Corporation.

Keywords: Land Bank,geoinformatics, World View, Cartosat-II, IRS P6 LISS IV, Autocad, Arc GIS 10.2,RoR

Introduction

The Goal no eleven of the total seventeen Sustainable Development Goals set by United Nations gives emphasis on making cities and human settlements inclusive, safe, regimen and sustainable. Sustainable human settlements development was also discussed at the second and third sessions of the Commission on Sustainable Development. "Promoting sustainable human settlements development" is the subject of Chapter 7 of Agenda 21(Göran *Finnveden*, 2016).While discussing the sustainability of cities in Odisha state of India ,it is observed that ,urban areas in Odisha state face numerous, varied, and evolving problems to housing, traffic, scarcity of free space for recreational activities, disruption of water supplies, extreme weather events and socio economic conflicts. Many of these problems have an important spatial component, and understanding where exactly something is, what it is, and why it is important is the job of the Geospatial-Intelligence. Effectively managing these problems requires geospatial intelligence that not only assesses and where and what is happening now, but that also prepares potential future plans. Geoinformatics has made a paradigm shift in urban planning and management providing pathway to the urban planners in understanding the problems and potentials of one urban development region through identification of individual cadastral and assets.Urban Land Bank information generation through use of high resolution satellite imagery,digital cadastre and geoinformatics provides authentic and updated vital input to the planners in identifying potential sites of development like parks,parking sites,waste water management sites, new bus terminals, etc in the urban administrative areas. One such attempt has been made to create the urban land bank for Berhampur Municipal Corporation of Ganjam district of Odisha state, India.

Objectives

Following are the major objectives of this study:

1. to create one georeferenced seamless digital cadastre of the Municipal Corporation incorporating all hierarchical administrative boundaries like corporation boundary, ward boundaries/mouza boundaries, Plot boundaries with plot numbers
2. to link the Record of Right (ROR) information of individual cadastral(plot) with the spatial cadastral database in GIS platform

3. to identify, map and generate the geo -spatial database on different urban vacant land categories like Government and Private inside the Municipal Corporation as per the Government land records
4. to generate the geospatial database of urban land bank of theBerhampur Municipal Corporation

Study Area

Berhampur Municipal Corporation (BeMC) consisting of 40 no of wards is situated between 19° 16'31.814" N to 19° 20'27.068" N Latitudes and 84° 44' 41.695" E to 84° 52' 12.077" E longitudes. The total area of BeMC is 3335.33 Hectare. Its average elevation above Mean Sea Level is 24m. It is the fourth largest city of Orissa with population of 210418 in 1991 & 307792 in 2001. The present population (2009) is estimated to be 0.38 million. It has been declared as a Class-I Town Category as per 2001 Census.The geology of the Berhampur Municipal Corporation (BeMC) is Eastern Ghats with plains and rock exposures of Granitic origin. The Howrah-Chennai Railway line of South-Eastern Railway/ East Coast Railway passes through the city making Berhampur as the busiest station in this region. Similarly N.H. 5 runs close to the city providing direct linkage to Kolkata, Vishakhapatnam & Chennai. N.H. 217 also runs through this city.

The city is well connected with districts through S.H. No.7, 17 & 65. River Rushikulya flows at a distance of about 30 kms from the city and discharges into the Bay of Bengal near Gopalpur port. The city has a good number of big Tanks/Lakes. High humidity prevails in the atmosphere both in summer & rainy seasons. Maximum summer temperature is 40o C whereas minimum winter temperature is 22o C. The mean daily temperature varies from 33o C to 38o C.

Data Used and Methodology

Data captured for this study involves both insertion of spatial data from digital cadastre and high resolution satellite images as well as assigning spatial data with respect to attributes. The following data sets have been used in this study.

1. Digital cadastral datasets of 42 villages surveyed in year 1978-79
2. World View-2 orthorectified Panchromatic image of October,2010 of 50 cm spatial resolution
3. Cartosat-II and LISS IV fused ortho rectified images of 1 metre spatial resolution-2016-17
4. Record of Right information as downloaded from Bhulekhwebsite ofNational Informatics Centre

Geoinformatics Methods

The cadastral maps for all 42 villages were available on larger scales like 1:2000 to 1:4,000. These maps depict the survey boundaries with survey numbers, cultural features like household, transport network natural features like drainage tank/ponds etc. The cadastral maps were generally prepared using plane table surveying and chain surveying. These maps were drawn to a true area projection or Cassini projection. These maps were brought under standard projection / coordinate system(UTM/WGS 84) for effective linkages in the GIS environment in this study.

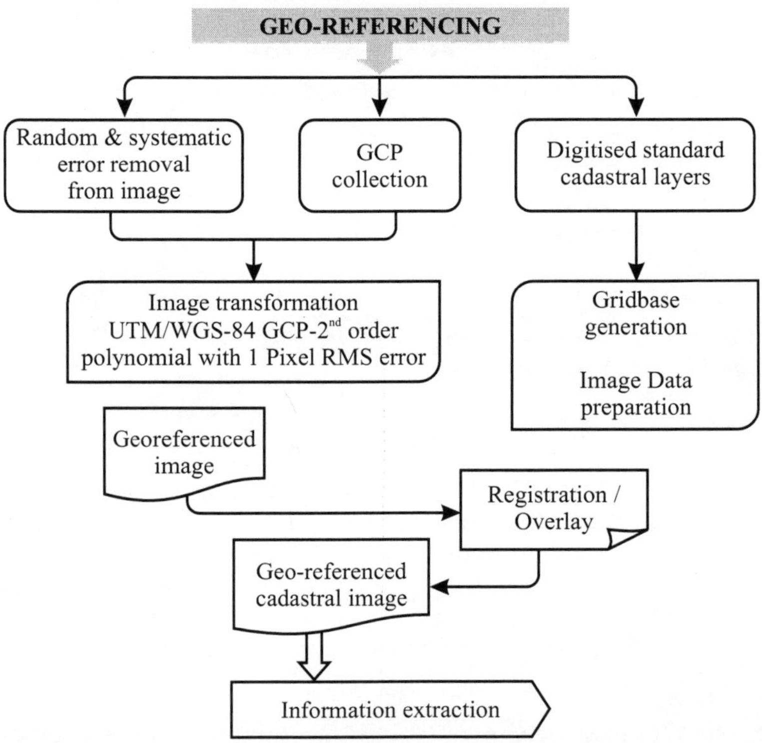

Chart 1

The high resolution satellite image depict field bunds, cart tracks, small nallas, settlements, tanks and other cultural features like roads, railway network, canals, buildings, etc. This gave an advantage in identifying ground control points for developing transformation model for image-image tie down.

The cadastral maps have been digitally scanned .Specific s/w i.e. Auto CAD and Arc GIS 10.2 are used for generating the digital cadastral database and subsequent overlaying of cadastral images on satellite image data. The cadastral image is registered with rectified satellite data using image to image transformation model. A registration accuracy of less than two pixels of standard and residual errors is achieved while image to image tie down. Arc-GIS software is used for image to image registration without artifacts and null points, a kernel-based line thinning, followed by editing and polygon labelling. The registered parcel boundaries are overlaid on satellite data in the form of vectors. The geo-referenced digital cadastral datasets developed by the above procedure is used as base for generating other datasets(flow chart 1 & 2)

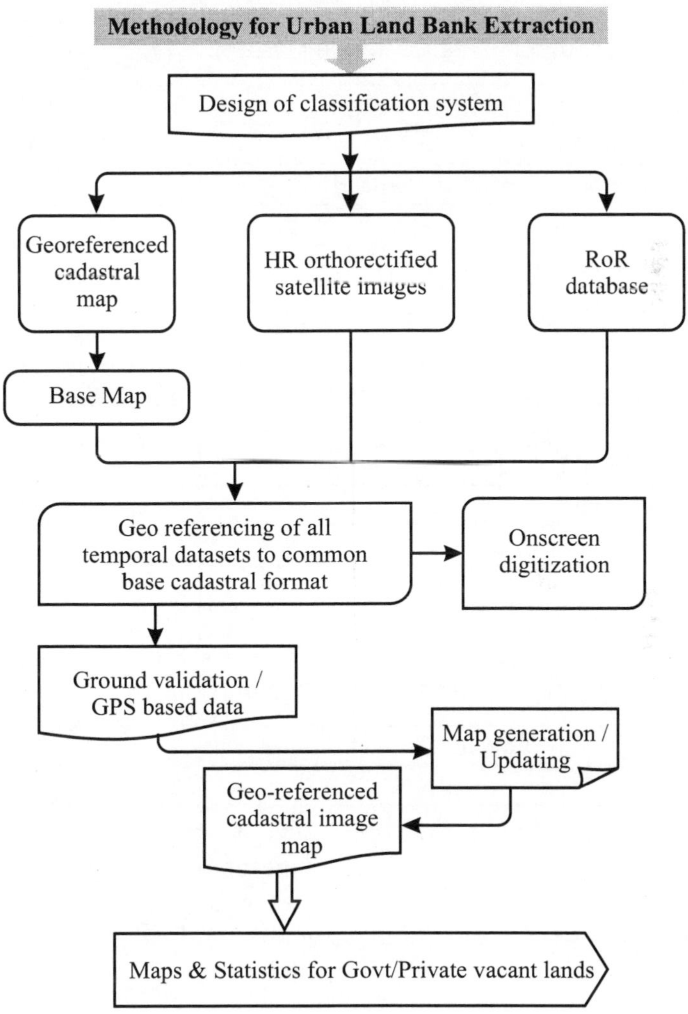

Chart 2

Thematic features on all types of vacant lands have been extracted from high resolution satellite images. The distinction between government and private has been made after integration of ROR database with the digital spatial cadastral database. All six types of government vacant land have been identified based on the land type (Kisam) as per the ROR.

Result & Analysis

Plot wise identification of all types of vacant lands inside Berhampur Municipal Corporation has been carried out during this study and the findings is depicted in the following Table 6.1.

Table 6.1: Categories of different land use classes under vacant land as identified from satellite image in BeMC

Sl. No.	*Land Use classes*	*Area in Hectare*
1	Construction sites	16.37
2	Cremation ground/Burial ground	11.15
3	Embankment	29.03
4	Grazing land(Gochar)	12.06
5	Land with and without scrub	35.01
6	Others	2.97
7	Marshy/Swampy area/Waterloged Area	20.58
8	Plotted Layout	770.46
9	Reclaimed Land	5.49
10	River sand	1.92
11	Rock outcrop areas	0.03
12	VL within industrial area	0.86
13	VL within institutional area	39.11
14	VL within other urban area	72.6
15	VL within residential area	53.5
16	Waste Dump/Dumping Ground	1.5
Grand Total		1072.64

In total, 1072.64 hectare of lands seems to be lying vacant inside the Municipal Corporation area, i.e; 32.15 percent of total geographical area. However out of this 1072.64 hectare of lands, the spatial extent of plotted layout lands is 770.46 hectare which cannot be considered as a vacant land in practical sense. The spectral signature of these lands though give impression of vacant lands, in ground reality, these lands can be considered as a landuse sub category of residential class. Hence, in reality only 302.18 hectare of lands can be considered as vacant land (VL) inside the Municipal Corporation area (Fig 6.1).

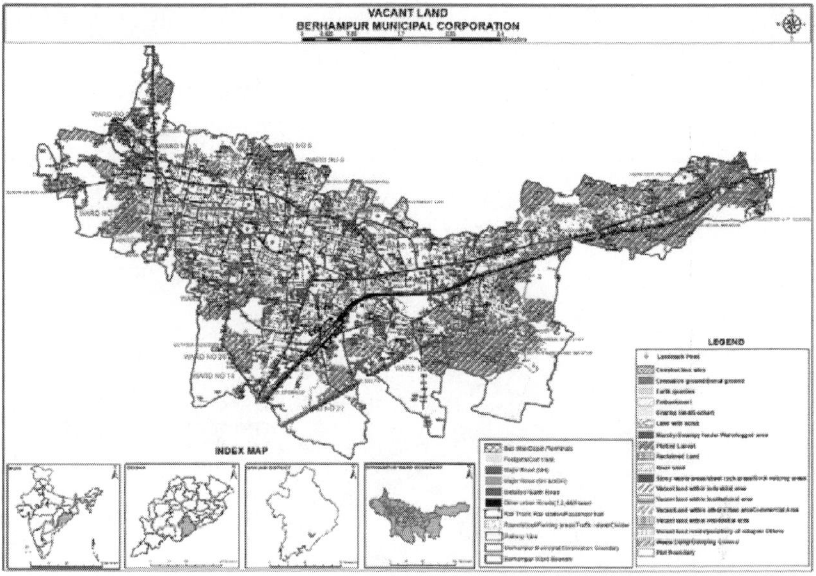

Fig. 6.1

The linking of RoR with the spatial geo-referenced cadastral distinguishes the vacant lands into government and private category (Fig. 6.2). The following table depicts the spatial extent of government vacant lands inside the Berhampur Municipal Corporation. Nearly six types of government vacant lands have been identified (Table 6.2).Only 4.61 percent of the total geographical area of the BeMC now has vacant lands which can be utilised for specific developmental purposes. Plot wise geospatial information of each piece of vacant land has been generated under the study and the details of which can be inferred from the Geodatabase either using any GIS platform or using the KML format (Fig. 6.3 as an example for Ward 40 of BeMC). Specifically the Protected lands, (Public Lands and Lands reserved for public use of total extent 78.33 hectare of lands can now seem to be used by Government either for new public bus stand, park, parking sites, etc inside BeMC.

Table 6.2: Government Vacant Lands in side Berhampur Municipal Corporation Area

Sl. No	*Government Vacant Land Category*	*Total Area in Hectares*
1	Unculturable Wasteland (Abadi AjogyaAnabadi)	38.53
2	Culturable Wasteland (Abad JogyaAnabadi)	15.39
3	Protected Lands (Rakhita)	44.36
4	Public Lands (Sarbasadharana)	17.7

Sl. No	*Government Vacant Land Category*	*Total Area in Hectares*
5	Lands Reserved for Public Use (Sarbasadharana sarankhita)	16.27
6	Railway	21.68
Grand Total		153.93

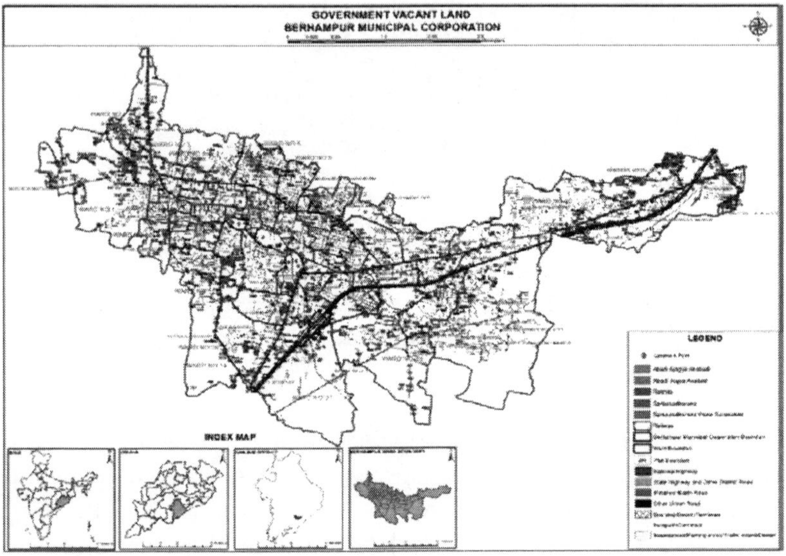

Fig. 6.2

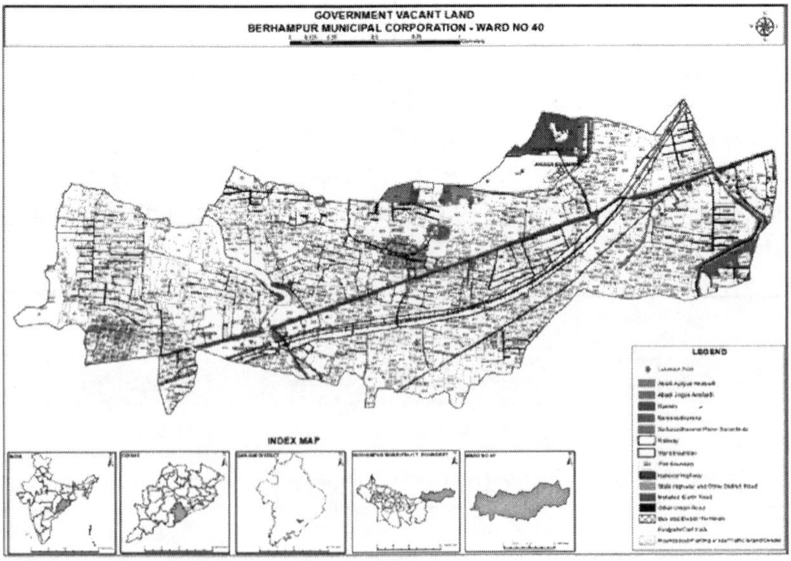

Fig. 6.3

Conclusion

The Geoinformatics based approach using orthorectified High Resolution satellite image and digital georeferenced cadastral data base with RoR is very simple and flexible which can be used to use to create land bank information for entire Berhampur Development Authority which is the larger administrative region for Berhampur Municipal Corporation.It provides comprehensive and satisfactory plot wise database of availabity of vacant lands for developmental work which in turn will help in solving any specific problem.This model can also encourage participation of planners and administrators in decision making process for sustained development of the region.

References

1. Chapter13 of Agenda 21 of the UN Conference Environment and Development (UNCED), in Rio de Janeiro, Brazil on 1996
2. ESRI,Environmental Systems Research Institute,Inc,(2018).Working with the Arc GIS Spatial Analyst,Redlands,USA:ESRI Inc
3. Göran Finnveden,et al,2016 JPI Urban Europe Symposium "Shaping common ground in urban sustainability?", Brussels 2016

Urban Environment and Spatial Science
Dr Mohd Akhter Ali, Dr. Kabir Mohan Sethy, Dr Muzafar Wani and M.Kamraju
Ane Books Pvt. Ltd. 2021, , ISBN : 978-93-90658-28-2, P.P. : 83 – 93

7

A Qualitative Study on Role of Satellite Cities in India

P.Manisha, Sanja Devi, M.Kamraju
M.Sc.,
Osmania University, Hyderabad
manishapendyala95@gmail.com,
valmikisandhya14@gmail.com,

Abstract

Satellite Towns were there for about 2 billion people on Earth in 1927, but our population is almost 7 billion today. This enormous increase in the human population has brought crowded metropolitan areas. We created satellite towns in order to create planned towns and houses. These towns have begun to be built in our country as well. It might therefore be a good idea to consider its benefits and disadvantages. The primary benefit of a city with skyscrapers is its modernity. Since we've had a terrible earthquake disaster in the past, it's important that our country has durable and secure homes, and modern homes have these qualities.

Furthermore, satellite towns include supermarkets and shopping malls. It means that nearly all our needs can be found close to home. Safety for young people is another important advantage of satellite towns. There are game areas for young people in the satellite towns to illustrate the point; however, kids play on the dangerous roads and streets in a casual city. It is clear that satellite towns are safer when we compare these two cases. In addition to their advantages, satellite towns also have several disadvantages. The major drawback is being located far away from the centre of the city. Therefore, commuting becomes more difficult and fatigue can be caused. Expensive houses are another important drawback of modern towns. They are really expensive, despite the

Corresponding Author: P.Manisha

fact that houses are smaller than casual homes. The modern cities are safer than old cities. Additionally, nearly every need we can find close to home. The central idea of this paper is to study the role of Satellite cities in growth of core city. Mostly secondary data has been used to formulate this paper.

Keywords: Satellite Towns, metropolitan areas, supermarkets, shopping malls, skyscrapers

Introduction

More than ever, the planet has become urbanized, and there is a massive spatial expansion of global centres. The number of cities and cities is on the increase forever. The world's landscape is dotted with cities in both parts of what is known as the North and the South (US State).

The study of cities has been linked directly with the world economy. This approach provides insights into urban change processes (Friedmann, 19863) because the strengthening or weakening of the economy is bound to have an impact on urban centres.

The planned satellite cities are towns adjacent to a major city. These cities control or contain urban sprawl. In all possible ways, they are designed to help a major city expand. Satellite cities could be entirely independent cities, developed outside the metro. Unlike a suburb or a subdivision, they are self-contained, independent towns. The aim of satellite cities is to ensure a perfect balance between population and resources in terms of environmentally friendly development. The goal is to create affordable housing for a large part of the community.

India has also seen the mushrooming of global cities like Bangalore, Hyderabad, Chennai, Kolkata, Delhi and Mumbai. These have made the World Economy and World Map a niche for them. A suburb of Delhi-'Gurgaon 'is the new one to have carved space for it on the World Map. And, as the 2007 State of the World Cities Report(UNFPA 2007) points out, the growth potential in small and intermediate cities is much greater.

Objective

The main aim of this paper is to study the role of satellite cities for the growth of core city (Central Business District).The paper also puts emphasis on the role of satellite towns in the growth of city/town.

Methodology

For our study we mostly relied on secondary data from various government reports, authentic websites, books, journals, etc

Discussion

Due to rapid urbanisation, major cities across India are facing a mammoth challenge on many fronts. One of the pressing problems these cities face is massive population growth. In metro towns such as Delhi, Mumbai and Bangalore, population growth has reached alarming proportions that can be said to be brimming to the rim (J, R. 2014). An influx of migrants from different parts of the country has resulted in the availability of job opportunities and better living conditions. This has resulted in cities reaching a point of saturation in terms of developable space available. This lack of space has led to the sale of developable land at exorbitant prices, which has led buyers to rethink their property purchasing plans. On the other hand, city planners must come up with solutions where they have to strike a balance between the development of infrastructure and the approval of residential areas within the urban developable area available (J, 2014).

In and around such cities, the development of satellite cities is good for real estate growth. They also provide most of the conveniences and facilities that major cities provide, in addition to being in the vicinity of major cities. Based on the integrated township model, satellite cities are developed to offer residents easy access to all the amenities and infrastructure facilities they would experience in major cities. In addition to the main city's decongestion, satellite cities serve a larger purpose. It offers a feasible option for citizens working in the main town to make use of affordable housing options. In addition, a satellite city alone provides its residents with employment opportunities, infrastructure, as well as commercial and residential spaces (J, 2014).

Major Satellite Cities in the World

- In Australia, Gold Coast in Queensland is a satellite city of Brisbane, Wollongong and Gosford is a satellite city of Sydney (Ansumant, 2020).
- Satellite cities are a major factor in urban regions of the United States and Canada. Some major satellite cities in the U.S include Bel Air, Bridgeport, Fort Collins, Fort Lauderdale, New Haven, Rockford, Riverside, San Bernardino, Santa Cruz, Tacoma, Worcester and Brentwood among others. In Canada, some satellite cities include Hamilton, Kitchener, and Sorel-Tracy among others (Ansumant, 2020).
- Satellite cities are there all over the world in Asia, Europe, South America and Africa wherever there are major cities and urban areas (Ansumant, 2020).

Major Satellite Cities in India

In India, there are many renowned satellite cities that have gained prominence due to the development of their infrastructure and the potential for real estate growth. Gurgaon, Noida, Ghaziabad and Faridabad are prominent satellite cities near Delhi. Some renowned satellite cities, such as Navi Mumbai, Dombivli, and Thane, are also in Mumbai (J, 2014).

Kanchipuram, Mamallapuram, Sriperumbudur and Tiruvallur, among others, are important satellite cities of Chennai. There are also a few prominent satellite townships in Bangalore, like Kengeri and Yelahanka. Other renowned satellite cities are Hitech City in Hyderabad, Salt Lake City in Kolkata, Pimpri-Chinchwad in Pune and Mohali in Chandigarh (J, 2014).

Importance of the Satellite cities

Satellite cities are gaining more popularity among the population today. The solution to the problem is provided by satellite towns. It is part of the larger cities of the metropolitan area, but completely independent of the urban area. Satellite cities provide living space and commercial space. It provides residents with a shopping mall, an education centre, and others.

The services, self-contained economies and others are maintained by the satellite towns while being interconnected with the closely located metropolitan areas. Through suburban sprawl, the bedroom communities, suburban areas and others are less self-contained. With the enormous variety of nodes, urban areas exist.

The satellite town provides residents with the luxury and security of living space. Advanced facilities are available for the upcoming satellite cities. The satellite cities are helping to reduce suburban sprawl with unique urban planning.

Characteristics of a Satellite City

The basic feature is that it is a smaller city in the vicinity of a large metropolitan city with its own local government and economy, independent of the surrounding big city. There are a lot of influences from the big city nearby on the satellite city. Satellite cities have their own culture, their own history, and their own independent economic infrastructure (Ansumant, 2020). The satellite towns are linked to the larger towns, but are entirely independent of the nearby big city. The nearby large city is sometimes called the parent city, and these satellite cities are known locally within the state but are not as famous around the world as the nearby larger parent city (Ansumant, 2020).

They are not an extension to the nearby large city. There is a clear distinction geographically between a major parent city and a satellite city. This implies that the two cities have some area or a few miles between them. Generally, there is a small rural area between the large parent city and the satellite city that separates the two cities completely (Ansumant, A. 2020, September 03).

These are not as advanced as the neighbouring larger cities. The population of the towns is much smaller than that of the nearby larger towns. In the satellite cities, many amenities and infrastructure facilities available in large cities nearby are not as prominent. Satellite city residents are known to travel regularly to the nearby big city for work, recreational and other reasons (Ansumant, 2020).

For work purposes, the labour force living in the satellite city travels daily to the big city, and satellite cities provide the major cities with manpower. As property rates and living costs in satellite cities are often lower compared to the parent city, many individuals find it affordable to live in the small satellite city and work in the nearby larger metropolitan area of the big city (Ansumant, A. 2020, September 03).

Students often travel to the parent city's higher education institutions, as quality educational institutions are often located in nearby large cities and not in satellite cities.

A satellite city's development and size are limited and limited and it never matches or exceeds the size of the nearby large city. Historically, they have evolved on their own and are not just an extension created to meet the need for a growing population for a large town. This implies that these towns have their own history, their own downtown or historic areas of the old city, and their own cultural identity (Ansumant, 2020).

Many times, along with the large cities nearby, products and brands are marketed to these cities. This means that these satellite cities in the zone or jurisdiction of the nearby large metropolitan area are often included in the telephone companies and other goods and services companies.

Between the satellite city and the large parent city nearby, there are often good transport services. Between these two types of cities, trains , buses and road transport are swift, efficient and on time, as commuters from satellite cities often travel daily to the nearby large city for work, education and other economic, recreational and social activities (Ansumant, A. 2020, September 03).

Ten Satellite Cities in India

India is one of the world's fastest-growing economies and the world's biggest democracy. Here, in terms of infrastructure, social and political standards, every major town is at the peak of development. The needs of existing metropolitan cities have risen with the boom in education and employment. These satellite cities were born or planned to support the country's major metropolitans because of the large influx in the neighbouring metro cities.

Haryana, Gurugram

Gurugram is a major satellite of New Delhi, located about 30kms southwest of the nation's capital. After Mumbai and Chennai, it is the third financial capital. It is spread over 732 sq km, with a population of 876,900 in total. It arose primarily when Maruti-Suzuki set up its plant in the 1970s and the city is booming today. It is the third town with the highest per capita income in the nation.

Uttar Pradesh, Noida

Noida (New Okhla Industrial Development Authority), located in the neighbouring state of Uttar Pradesh, is a planned satellite city of New Delhi. It is spread over 203 sq km, with a population of 637,272. It falls within the Yamuna River catchment area. The streets are planned adjacent to trees that increase the green cover of the city and are also regarded as the nation's greenest city with about 50 percent green cover.

Gujarat, Gandhinagar

Gujarat's state capital, Gandhinagar, is a planned satellite city of the city of Ahmedabad. It was designed by H.K Mewada, the architect, assisted by Prakash M Apte. It is spread over 177 square km. Since it is in the birthplace of Mahatma Gandhi, as a result of planning & infrastructure to metro everything is handled by Indian companies only, the authorities wanted to be purely an Indian enterprise.

Gurgaon City, India

View of Noida City

Gandhinagar

Hitech-City

Navi Mumbai

Fig. 6.7

Source: *www.re-thinkingthefuture.com*

City of Hitec, Telangana

Far as the country's economy and technology were simultaneously booming, the urge for IT hubs also emerged in the country's different pockets. HITEC City (Hyderabad Information Technology and Engineering Consultancy) was established to support Hyderabad and make it the country's major IT hub. It is an amalgamation of five sectors that make up a city. There are several major campuses, such as L&T Info City, Laxmi Cyber City, etc.

Navi Mumbai, Maharashtra

Navi Mumbai, designed by the visionary architect Charles Correa, is also regarded as Correa 's vision of the country in the 1960s. The country's economic capital was also growing at a rapid pace as the country progressed, and as a result, Charles Correa proposed Navi Mumbai to Mumbai as a satellite. CIDCO (The Corporation for the City and Industrial Development). Its planning began in 1971, and Navi Mumbai is today one of the country's most efficiently planned cities. The city's scenario has changed topsy-turvy after the proposal of Navi Mumbai International Airport

Newtown, West Bengal

It is a planned Kolkata satellite city and is managed by the Development Authority of Newtown Kolkata (NKDA). A 10.5 km stretch of Wi-Fi zone and also India's first Wi-Fi connectivity road are enabled. It is also known as the West Bengal state's IT hub.

Thane, Maharashtra

Besides Udaipur, as it is surrounded by 35 small and large lakes, Thane is also known as the City of Lakes. Thane is not a planned city, unlike other satellite cities, but because of its provinces to the city of Mumbai and suburbs, along with Navi Mumbai, Thane became the satellite city of Mumbai. Today, with well-developed residential areas and hubs of major businesses like TCS, L&T etc., it is spread over 147 sq km. It was also the first-ever passenger train station on the Asian continent.

New Kanpur City, Uttar Pradesh

Like every other satellite city , the city of New Kanpur is the Kanpur satellite. For the city, around 10,000 acres of land is proposed. The city will be connected via the metro, rail and expressways to Kanpur. Because of its proximity to IIT Kanpur (one of the nation's top engineering institutes), the government has planned to make Kanpur and Lucknow the state's IT hubs, increasing the city's potential. The majority of its land will be allocated to cooperative housing and the remainder will be allocated to private developers, with only 25 % of the total area covered by the land.

Mohali, Punjab

Mohali is the satellite city of Chandigarh, renowned for its sporty spirit of cricket and hockey. Politically located in Punjab, it is the state's IT hub as well. It was originally an extension of Chandigarh, but it is gaining its own identity as a city because of its rapid development in different sectors.

Amravati ,Andhra Pradesh

Amravati is an upcoming satellite that will also be Andhra Pradesh State's capital. The town is being prepared by Ar. Foster and Associates, and Ar. handles the infrastructure. Contractor for Hafeez. It is spread over 217.23 sq kilometres. The city is currently under development and soon it will be one of the nation's major cities.

Newton

New Kanpur City

Mohali

Thane

Amravati

Source: *www.re-thinkingthefuture.com*

Features of Satellite Cities

Satellite townships have local government and corporate life of their own. With the exception of a few purposes, such as employment and sometimes education, they have all the necessary amenities and facilities within their limits, they have to depend on the parent city's main city. Transportation means connecting the various satellite townships to the main city, such as buses, trains, etc., so it is not a problem to travel to the main city for work. It is free to decide the economic, social and cultural nature of its. Generally, satellite townships develop beyond the city's green belt. Like we discussed earlier, people are well equipped with different amenities and facilities, but for work or higher education, they have to depend on the parent city. The reason why people have to depend on the parent city for work is that in satellite townships it is prohibited to set up industries. It is mainly a residential area with only local shops, children's schools. Because their size and growth is restricted and controlled, these townships never become a rival to their parent city. Sometimes, for some goods and services produced in the parent city, satellite townships are considered as part of the market. Workers living in a particular satellite may belong to a particular industry's labour force and, in that case, the employers of such industries will be given a broader choice to find the best man for the job.

Advantages of Satellite Cities

Satellite cities offer multiple advantages, more than just mixed-use realty developments. It also helps to boost the local economy, in addition to providing its residents with superior quality of life in the form of road connectivity, electricity, water, drainage and other significant facilities. This leads to price increases in land and residential property prices in and around the satellite city. It provides them with a viable alternative for residents in the main city who want to escape from the stress, pollution and hassles of city life. In addition to providing its residents with easy accessibility, the transport infrastructure developed in satellite cities also allows the decongestment of traffic in the main city. In addition, satellite cities provide a scientific balance between the population and the resources it needs, leading to sustainable and eco-friendly development.

Satellite cities are the perfect choice for individuals who are looking to invest in the real estate sector. The workspace, social infrastructure and others are closely located to it. The benefits of investing in satellite cities, such as affordable housing, well-infrastructure and others, are vastly diverse. It provides the residents with a high quality of living experience. It provides access to roads, water , electricity, drainage and important facilities.

This city offers the inhabitants the stress and pollution free lifestyle. In satellite towns, transport infrastructure is developed that not only offers comfortable accessibility to residents, but also reduces traffic in the big city. It provides the residents with high quality water. The satellite town provides great facilities for affordable housing. The scientific balance between resources and populations is offered by satellite cities. It supplies the eco-friendly environment

Conclusion

The purpose of satellite cities is to provide the population and resources with a perfect balance in terms of environmentally friendly development. The goal is to create affordable housing for a large part of the community. The development of satellite cities into smart cities is an underlying need. A satellite city should be able to accommodate a smarter generation without compromising on the ecology of the area in order to ensure planned urbanisation and systematic development.

Some key considerations need to be kept in mind by policymakers and government agencies:

- **Rounded plan:** Demographic factors are a few things that need to be taken into account when planning a satellite city, such as socio-economic conditions, education centres, and population dialect.
- **Safety:** The safety of its inhabitants must be of primary concern to planners. Security issues in the planning process need to be carefully considered and integrated.
- **Heavy capital:** It requires enormous capital to build a city. The acceptability of the upcoming satellite city and its growth would depend on how early it can become a self-sustaining unit, aside from sourcing the required funds.

References

1. Ansumant, A. (2020, September 03). Satellite City: Meaning, Characteristics, & Examples. Retrieved September 31, 2020, from https://planningtank.com/settlement-geography/satellite-city
2. Kishan, A. B., Ali, M. A., & Kamraju, M. (2019). Impact of Urban Growth on Land Use-Land Cover in Hyderabad City.
3. J, R. (2014). Significance of Satellite Cities in India. Retrieved October 31, 2020, from https://www.commonfloor.com/guide/significance-of-satellite-cities-in-india-47384.html
4. Kamraju, M., & Kamraju, M. (2018). Changing Pattern of Urban Growth in Hyderabad City: A Study. Jai Maa Saraswati Gyanadayani, 3, 483-503.
5. P., N. (2007). Impact of Migration on Urbanization In India A Statistical Analysis. Retrieved August 25, 2020, from https://shodhganga.inflibnet.ac.in/handle/10603/161997
6. Satellite Townships: Town Planning and Design. (2011, July 15). Retrieved September 01, 2020, from http://www.architecture-student.com/town-planning/satellite-townships-town-planning-and-design/

7. Sen, A. (2016, June 10). Satellite Cities India: Why Satellite Cities Are Become More Significant. Retrieved October 11, 2020, from https://www.proptiger.com/guide/post/how-the-concept-of-satellite-cities-is-gaining-ground
8. State, U. D. (n.d.). The North-South Dialogue and Economic Diplomacy The North-South Dialogue refers to the process through which the developing and newly independent nations of the "third world. Retrieved October 01, 2020, from http://history.state.gov/
9. UNFPA (United Nations Population Fund), 2007. Op. cit.
10. Venkatesh, K., & Kamraju, M. (2018). Urban Sprawl and Sustainable Development in Hyderabad: A Geoinformatic Approach. *International Journal of Creative Research Thoughts (IJCRT)*, *6*, 1285-294.
11. 10 Satelite Cities in India. - RTF: Rethinking The Future. (2020, May 27). Retrieved September 01, 2020, from https://www.re-thinkingthefuture.com/fresh-perspectives/a899-10-satelite-cities-in-india/

Urban Environment and Spatial Science
Dr Mohd Akhter Ali, Dr. Kabir Mohan Sethy, Dr Muzafar Wani and M.Kamraju
Ane Books Pvt. Ltd. 2021, , ISBN : 978-93-90658-28-2, P.P. : 95 – 104

8

Coastal Cities and Erosion Issues: A Study Along The Coast of Puri Town, Odisha, India Using Remote Senisng & Gis

Ms. Prachi Prava Panda, Prof. Manas Ranjan Das,
Dr. Nihar Ranjan Das
Dept. of Civil Engineering, ITER (FET),
S.O.A. (Deemed to be University), Bhubaneswar

Introduction

Coastal zones are unique ecosystems. Now a days, these coastal areas are under sever threat due to imbalance in their ecosystems caused by human interventions primarily in the form of rapidly changing landuse. In fact a major part of the world's population is now living in urban areas and also most of the world's cities have been grown along the coasts. The most important issue faced by these coastal areas now is coastal erosion, which results from a combination of natural factors intensified by human activities.

In the process of monitoring the change in shoreline Remote Sensing is most important tool gives more reliable, accurate and synoptic result. The application of remote sensing and GIS has an important role in change analysis study of coastal shoreline providing synoptic views. Today, the most common shoreline detection technique has been subjective visual interpretation. Recent topographic data collection and digital image-processing techniques are more convenient for the coastal investigator to use objective shoreline detection methods. This study attempted to find the trend of shoreline changes, quantify the shoreline erosion and accretion and the factors attributed to the changes. The satellite imagery has been used in monitoring shoreline changes as this gives wide coverage.

Corresponding Author: Ms. Prachi Prava Panda

Study Area

Odisha is one of the eastern coastal States of India. It is located between the 17.49 N to 22.34 N latitudes and 81.27 E to 87.29 E longitudes. The length of coastline along Odisha state is 480 km. It is bounded by the Bay of Bengal on the east. It consists of 30 districts, out of which 06 are coastal districts. Puri district is one of these 06 coastal districts, liying between 85° 09' to 86° 25' East longitude and between 19° 28' to 20° 10' North latitude. In the present study, around 07 km of coastline along Puri town (Fig. 8.1) has been considered for study of shoreline mapping and decadal monitoring of erosion and accretion from the period 1970 to 2020. The district is bounded by the Khurdha district in north, Bay of Bengal in south, Jagatsinghpur district in the east and Ganjam district in the west. The climatic condition of Puri district is normally hot with high humidity. Summer feels during April to May with maximum temperature between 35°c - 40°c. and winter feels from November to January with minimum temperature within 20°c.

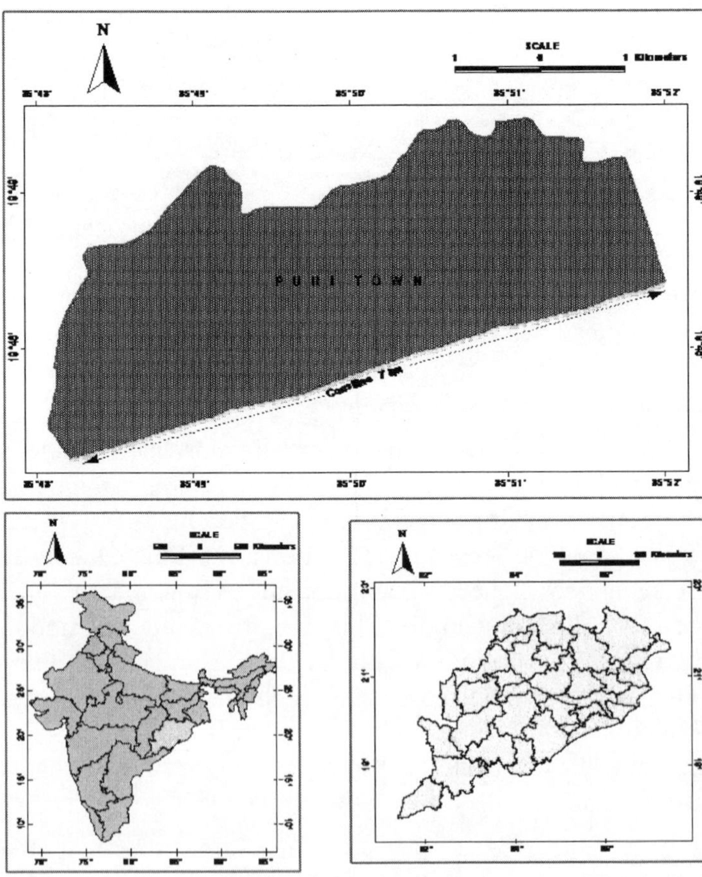

Fig. 8.1: Map Showing Location of Study area (Puri Town)

Puri town is well known as *Shri Jagannath Dhama* (the abode of Lord Jagannath). This place is considered as famous heritage site in Odisha as well as a famous pilgrimage site in Hindu culture. There are various sand dunes of about 10-15 m height near to Puri sea beach. As it has been observed during several earlier studies, ther is large scale shore erosion in parts of the coastal zone of odisha between Chilika lake on south to Subarnarekha river mouth on north, with a very pronounced impact along the coast of Puri town. Puri town beach is getting eroded particularly during the south west monsoon season (June to October), when wave action is significantly increased during the low pressure/depression/cyclones in Bay of Bengal. Encroachment of human activities in to the beaches is aggravating this issue.

Most often during October – November and April – May the tropical cyclones have been occurred in the Bay of Bengal, due to which enormous devastation fell out along Puri coast (Fig. 8.2). It has been noticed that Coastal degradation, coastal flood, sea level rise and inundation along coast arose due to cyclone and storm surge. Along the coast of Odisha, the Puri coast has also remained highly vuolnerable to these tropical cyclones (Fig. 8.3).

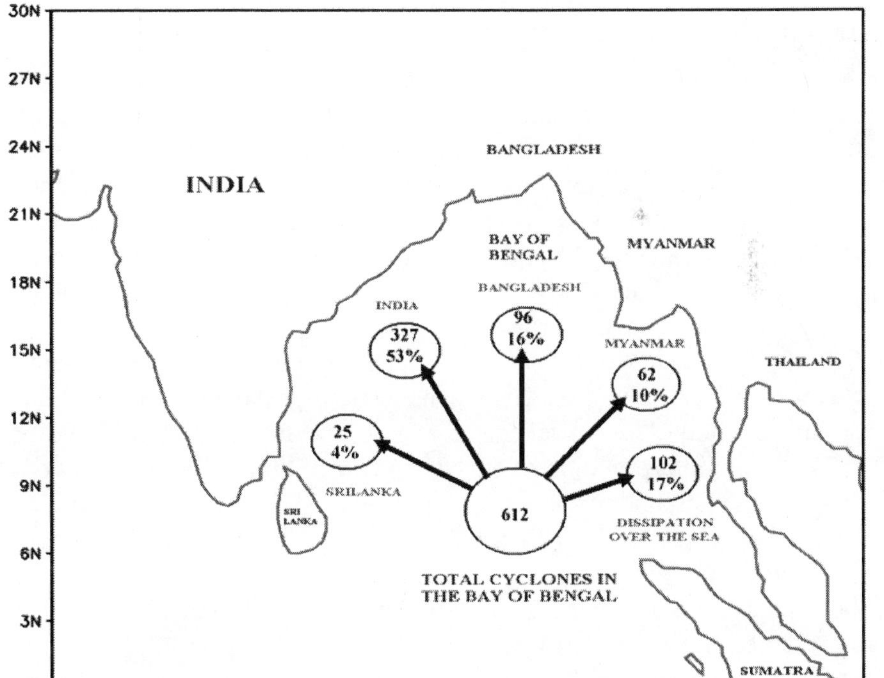

Fig. 8.2: Number of Tropical cyclones crossing different Countries surrounding Bay of Bengal (1890 – 2012)

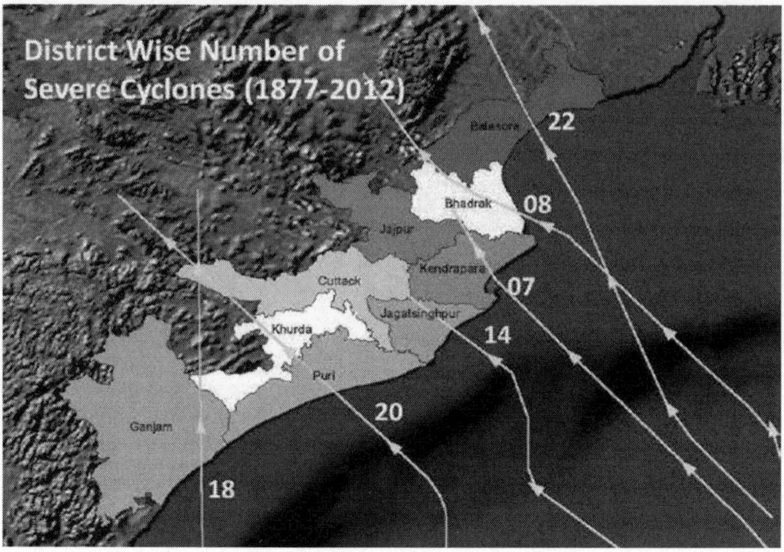

Fig. 8.3

Material And Methodology

As the primary objective of the study was to identify decade wise shoreline change along Puri coast, remote sensing data for the years of 1972, 1980, 1990, 1999, 2012 and 2019 have been used based on availability for the study area. The satellite images used in the study have been described in the below given Table 1. To extract position of shoreline the LANDSAT satellite image (L1 MSS, L5 TM, L7 ETM+ and Sentinel) has been downloaded from earth explorer and used. This study is a comparative study in which change of shoreline has been analyzed for different years i.e. 1972-1980, 1980-1990, 1990-1999, 1999-2012 and 2012-2020. Each image is geo-rectified and the study area was masked before using the image through Arc GIS 10.1. The image processing methods like visual interpretation and band rationing have been used. The visual interpretation of LANDSAT- MSS images was carried out to quantify the erosion and accretion. The year wise shoreline has been digitized from satellite imagery in line feature. Then overlay of different years data has been done to identify differences and year wise increase and decrease in length has been measured. Again the quantity of shoreline erosion and accretion has been measured in time series format. In this study the specific model Digital Shoreline Analysis System (DSAS) has been used for measurement of erosion and accretion in ARC GIS software. In this model the net shoreline movement (NSM), end point rate (EPR), linear regression rate (LRR) can be identified which helps in delineation of change in shoreline. It is an automated method. It is helpful to user to calculate the change from multiple historical shoreline position. For this study the transect layer has been created by considering 50 meters of spacing as fixed distance. In this method the uncertainty of results increases by high spacing of transects and massive data values occurs along low distance spacing. So here by 50 m spacing has been taken for the study. In this work these results has been calculated for 1972 - 2019. Coast under study area shows different behaviour under different time scale.

Table 8.1: Details of Satellite Image Used in the Study

Date and Year	*Path/Row*	*Satellite ID*	*Sensor*	*Resolution (m)*
07-11-1972	150/046	Landsat 1	MSS	80
18-01-1980	150/046	Landsat 3	MSS	38
13-02-1990	140/046	Landsat 5	TM	30
29-11-1999	140/046	Landsat 7	ETM+	30
12-07-2012	140/046	Landsat 7	ETM+	30
19-07-2019	140/046	Sentinel	Sentinel	30/ 10

Results And Discussion

Shoreline change mapping for Puri coast has been done at a temporal scale of 50 years. Detailed lengths of shoreline are given below in Table- 2 below.

Table 8.2: Shoreline Length in km along puri Town in Different Years

1972	1980	1990	1999	2012	2019
7.02	7.08	7.02	7.04	7.11	7.12

Fig. 8.4: Map showing shoreline Along Puri Town during various Years from 1972 to 2019

The above study reveals that the shoreline change has dynamic behaviour which has been influenced by the occurrences of cyclonic storms and wave height. In Puri coast there is 100 m increase in length of coastline in 50 years of period for the year from 1972-2019. In this study DSAS tool has been used for measurement of erosion and accretion. For this the transect layer has been created by considering 50 meters of spacing as fixed distance. In this method the uncertainty of results increases by high spacing of transects and massive data values occurs along low distance spacing. So here by 50mtr spacing has been taken for the study. In this work these results has been calculated for 1972- 2019. Coast under study area shows different behaviour under different time scale.

Map (Fig. 8.5) depicts that a maximum erosion of 50.6 m and accretion of 50.14 m has been observed at transect id 5 and 26 respectively in the year 1970-1980 at Puri coast. In the shoreline mapping of year 1980-1990 (Fig. 8.6), transect id 9 shows 47.7 m of erosion and at transect id 27 accretion of 49.03m has been identified. The map of the year 1990-1999 (Fig. 8.7) depicts that at transect id 16 there is maximum erosion of 28.3m and maximum accretion of 46.18m has been observed at transect id 18. In the map of year 1999-2012 (Fig. 8.8), transect id 22 shows maximum erosion of 64.19 m and at transect id 25 accretion of 65.8 m has been identified. From the shoreline map of year 2012-2019 (Fig. 8.9), a maximum erosion of 59.76m has been assessed at transect id 25 and at transect id 22 accretion of 64.19m has been identified.

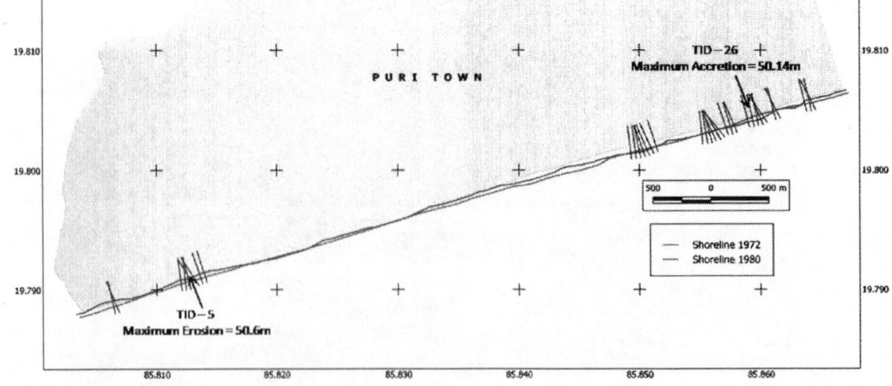

Fig. 8.5: Erosion and accretion mapping for Puri coast for years 1972-1980

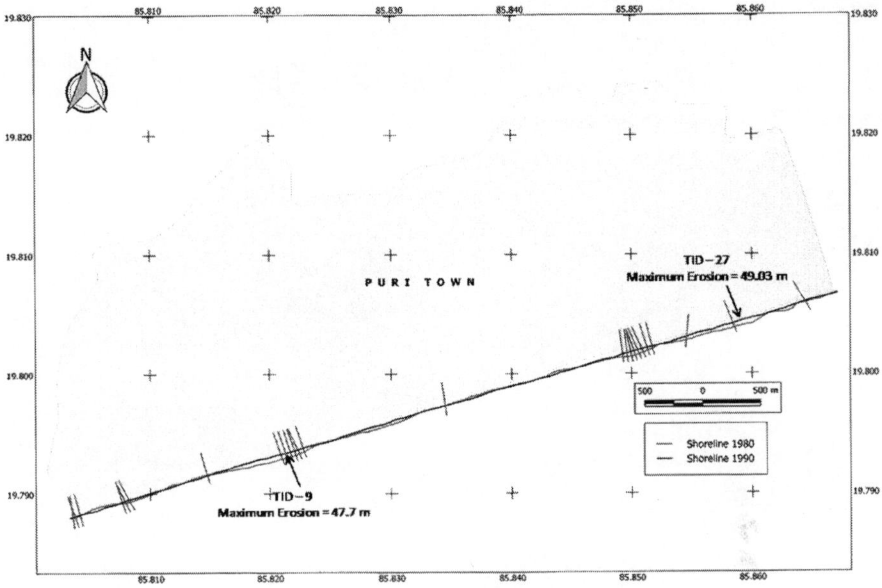

Fig. 8.6: Erosion and accretion mapping for Puri coast for years 1980-1990

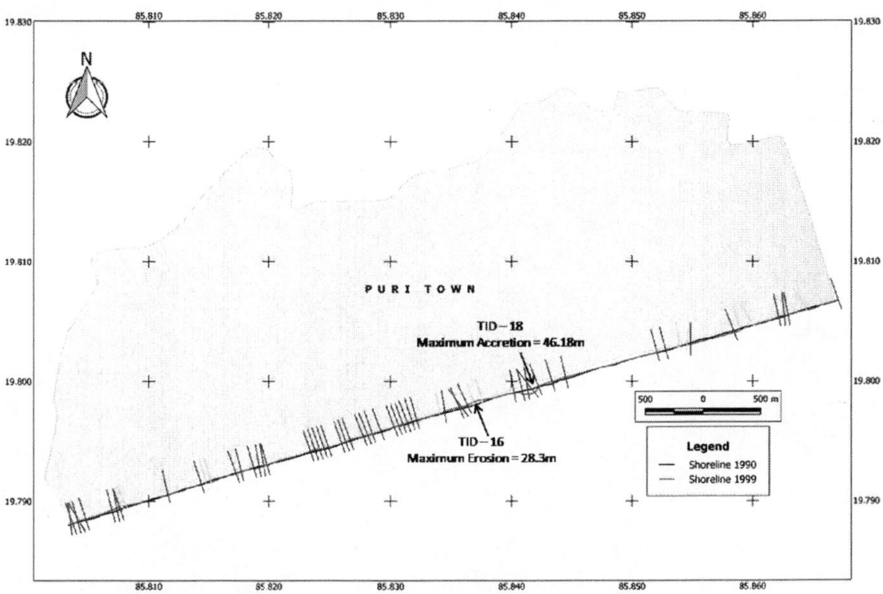

Fig. 8.7: Erosion and accretion mapping for Puri coast for years 1990-1999

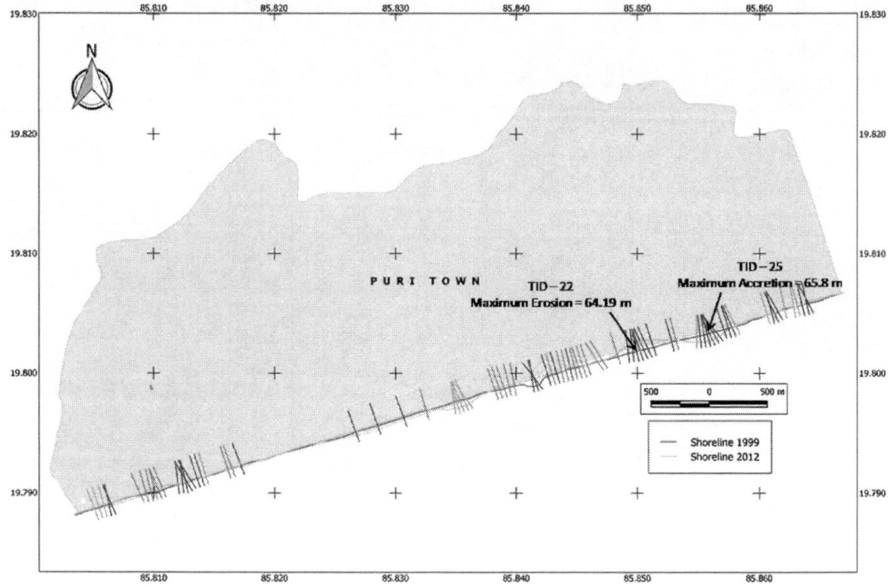

Fig. 8.8: Erosion and accretion mapping for Puri coast for years 1999-2012

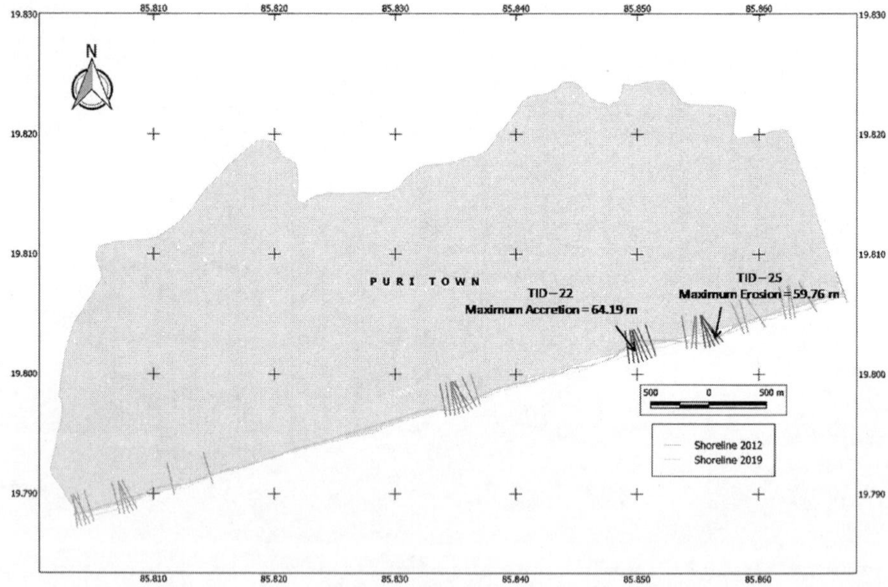

Fig. 8.9: Erosion and accretion mapping for Puri coast for years 2012-2019

As a result of the present study, at Puri coast an average erosion of 5.06 m/year from 1972 to 1980 has been observed which is decreased in next during 1980-1990 i.e. 4.9 m/year, then in the year of 1990-1999 average erosion is

2.83 m/year and in decade 1999-2012 the average erosion is increased and is about 6.41 m/year ând in last decade it has been found that 5.9 m/year. From the shoreline map of year 1970-2019 (Fig. 8.10), a maximum erosion of 68.6 m has been assessed at transect id 18 & 21 in central part and at transect id accretion of 31.79 m has been identified in northern part. The coast may be affected due to storm surge generated by the cyclones and the depressions in the Bay of Bengal. Here maximum erosion occurred at northern part of Puri coast. Somehow Central part of the Puri coast is accreted and erosion is mostly observed in northern and southern part.

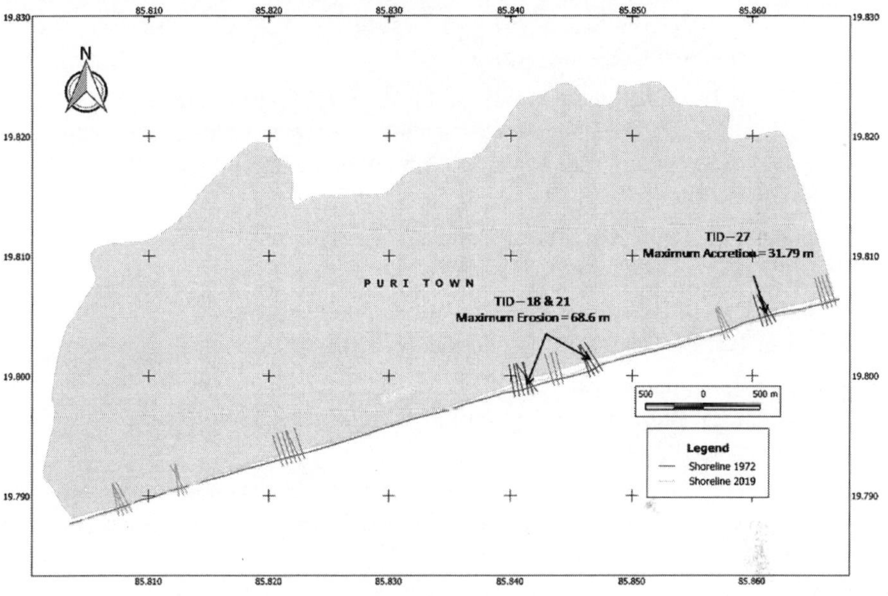

Fig. 8.10: Erosion and accretion mapping for Puri coast for years 2012-2019

Conclusion

It is observed from the present study that the coastline along Puri town coast in Odisha has undergone high erosion mostly may be due to tropical cyclones and anthropogenic activities. There is increase in coastal erosion during these recent years as compared to the last few decades. These might be due to some natural causes like increasing number of tropical cyclones and depression in Bay of Bengal, floods in coastal plains, wave height and deltaic behaviour of rivers in this area. Puri coast has undergone accretion in central to southern direction and erosion is in northern direction, which seems the ocean current is northward flowing. It is noteworthy that the Puri town is a major tourist destination contributing to states economy and most of the tourist infrastructure and hotels are existing along the shoreline of this town. So this study may help in identifying precise vulnerable locations along the coast of Puri town.

References

1. Bagdanaviciute I, Kelpsaite L, Daunys D (2012) Assessment of shoreline changes along the Lithuanian Baltic Sea coast during the period 1947–2010. Baltica 25(2):171–184
2. Bedini E (2007). Use of GIS and remote sensing to detect change along the coastline segment between Shkumbini and Semani rivers, central Albania. Bulletin of the Geological Society of Greece vol. XXXVII, Proceedings of the 11th International Congress, Athens
3. Khalid M. Dewidar and Omran E. Frihy (2010). Automated techniques for quantification of beach change rates using Landsat series along the North-eastern Nile Delta, Egypt. Journal of Oceanography and Marine Science, Vol. 1(2) pp. 028-039, February 2010.
4. Kumar A, Jayappa KS (2009) Long and short-term shoreline changes along Mangalore coast, India. Int J Environ Res 3(2):177–188
5. Kuleli T (2010) Quantitative analysis of shoreline changes at the Mediterranean Coast in Turkey. Environ Monit Assess 167:387–397
6. Mujabar PS, Chandrasekar N (2011) Shoreline change analysis along the coast between Kanyakumari and Tuticorin of India using remote sensing and GIS. Arab J Geosci 4:394
7. Murali RM, Shrivastava D, Vethamony P (2009) monitoring shoreline environment of Paradip, east coast of India using remote sensing. Curr Sci India 97:79–84
8. PINTO , P., CABRAL , P., CAETANO , M. and ALVES , M.F., 2009. Urban growth on coastal erosion vulne rable stretches. Journal of Coastal Research, SI 56 (Proc eedings of the 10th International Coastal Symposium), Lisbon, Portugal

Urban Environment and Spatial Science

Dr Mohd Akhter Ali, Dr. Kabir Mohan Sethy, Dr Muzafar Wani and M.Kamraju

Ane Books Pvt. Ltd. 2021, , ISBN : 978-93-90658-28-2, P.P. : 105 – 118

9

Impact Assessment of Anthropogenic Stress on Green Spaces of Srinagar City, Jammu & Kashmir

[1]Saleha Jamal
Associate Professor, Department of Geography, Aligarh Muslim University Aligarh, India.

[2]Wani Suhail Ahmad
Research Fellow, Department of Geography, Aligarh Muslim University Aligarh, India.

[3]Shahnawaz Ahmad Baba
Contractual lecturer, Department of Geography and Disaster Management, University of Kashmir.

[4]Md. Sarfaraz Asgher
Associate Professor Department of Geography, University of Jammu, J&K, India

[5]Umar Amin Reshi
Research Fellow, Department of Geography, Aligarh Muslim University Aligarh, India.

[6]Md Ashif Ali
Research Fellow, Department of Geography, Aligarh Muslim University Aligarh, India.

Corresponding Author

Wani Suhail Ahmad;
wanisuhailgeo@gmail.com

Introduction

Globally, urban expansion has increased over recent decades (Cohen, 2006). This is estimated that urban areas are attracting and will attract most of the world population growth in the coming decades (United Nations Department of

Corresponding Author: Saleha Jamal

Economic and Social Affairs UNDESA, 2012). Cities have developed swiftly in size and density (Turrini and Knop, 2015) and cities have tripled in size in some developing nations throughout the globe (Seto et al., 2012), also termed as speedy urban expansion. As compared to the other urbanised part of the world, the expansion rate (2.8%) of Southeast Asia is higher (United Nations Department of Economic and Social Affairs UNDESA, 2012). As a result of this phenomena's, process of urbanisation inversely affects the ecology and ecosystem services, social and cultural associations, physiological well-being and health of inhabitants in its vicinity. Moreover, the urbanisation processes create much more pressure on water bodies and green spaces if unplanned (Tian et al., 2011). The transformation of green spaces into concrete jungles has become one of the devastating factor for habitat degradation throughout the planet earth (Shafiq et al. 2019, Turrini and Knop, 2015) and in order to check this damage, it requires that such portion of green spaces can be reserved, protected and recovered, then only we can observe and understand these urban ecosystem, which are vulnerable under the pressure of rapid urbanisation and urban expansion. The primary aim of this study is to measure the effect of urbanisation on one of the essential urban service that is mostly unequally distributed viz; green spaces. This research paper focuses on the importance of green space through multidisciplinary structure that gives linkages between the various social, ecological, and financial advantages of improving the quality and amount of urban green spaces and providing some suitable suggestion for their recovery and sustainability.

Study Area

The study area (Srinagar City) which is the summer capital of Union territory J&K lies between geographical coordinates 74°43′-74°52′E longitude and 34° 0′- 34°14′N latitude (Fig. 9.1). It is about 5200 feet above mean sea level. The city is famous for its unique physiographic setup famous Dal Lake is situated in the heart and steep hills in the East and North east. River Jhelum flows through the city and unfortunately is became a dumping site for the city where all faeces, garbage and other pollutants are finding their way into the river. Mediterranean type of climate is found in City of Srinagar with most of the precipitation in winter season in the form of rain and snow. It is the only primate city in Himalayas acting as a hub of business, infrastructure, administration, tourism and also for health facilities. The city has been growing at an alarming pace and the changes in its demographic dimension have been very fast (Bhat, 2008). The city is among the 100 fastest growing Urban Centres of the world (City Mayor, 2013). The natural vegetation in the area has been considerably altered by urbanization and cultivation over the period of last fifty years (Kuchay and Bhat, 2011).

Population growth in Srinagar City

Over half of the world's population live in urban areas (UNFPA, 2007). Recently, urban centre attracts most of the population by giving many economic opportunities. It has been estimated that by 2030, nearly 80% population will live in urban area in developing countries. As shown in figure 2, over half of the world population lives in the urban areas in 2008 and by 2050 it will be over 70% (UNFPA, 2007).

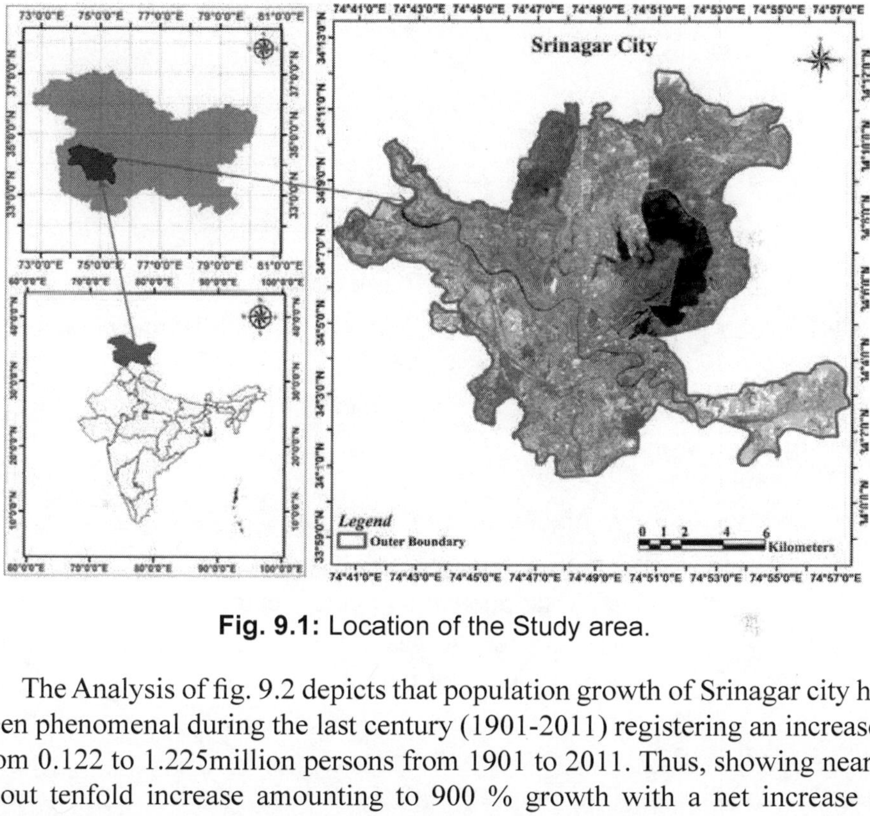

Fig. 9.1: Location of the Study area.

The Analysis of fig. 9.2 depicts that population growth of Srinagar city has been phenomenal during the last century (1901-2011) registering an increased from 0.122 to 1.225million persons from 1901 to 2011. Thus, showing nearly about tenfold increase amounting to 900 % growth with a net increase of 1.103million persons. The decadal growth pattern of Srinagar city, is found to be non-uniform and was slow and declining in the early decades from 1901 to 1961 (22.46 percent in 1931 to 15.71 percent in 1961). This decline could be attributed to the large-scale migration due to the partition of the subcontinent in 1947 and political unrest (Bhat, 2008). It was after 1961 that factors like in-migration, increase in birth rates and fall in death rates city population has increased from 0.285 to 0.606million persons from 1961-1981. Besides this, the other factor for this phenomenal growth was the introduction of urban agglomeration concept in the city which lead to merger of 62 villages in 1971 under the jurisdiction of Srinagar city. Because of political turmoil in the Valley in 1991 no census was conducted in Jammu and Kashmir. Subsequently, in the year 2001, the population of the city increased to 0.971 million persons, 1.225 million persons according to Census 2011. The projected population of the city was calculated using the equation given below (Zimstat 2012, Tendaupenyu et al. 2017, Ganaie et al. 2020):

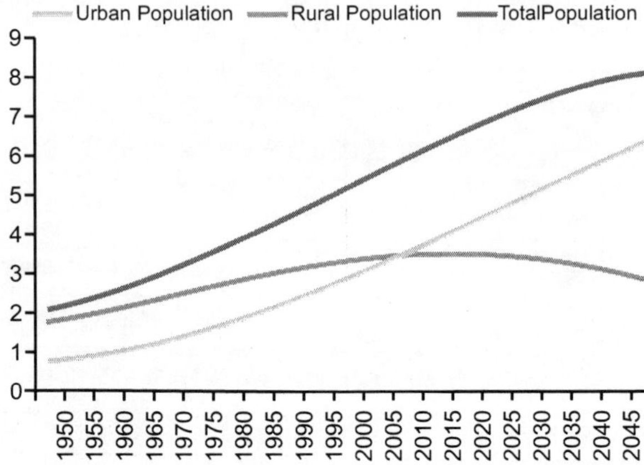

Fig. 9.2: Global population, including the portion of rural and urban populations, from 1950 to predicted levels in 2050.

$$Pp = P_1 + \frac{n(P_1 - P_2)}{N}$$

Where:

P_p = the Projected Population;
P_1 = present population according to the recent census;
P_2 = Total population in the previous census;
n = Number of years from projection year and the previous census; and
N = Total number of years between the recent and previous census

The derived population figures for different decades of Srinagar city were plotted on the graph (Fig. 9.3)

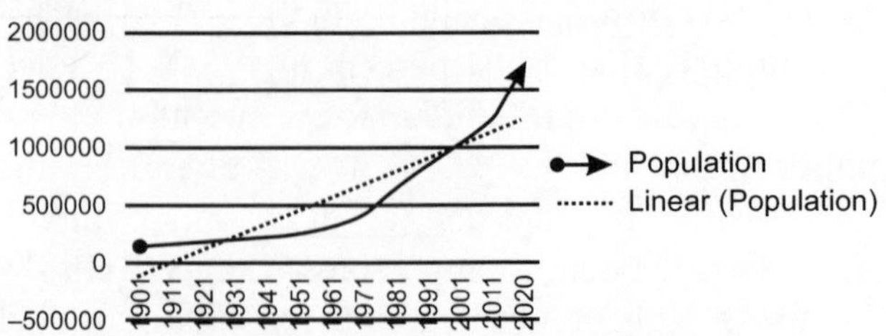

Fig. 9.3: Human population growth in Srinagar City, J&K*

****Source:*** Census of India, 2011

Data Base and Methodology

To justify the objectives of the study, data has been gathered from Satellite images Landsat 7 ETM+ for month of September 2000 and Landsat 8 OLI for September 2020 downloaded from United States Geological Survey (USGS-Earth Explorer) and Census of India were used for the Study. The collected secondary data from the above sources were analysed, and the relationship among the related variables was established. To classify and process the data of imageries of the study area, satellite image processing software Arc GIS 10.2 and Erdas Imagine 14 were used. Similarly, ground validation and Google earth were also taken into consideration in order to inquire different points for the purpose of better accuracy assessment. Firstly, layer stack was done by using red, green, blue, and near infrared band of Landsat 7 ETM + and Landsat 8 OLI. Secondly pan chromatic band was used to get images pan sharpened and to get a better spatial resolution of 15 meter in both images. Subset of the area was done in Erdas Imagine 14 using shape file of Srinagar city. Signature class was created by taking about 50-60 samples for each category in both the satellite images. For water body delineation and to get the maximum accuracy AOI layer was being prepared in both the satellite images which were then recoded. Mosaic processing was done to get the different categories interpolated in Eardas 14. and Supervised Maximum Likelihood Classification technique was adopted for preparation of raster layers (Jamal et al. 2019, Khan et al. 2020). Finally, layout of the processed maps was done in Arc GIS 10.2.

Urban Amenities – Green Space and Water Resources

As earlier mentioned, rapid urbanization is posing some barriers to the researchers and planners to provide some of the basic services of urban amenities as well as natural landscapes such as green space and water bodies. It is a fact that urbanization and urban development causes environmental problems, resulting from this fragmented and conversion of mostly green spaces and water bodies, and land intensive development pattern. It is quite imperative to save and maintain these natural resources found in urban areas because more unplanned development and urbanization, negatively affect the human health (Taqi et al. 2017, Liu et al., 2007). Indeed, these natural resources and habitats have been depicted as "restorative environments "due to their capacity to help in psychological wellbeing (Barton et al., 2010).

Importance of Green Spaces

Various studies have signified the social, ecological, and economic importance of urban green space (Chiesura, 2004; Crompton, 2001; Wright Wendel et al., 2011b). Urban occupants utilize these green spaces as an approach to get away from the everyday stresses, to keep fit their health by walking in morning and evening timings, as recreation sites and demands of city living (Maller et al., 2006).

Further, it is found that overall health condition was seen better for individuals living in a green environment in comparison to congested areas with less or no available green spaces (Southworth, 2005). However, within industrialized nations, it has been observed that females, older and less educated people have lower green space use and adults living below the poverty line were three times less healthy than those who have higher income (Lindsey et al., 2001; Sherer, 2006). The advantages of exposure to open space environments for inhabitants working on daily bases in any area the reawakening of a sense of possibility, relief from daily struggles; empowerment, and the enabling of environmental stewardship. This has significant ramifications for urban areas around the globe that are encountering an enormous flood of migrants, if proper checks are not undertaken (GMSC, 2007).

While seeing numerous advantages related with urban green space, negativity may also develop if these urban green spaces are mismanaged, over populated, ignored or unplanned. Improper waste management can harm the green environment or the green space can result in potential users of park to face the problems of unpleasant, irritating, polluted environment which decline the use, and may be avoided by the inhabitants which were seeing them as a resource of pleasure and health boom (Boone et al., 2009).On the other hand, if the green spaces fail to accommodate the preferences of different user groups then its usage can be decreased. Some of the following factors are found to be vital in influencing the use of green spaces namely, user socio-demographic characteristics, capability for amenities, quantity and quality of spaces, maintenance and security, access to competing facilities to fulfil the needs of users (Giles-Corti et al., 2005). When all the above-mentioned services are available then green space clients were found to get attracted toward the green spaces by their closeness (walking distances), size of the park, diversity in the park. This is a result of the perception that larger parks have more amenities. These studies have identified many benefits of green space, which have been summarized and grouped according to the three pillars of sustainability: social, environmental, and economic benefits are given below:

Social Benefits:

- Enhanced recreational opportunities
- Increased levels of physical activity
- Increased sense of security
- Improved mental health
- Reduced crime and juvenile delinquency

Environmental Benefits

- Improved air quality
- Water pollutant filtration
- Increased control of storm water runoff & flooding
- Reduced loads on storm water systems
- Groundwater recharge
- Reduced heat island effect Wildlife habitat

Economic Benefits

- Increased property values
- Improved ability to attract and retain businesses and residents Tourism
- Decreased needs for police and prisons
- Reduced pollution prevention measures

Results and Discussions

Usually, the degree of urban expansion is carried out by measuring the built-up area in any geographical region by superimposing multi-date geospatial data (Barnes et al. 2001; Galster et al. 2001; Epstein et al. 2002; Koomen and Stillwell 2007). The pattern of urban expansion can be characterised by the spatial extent of the built-up and associated process that explain sprawl (Maryama and Thappa 2010). One of the chief determinants of urban development is consuming the nearby open spaces within the landscape. With the increase in population growth rate in the study area, the built-up also reveals a significant improvement. Satellite images for different periods (1998-2018) clearly demonstrate the drastic pattern of landscape transformation and the typical urban growth in the study area (Fig. 9.7, 9.8, 9.8, 9.9). The analysis of the classified raster maps of the city depicted that there is a significant transformation of land use, where built-up is encroaching in all other class of land cover. Built-up in the study area is registering a web like pattern of sprawl i.e. spreading horizontally in almost all directions. In the study year 2000, the area under built-up was about 32.53 sq. km (13.53%) of the total geographical area of the city (Table 9.1, Fig. 9.4). However, due to increasing population in the city reinforced by immigration from all corners of the valley, it showed a phenomenal growth in built-up area, accounting about 62.07 sq. km in 2020 (24.17%) (Table 9.1, Fig. 9.5). Thus, it reveals that the city is facing the over burden on its natural resources. Built-up area depicts a positive growth rate of 90.81% from 2000- 2020 (Table 9.1, Fig. 9.4 and 9.5). This expansion of built-up has resulted in decrease of green spaces in the city area. Where in 2000, the total area under green spaces was registered about 45.65 sq. km (17.64%) (Fig.

9.6). This area demarcated a negative change in its area where in 2020, the area under this class as revealed by satellite data is about 26.27 sq. km (10.04%) (Fig. 9.7). Thus, green spaces of Srinagar city depicted a negative growth rate of -42.45% from 2000-2020 (Table 9.1, Fig. 9.6 and 9.7). From the results of our study we are now in a position to describe the state of the city in terms of environmental sights. The city is under the grip of anthropogenic stress, from all sides due to increasing population in the city, urbanization and concretization, untreated waste, pollution, congestion, poverty, increased volume traffic on poorly maintained roads, lack of drainage, lack of governmental policies and checks, thereby jeopardizing the environmental stability of the city. The city needs proper and quick attention to check the anthropogenic stress so that its equity and sustainability can be saved. Following are some of the suggestion for city's healthy recovery and to save it from further degradation:

- Strengthening and promoting its long term and sustainability perspectives.
- Promoting and better understanding overall holistic overview of urban green spaces.
- By developing green space potentials and discovering effective ways to solve its problems.
- Compulsory education delivering knowledge at school, higher secondary's, college and even at university level about the importance of green spaces.
- Mass awareness among the people regarding the benefits of green spaces.
- Improving the cities quality of life by maintaining proper infrastructure, health facilities, cleanliness and proper management.
- Incorporating issues of green spaces in legislation and planning systems.
- General public participation and political awareness for protection of green spaces.
- Coordination of NGO's, general public, inter-departmental coordination and generation of stakeholders for green space development.

Table 9.1: Land Use Statistics of Green spaces and Built-Up, 2000-2020*

Class	*Landsat 7 ETM+ 2000 (Area Sq. Km)*	*Area (%)*	*Landsat 8 OLI 2020 (Area Sq. Km)*	*Area (%)*	*% Change (2000-2020)*
Built-Up	32.53	13.53	62.07	24.17	90.81
Green Spaces	45.65	17.64	26.27	10.04	-42.45

Source: Compiled by researchers from raster layers 2000 and 2020

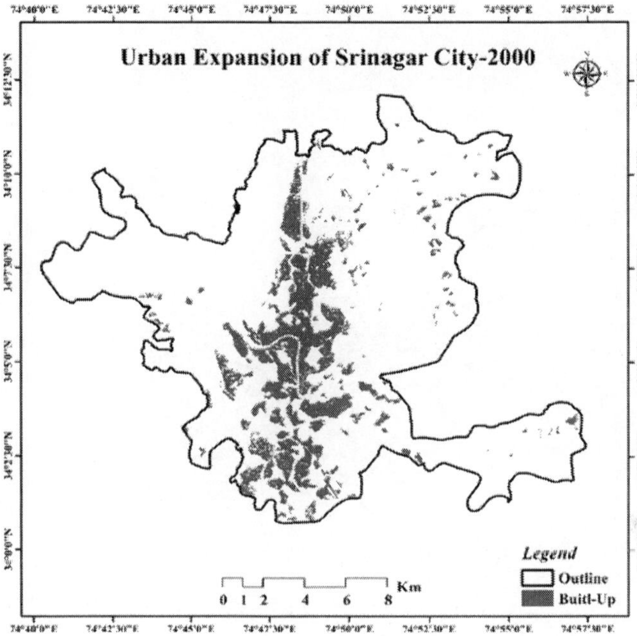

Fig. 9.4: Area under Build-Up, 2000*

****Source:*** Computed by Researchers form Raster layers of Landsat 7 ETM+, 2000

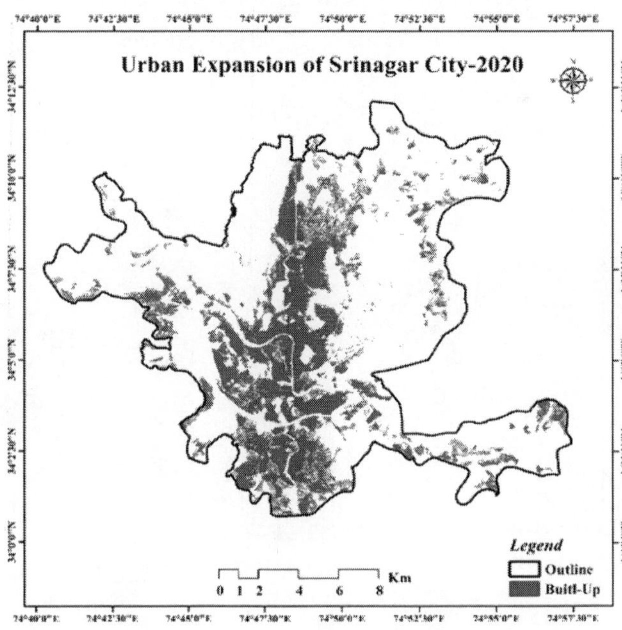

Fig. 9.5: Area under Build-Up, 2020*

****Source:*** Computed by Researchers form Raster layers of Landsat 8-OLI, 2020

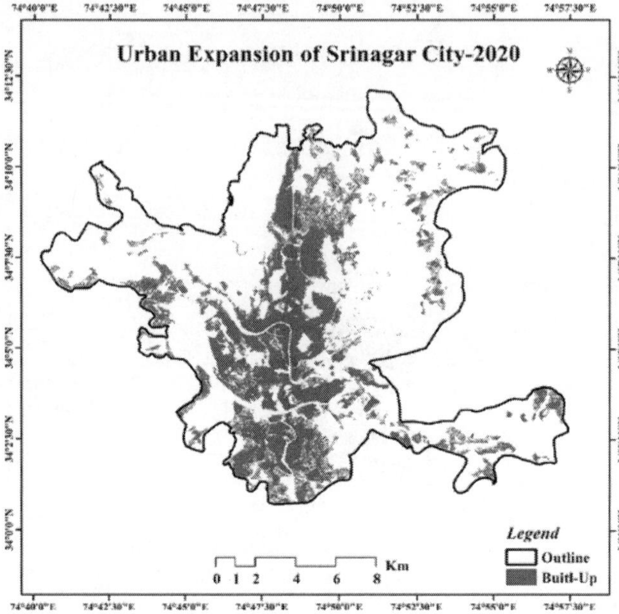

Fig. 9.6: Green spaces figure

Source: Computed by Researchers form Raster layers of Landsat 7 ETM+, 2000

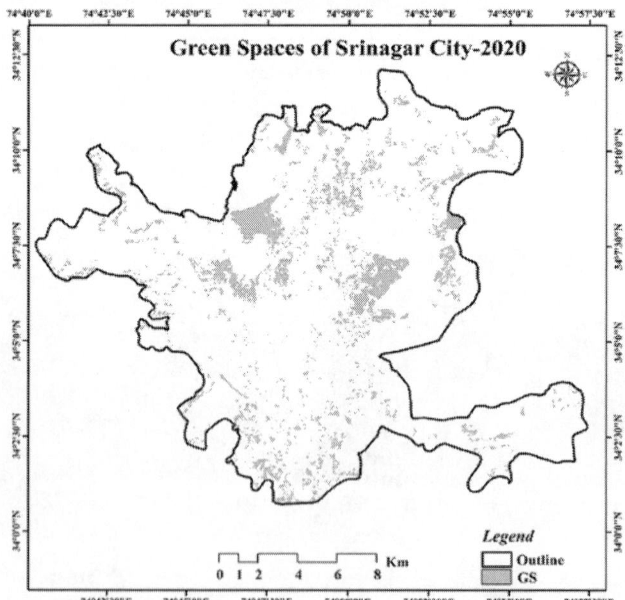

Fig. 9.7: Area under green spaces, 2020*

Source: Computed by Researchers form Raster layers of Landsat 8-OLI, 2020

Conclusion

Urban centre attracts most of the population by giving many economic opportunities. It has been estimated that by 2030, nearly 80% population will live in urban area in developing countries. This phenomena's, process of urbanisation inversely affects the ecology and ecosystem services, social and cultural associations, physiological well-being and health of inhabitants in its vicinity. Moreover, the urbanisation processes create much more pressure on water bodies and green spaces. Urban green spaces have significant importance socially, ecologically, and economically particularly found in city areas. It is quite imperative to save and maintain these natural resources found in urban areas for sustainability of city and fauna residing therein. The study reveals that Srinagar city if facing acute shortage of green space and are day by day losing their ground due to alarming anthropogenic stress. It is found that in last two decades the city of Srinagar city lost an area of about 28 Sq. Km of green spaces. This means that there will severe ramification in response to this negative growth rate of 42.45% in case of green spaces. They are being encroached and converted to settlements, plantation and for other infrastructural activities, thereby, disturbing the equilibrium of ecosystem of the city. At the same time, it has been found that the city is expanding a web like pattern in built-up class through its length and breadth. The urban expansion is mostly of horizontal in nature and expanding at a very fast rate depicting a positive growth rate of about 90% from 2000-2020. Most of this expansion is unplanned, which is posing an addition threat to the city sustainability. Built-up category according the Landsat data registered an additional area of about 30 Sq. km from 2000-2020. This wild urban expansion in Srinagar, which is by and large unplanned, will have further detrimental impacts on the environment, and is never a neutral phenomenon until checked with priority. The examination of results of our study brings to light the pattern and process of rapid urbanisation in city environment and calls for the speedy attention of researchers, planners and government officials to conceive a comprehensive land-use plan for the balanced and sustainable urban development in the city. Otherwise, the city environs may find in near future at a state of an unmanageable municipal complex with severe social and ecological implications and, further in the near future, it may be a massive sprawl associated with harmful consequences and connotations.

References

1. Barnes, K., Morgan, J. I., Roberge, M., & Lowe, S. (2001). Sprawl development: Its patterns, consequences, and measurement. Towson University.

2. Barton, J., & Pretty, J. (2010). What is the Best Dose of Nature and Green Exercise for Improving Mental Health? A Multi-Study Analysis. *Environ. Sci. Technol.,* 44(10), 3947-3955.
3. Bhat MS (2008) Urban System in Himalayas- A Study of Srinagar City Region. Arina Publishers, New Delhi.
4. Boone, C. G., Buckley, G. L., Grove, J. M., & Sister, C. (2009). Parks and People: An Environmental Justice Inquiry in Baltimore, Maryland. *Ann. Assoc. Am. Geogr.,* 99(4), 767-787.
5. Chiesura, A. (2004). The role of urban parks for the sustainable city. *Landscape Urban Plan.,* 68, 129-138.
6. City Mayor (2013). Urban areas ranked 1 to 100.The world"s fastest growing cities and urban areas from 2006 to 2020.
7. Cohen, B., 2006. Urbanization in developing countries: current trends, future projections, and key challenges for sustainability. Technol. Soc. 28 (1–2), 63–80. Eastman, J.R., 2006.
8. Crompton, J. L. (2001). The Impact of Parks on Property Values:A Review of the Empirical Evidence. *Journal of Leisure Research,* 33(1), 1-31.
9. Epstein, J., Payne, K., & Kramer, E. (2002). Techniques for mapping suburban sprawl. Photogrammetric Engineering and Remote Sensing, 63, 913–918.
10. Galster, G., Hanson, R., Wolman, H., Coleman, S., & Freihage, J. (2001). Wrestling sprawl to the ground: Defining and measuring an elusive concept. Housing Policy Debate, 12(4), 681–717 (Fannie Mae Foundation).
11. Ganaie, T. A., Jamal, S., & Ahmad, W. S. Changing land use/land cover patterns and growing human population in Wular catchment of Kashmir Valley, India. GeoJournal, 1-18.
12. Giles-Corti, B., Broomhall, M. H., Knuiman, M., Collins, C., Douglas, K., Ng, K., et al. (2005). Increasing Walking -- How important is distance to, attractiveness, and size of public open space? *Am. J. Prev. Med.,* 28(2), 169-176.
13. GMSC. (2007). *Plan Estrategico de Desarrollo Municipal*: Gobierno Municipal Autónomo de Santa Cruz de la Sierra.
14. Jamal, S., Ahmad, W. S., Ali, M. A., & Sharma, A. Monitoring Land Use/Land Cover Change Detection and Urban Expansion with Remote Sensing and GIS techniques in Anantnag District of Kashmir Valley. The Geographer, Vol. 66 No. 1, 60-69.
15. Khan, T. A., Ahmad, S. A., Tariq, S., A Multi-Temporal Land Use and Land Cover Change analysis of Delhi NCT, using remote sensing and GIS. Bhugol Swadesh Charcha (Multidisciplinary International Journal). Vol. 16, Issue 1, Jan 2020, 1-11.
16. Koomen, E., & Stillwell, J. (2007). Modelling land-use change; progress and applications Dordrecht: Springer, 1–21.

17. Kuchay NA, Bhat MS (2011). Mapping and Modelling the Land use Dynamic in Srinagar City- A Geo-spatial Approach. Unpublished Thesis.Department of Geography, University of Kashmir.
18. Lindsey, G., Maraj, M., & Kuan, S. (2001). Access, Equity, and Urban Greenways: An Exploratory Investigation. *Prof. Geogr.,* 53(3), 332-346.
19. Liu, G. C., Wilson, J. S., Qi, R., & Ying, J. (2007). Green Neighborhoods, Food Retail and Childhood Overweight: Differences by Population Density. *American Journal of Health Promotion,* 21(4), 317-325.
20. Maller, C., Townsend, M., Pryor, A., Brown, P., & Leger, L. S. (2006). Healthy nature healthy people: 'contact with nature' as an upstream health promotion intervention for populations. *Health Promotion International,* 21(1), 45-54.
21. Maryama and Thappa (2010). Urban sprawl and public health: designing, planning and building for health communities Washington DC: Island Press, 279 p.
22. Seto, K.C., Güneralp, B., Hutyra, L.R., 2012. Global forecasts of urban expansion to 2030 and direct impacts on biodiversity and carbon pools. Proc. Natl. Acad. Sci. U.S.A. 109 (40), 16083–16088.
23. Shafiq, M. U., Islam, Z.U., Abida, A.W., Bhat, M.S., & Ahmed, P. (2019). Recent trends in precipitation regime of Kashmir valley, India. Disaster Advances, 12 (4), 1-11.
24. Sherer, P. M. (2006). *The Benefits of Parks: Why America Needs More City Parks and Open Space.* San Francisco, CA: The Trust for Public Land.
25. Southworth, M. (2005). Designing the Walkable City. *Journal of Urban Planning and Development,* 4, 246-257.
26. Taqi, M., Bidhuri, S., Sarkar, S., Ahmad, W.S., & Wangchok, P. (2017). Rural healthcare infrastructural disparities in India: a critical analysis of availability and accessibility.
27. Tendaupenyu, P., Magadza, C. H. D., & Murwira, A. (2017). Changes in landuse/ landcover patterns and human population growth in the Lake Chivero catchment, Zimbabwe. *Geocarto international*, *32*(7), 797-811.
28. Tian, Y., Jim, C.Y., Tao, Y., Shi, T., 2011. Landscape ecological assessment of green space fragmentation in Hong Kong. Urban Forestry Urban Green. 10 (2), 79–86.
29. Turrini, T., Knop, E., 2015. A landscape ecology approach identifies important drivers of urban biodiversity. Global Change Biol. 21 (4), 1652–1667.
30. UNFPA. (2007). *State of world population 2007: Unleashing the Potential of Urban Growth*: United Nations Population Fund.
31. United Nations Department of Economic and Social Affairs [UNDESA], 2012. Nations Department of Economic and Social Affairs [UNDESA]

32. Wright Wendel, H. E., Downs, J. A., & Mihelcic, J. R. (2011b). Assessing Equitable Access to Urban Green Space: The Role of Engineered Water Infrastructure. *Environ. Sci. Technol.,* Article in review.
33. Zimstat, I. (2012). Zimbabwe Demographic and Health Survey 2010–2011. *Calverton, Maryland.*

Urban Environment and Spatial Science
Dr Mohd Akhter Ali, Dr. Kabir Mohan Sethy, Dr Muzafar Wani and M.Kamraju
Ane Books Pvt. Ltd. 2021, , ISBN : 978-93-90658-28-2, P.P. : 119 – 132

10

Air and Noise Pollution Status in Osmania University Campus

Syeda Azeem Unnisa, Vattikoti Praveen,
Akhtar Rasool, Bharath Raj[3]
Department of Environmental Science,
Osmania University, Hyderabad,
Telangana-500007, India
**syeda_30@yahoo.co.in*

Abstract

Osmania University Campus has several sources of air and noise pollution that can adversely affect human health, welfare and overall efficiency of the educational process. This study was aimed to assess the concentration of air pollutants, noise level and oxygen percentage in the Osmania University (OU) campus. Twelve different sites were selected for the study in the year 2018. The air pollutants CO (carbon monoxide), CO_2 (carbon dioxide), O_2 (oxygen), noise level, and temperature was measured at all selected sites at three different intervals of times on working and non-working days. The data was compared with Central Pollution Con0trol Board (CPCB) standards. The research results were statistically analyzed by the statistical package for the social sciences (IBM-SPSS version -20 software). The two air pollutants CO and CO_2 was measured on working days where the average concentration of CO ranged from 0.4-4.04ppm and CO_2 ranged from 393.5-445.2ppm where as on non-working days, CO ranged from 0.7-4.8ppm, and CO_2 379.1-506.5ppm. Oxygen(O_2) concentration on working days ranged from 18.30 -18.60% whereas, on non-working days 18.30-18.70%, noise on working days ranged from 53.8-67.8 dB where as non-working days 56.3-68.8 dB and temperature on working days 32.4-33.7°C and non-working days 32.0-33.2°C. Levels of air pollutants CO and CO_2, and noise level was high on both working and non-working

Corresponding Author: Syeda Azeem Unnisa

days at all three intervals when compared to CPCB norms. Whereas oxygen percentage was slightly fluctuated with the concentrations of air pollutants and temperature was within the guidelines. The statistical results revealed that positive correlation was observed between CO_2 and CO (0.6469), noise and CO (0.8845) on working days, where, as on non-working days noise and CO (0.7828), temperature and CO (0.9075), temperature and noise (0.8282) . The study revealed that university administrative polices and management procedures will lead to reduce and improve the ambient air quality and noise levels inside OU campus, by diverting the vehicles through other lanes and by lanes.

Keywords: Automobiles, air pollutants, noise, campus, impact.

Introduction

The content of oxygen (which is vital for human life) in the ambient air is the key factor determining the health status of a person. The mass concentration of oxygen on surface air which depends on the temperature, pressure, and humidity of air, under natural conditions which is described by classical thermodynamic formula. Over the last millennia, natural sources and sinks of oxygen have balanced the percentage of oxygen in the Earth's atmosphere at a level of 20.95%, which, at present, is practically the cosmological constant. However, the levels of both industrial and agricultural developments, the combustion of fossil fuels and other anthropogenic processes, natural and technogenic fires, and global climate changes affect the content of oxygen in the air over a certain location and time[1].

One of the significant sources of air pollution in urban areas, towns and cities of the developing countries is the emissions from motor vehicle exhausts[2]. India, one of the fast developing countries of the world, has registered a sharp increase in vehicular pollution, particularly, in the urban area[3]. In vehicular emissions carbon monoxide (CO), hydrocarbons (HC), oxides of nitrogen (NO_x), sulphur dioxide (SO_2), lead and particulates are the main pollutants. Recently, a few studies were carried out where in the investigators analyzed the diurnal and seasonal variations of O_3, SO_2, and NOx [4-5].CO is a colourless, odourless and chemically stable, but relatively inactive gas that has molecular weight close to that of air. In the urban centers, developing towns and cities vehicular exhaust is the major anthropogenic source for CO[6]. Thus CO levels in the ambient air play a role in determining the air quality of a region. The vehicle's exhaust as a result of incomplete combustion releases Carbon monoxide which is a colorless, odorless, poisonous gas. This gas interferes with the blood's ability to carry oxygen to the heart, brain, and other tissues. Unborn or newborn children and people with heart disease are in the greatest danger from this pollutant, but even healthy people can experience headaches, fatigue and reduced reflexes due to CO exposure. Carbon monoxide reduces the volume of oxygen that enters the bloodstream and can slow reflexes, cause drowsiness, impair judgment and vision and even cause death[7]. Noise pollution in India is assuming greater significance in urban environment due to its varying frequency and intensity. Presently in Chidambaram Town of Cuddalore District Tamilnadu, the noise levels have increased significantly due to increased vehicular density. Road traffic noise now produces serious community disturbance. Few studies have revealed that noise annoyance from transportation produces a variety of negative emotions including disappointment, anxiety, anger, unhappiness, and even depression[8-11].

Study Area

Hyderabad is the capital of the Indian state of Telangana, occupying 650 square kilometers (250 sq mi) along the banks of the Musi River. The population of Hyderabad city is about 6.9 million, making it the 4th most populous city and 6th most populous urban agglomeration in India. At an average altitude of 542 meters (1,778ft) and the latitude and longitude of Hyderabad is 17°22'31" N and 78°28'27"E. Hyderabad is situated on hilly terrain, artificial lakes, including Husain sagar predating the city's founding north of the city center. The study area is depicted in fig. 10.1. Osmania University is a public state university located in university town, Hyderabad, India which was founded in 1918.It is the third oldest university in southern India, and the first to be established in the erstwhile princely state of Hyderabad. As of 2018, the university hosts 3,700 international students from more than 80 nations. The OU is one of the largest university systems in the subcontinent with over 300,000 students on its campuses and affiliated colleges. The university has a huge campus of nearly 1600 acres. Osmania University has about 60 departments actively functioning. The campus is surrounded on two sides by main traffic roads, different type of vehicles daily passes through the campus. Air and noise pollution in OU campus is a result of traffic movement inside the campus, and transportation of air pollutants from adjacent roads. The sampling locations and distance of samples collected in OU campus is shown in table 10.1.

Table 10.1: Sampling locations and distance of sample collected in Osmania University campus

Sample code. No	*Sample collected from various Locations*	*Distance (Meters)*	*Sample interval periods*
01	Andhra Mahila Sabha (AMS)	200	3
02	University College of Engineering (EC)	150	3

Sample code. No	*Sample collected from various Locations*	*Distance (Meters)*	*Sample interval periods*
03	Science and Humanities (S&H)	400	3
04	Department of Genetics(DPT OF GEN)	500	3
05	Ladies Hostel (LH)	450	3
06	University Press (PRESS)	500	3
07	College of Commerce and Business Management (C&M)	150	3
08	University College of Law (LC)	450	3
09	Department of Geography (DPT OF GEO)	500	3
10	University College of Arts and Social Sciences (A C)	500	3
11	University College of Science (UCS)	200	3
12	Police Station(PS)	200	3

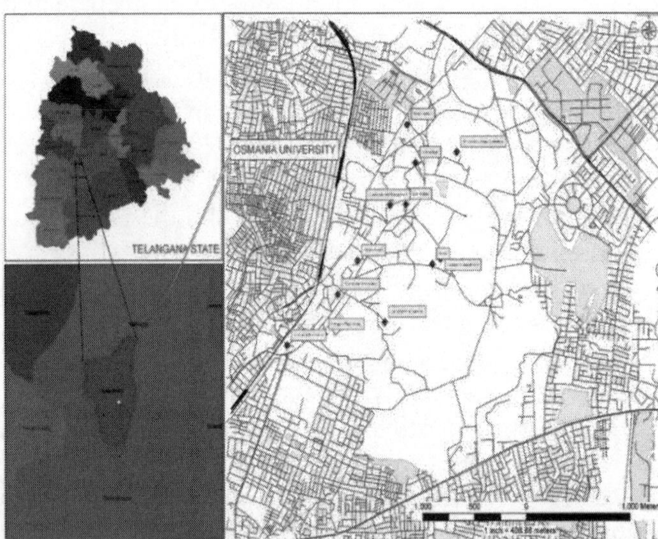

Fig. 10.1: Sampling Location in Osmania University Campus

Monitoring and Analysis

The aim of the study was to assess noise level air pollutants, (carbon monoxide, carbon dioxide), oxygen and temperature inside the Osmania University campus. Twelve different locations were selected for measuring all parameters during the study in 2018. Level of noise, carbon monoxide, carbon dioxide, oxygen and temperature were measured in free flowing traffic conditions at three different intervals periods from 8-10 AM (Morning), 12-2 PM (Afternoon) and 3-5 PM (Evening). The operation of the meters was followed as described in the manual. The CO meter, CO_2 meter, O_2 meter and noise meter were first switched on and were allowed to warm up where temperature was already available in CO, CO_2 meters. Using the meters the concentration of CO CO_2, percentage of O_2 and levels of noise at 12 different locations in the O.U campus was recorded. The above procedure was repeated for seven working and non-working days. The pollutants selected and their measurable principle is given in table 10.2. The air pollutants (CO, CO_2) were measured from the nearest distance, when they are released from vehicles.

Table 10.2: Pollutants selected for study and their measurement principle

S. No	*Parameters and Units*	*Equipment Description and Principle*
1	Carbon Monoxide(CO), ppm	• Model: Gco-2008 • Luthra Make • Two Functions: CO, Temperature • Range: 0-1000ppm • Sensor Based
2	Carbon Dioxide(CO_2), ppm	• Model: Gc-2028 • Luthra Make • Range: 0-4000ppm • Functions: CO_2, Temperature • Sensor Based
3	Oxygen(O_2), %	• Model: Po2-250 • Luthra Make • Range: 0-30.0% • Functions: O_2 and Temperature • Sensor Based
4	Noise,dB	• Model:Sl-4001 • Taiwan Make • Range:0-200 dB • Functions-Min and Max dB • Sensor Based

Statistical Analysis

The relationship between two or more variables in statistics comes under the broad class of statistical correlation. The correlation study is useful to find a predictable relationship which can be exploited in practical. It is used for the measurement of the strength and statistical significance of the relation between two or more air quality parameters[12].To study the correlation between various air and noise quality parameters, the statistical analysis was carried out by using IBM-SPSS version-20 software. Assessing the correlation analysis measures the closeness of the relationship between chosen independent and dependant variables[13]. If the correlation coefficient is nearer to 1 or -1, it shows the probability of linear relationship which is between the variables x and y. The parameters are characterized as strong ,moderate and weak based on correlation. The parameter is strong, when it is in the range of 0.8to 1.0 and -0.8 to -1.0, the parameter is moderate when it is having value in the range of 0.5 to 0.8 and -0.5 to -0.8, and the parameter is weak when it is in the range of 0.0 to 0.5 and -0.0 to -0.5.[14]. The correlation analysis attempts to establish the nature of the relationship between the variables which is based on correlation analysis which produced mechanism for forecasting and prediction[15]. In the present study, the Pearson correlation coefficient was used which a statistical formula that measures the strength between variables and relationship which is referred as Pearson R test. This coefficient correlation value was useful to determine how strong that relationship is between those two variables.

Results and Discussion

Traffic movement is considered as the primary source for measuring air pollutants and noise levels. The analyzed data was estimated for in the concentration of air pollutants (CO CO_2), noise levels, oxygen percentage and temperature which is depicted in the below figures.

Noise: From the study results it is revealed that the level of noise in the twelve sites of the OU campus on working and non working days was above the level prescribed by the CPCB guidelines. The results are depicted in fig. 10.2. The noise in decibels was recorded on working days as an average between, 53.8-67.8 dB and non working days 56.3-68.8 dB. Levels of noise pollution inside university campus vary depending on several factors such as outside activity, internal activity, period of the year, time of the day, and others[16]. OU campus is surrounded by traffic roads from all sides, one of them is considered the main coastal road with moderate and sometimes high traffic activity particularly in the morning rush hour.

The finding is in accordance with several studies in different cities of the world, for example the study which has conducted for quality assessment at the day time for urban noise in Kolhapur, where five critical zones noise levels ranged from 63.71-72.25 dB[17]. On the other hand the study on effect of high noise levels on people's health and welfare was evaluated in Varanasi, India, where results revealed that 85% of the people were disturbed by traffic noise, while about 90% of the people reported that traffic noise is the main cause for headache, high blood pressure, dizziness and fatigue[18]. Location of any university campus is a crucial factor in the noise pollution level inside the campus. Traffic movement inside the OU campus is the main source of the high noise pollution. Noise level inside the campus at 12 locations was higher than the recommended guidelines, which means that all occupants of the OU campus are exposed to the bad effects of noise pollution.

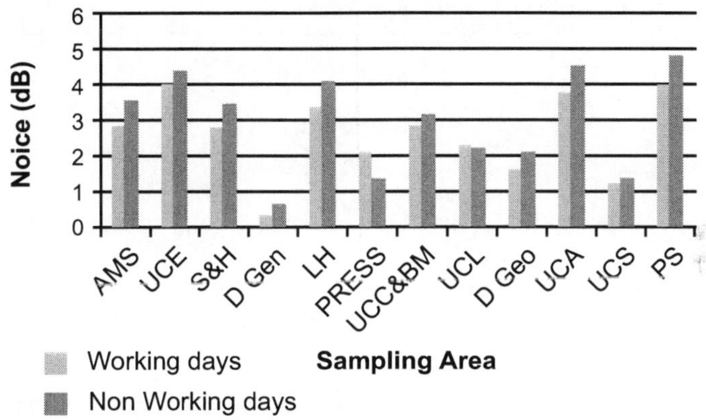

Fig. 10.2: Average level of noise on working and non-working days

Carbon Monoxide (CO): Emission of CO from vehicles contributes approximately, 60% of all emissions and thus high concentration of CO generally occurs in areas with heavy traffic and congestion[19]. The CO concentration was found high in all twelve sites on both working and non-working days. The CO levels on working days ranged from 0.4-4.04 ppm and non-working days 0.7- 4.8 ppm. Sampling locations-1, 2,3,5,7,8,9,10,12 on non-working days where above permissible limits, which is shown fig. 10.3.

It confirms that traffic movement inside the campus is strongly linked with the level of air pollution, which is concluded based on the difference in traffic activity in the morning, afternoon and evening on working and non working days. The different trends in air pollution levels is due to their location, high traffic road, down word and upward wind respectively[20].The CO exposure levels stipulated by the (Central Pollution Control Board (CPCB 1999b) are 2.4 ppm (personal), 3.4 ppm (occupational) and 2ppm (residential). Traffic affects the concentration of CO in the ambient air[21]. A modulation of CO concentration due to traffic was clearly seen in OU campus since the measurements sites were well inside the campus. The weekday-weekend effect was observed in the CO concentration, from earlier studies[22]. The results of the study can be summarized as CO levels at 12 sites on working and non-working days has shown them to be above CPCB levels. CO on working and non-working days were found to be higher, establishing clearly the effect of traffic on the ambient air[23].

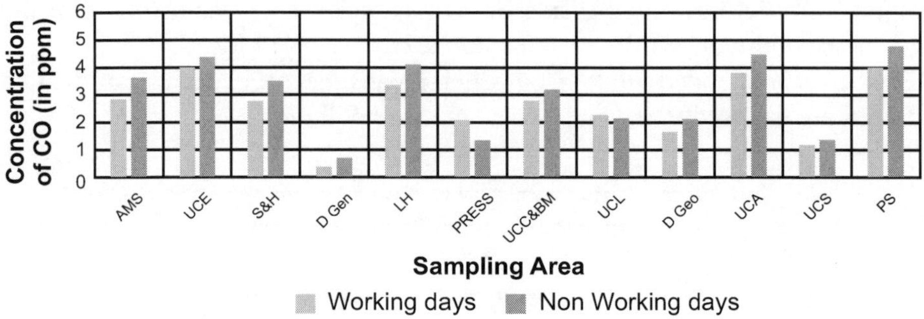

Fig. 10.3: Average concentration of CO on working and non-working days

Carbon Dioxide (CO_2): Concentration of CO_2 was measured at 12 different locations in Osmania University (OU) campus at different time intervals on both working and non-working days. On working days, in morning the concentration of CO_2 ranged from 237.7ppm to 463.7ppm with an average of 389.4ppm. The concentration of CO_2 was maximum at Police Station (463.7ppm) and minimum at Andhra Mahila Sabha (237.7ppm). In the afternoon, the concentration of CO_2 ranged from 375ppm to 434.2ppm with an average of 406.8ppm.The concentration of CO_2 was maximum at Police Station (434.2ppm) and minimum at University College of Science (375ppm). In the evening, the concentration of CO_2 ranged from 392.5ppm to 456.2ppm with an average of 424.4ppm. The concentration of CO_2 was maximum at Arts College (456.2ppm) and minimum at Department of Genetics (392.5ppm), which is shown in fig 10.4.

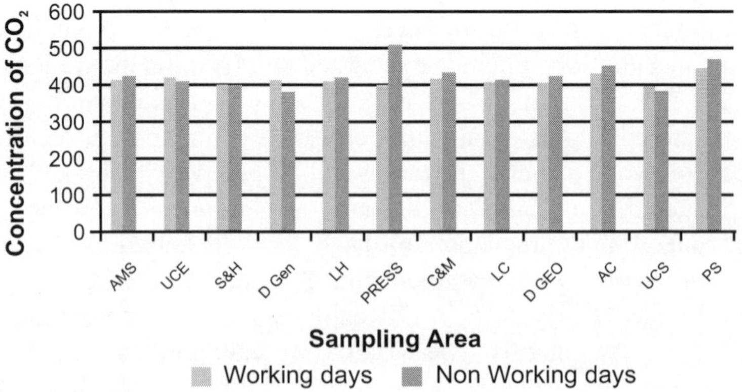

Fig. 10.4: Average concentration of CO_2 on working and non-working days

On non-working days, in the morning, the concentration of CO_2 ranged from 354.6ppm to 577.3ppm, with an average of 429.3ppm.The concentration of CO_2 was maximum at University Press (577.3ppm) and minimum at Engineering College (354.6ppm). In the afternoon, the concentration of CO_2 ranged from 351.3ppm to 467ppm with an average of 410ppm.The concentration of CO_2 was maximum at Police Station (467ppm) and minimum at University College of Science (351.3ppm). In the evening, the concentration of CO_2 ranged from 394.6ppm to 507.6ppm with an average of 495.7ppm. The concentration of CO_2 was maximum at Police Station (507.6ppm) and minimum at Department of Geography (394.6ppm).The average concentration of CO_2 on working days and non-working days was 412.6ppm and 424.8ppm respectively. The concentration of CO_2 was more on non-working days when compared to working days as frequency of vehicles was found to be more on non-working days. The concentration of CO_2 was maximum at police station on working days, as the main road of Tarnaka bifurcates near police station. The concentration of CO_2 was maximum at University Press on non-working days, as the movement of vehicles was observed more.

The emission of greenhouse gases is one of the causes for the global warming. 72% of the total emitted greenhouse gas is CO_2. CO_2 is inevitably created by burning fuels like oil, natural gas, diesel, organic-diesel, petrol, organic-petrol, and ethanol. Personal vehicles are a major cause of global warming, collectively cars and trucks which accounts for $1/5^{th}$ of all CO_2 emissions. CO_2 in its gas form is asphyxiate, which cuts off the oxygen supply for breathing, especially in confined spaces. Exposure to 10% or more of CO_2 can cause death, unconsciousness, or convulsions and damage a developing feotus. Exposure to lower concentrations of CO_2 can cause vision damage, lung congestion, central nervous system injury, elevated blood pressure. Exposure can also cause headache, sweating, fatigue, memory loss, nausea, vomiting, depression, skin and eye burns. The CO_2 normal outdoor level is 350-450 ppm and acceptable levels is <600 ppm.

Oxygen (O_2): The concentration of O_2% was measured at 12 different locations in OU campus at different time intervals on both working and non-working days. On working days, in the morning the percentage of O_2 ranged from 18.4% to 18.8% with an average of 18.6%. The concentration of O_2% was maximum at Department of Geography (18.9%) and minimum at University Press (18.4%). In the afternoon the percentage of oxygen ranged from 18.4% to 18.6% with an average of 18.5%. The concentration of O_2% was maximum at University College of Science (18.7%) and minimum at Police Station (18.3%). In the evening the percentage of oxygen ranged from 18.5% to 18.6% with an average of 18.5%.The concentration of O_2% was maximum at

Department of Genetics, Law College, University College of Science (18.7%) and minimum at Police Station (18.0%), which is shown in fig. 10.5.

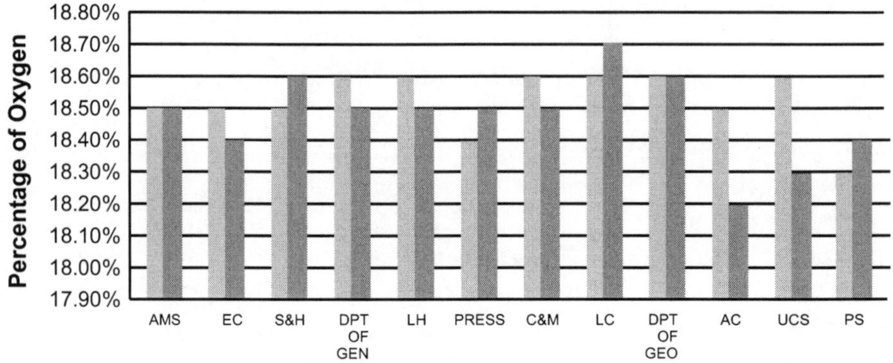

Fig. 10.5: Average percentage of oxygen on working and non-working days

On non-working days, in morning the percentage of oxygen ranged from 18.4% to 18.9% with an average of 18.4%. The concentration of O_2 was maximum at Department of Geography (19.1%) and minimum at Engineering College, Department of Geography, Arts College and University College of Science (18.4%). In the afternoon the percentage of oxygen ranged from 18.4% to 18.5% with an average of 18.4%. Engineering College and Department of Geography (18.7%) and minimum at University College of Science (18.1%). In the evening, the percentage of oxygen ranged from 18.3% to 18.4% with an average of 18.3%. The concentration of O_2% was maximum at Andhra Mahila Sabha, Science and humanities, Ladies Hostel (18.5%) and minimum at Police Station (18.1%). The average oxygen percentage on working days was 18.57% and on non-working days was 18.50%.The oxygen percentage was maximum at Department of Genetics, Law College, and Department of geography and University College of science (18.7%) and was minimum at Police Station (18.3%) on working days where as on non-working days the oxygen percentage was maximum at Department of Geography (18.7%) and minimum at University College of Science and Police Station (18.3%). The low level of oxygen can be attributed to the presence of other gases like CO, CO_2 and CH_4.

It is scientifically proved that oxygen deficiency causes hypoxia in humans (reduced oxygen content in the human body)[24]. People living in urban agglomerations experience oxygen deficiency caused by ecological factors and by increase in the atmospheric contents of carbon monoxide and suspended particles (aerosols), which block oxygen from being properly absorbed into the body. At present, the percentage of oxygen (O_2) in the dry air at the Earth's surface was considered practically constant (20.95%).It is assessed that possible decrease in the amount of oxygen due to an increase in the amount of green house gases. It is believed that the atmospheric content of CO_2 was about 260–280 ppm just before the Industrial Revolution in the 19th century, and it had changed slightly in the previous 10000 years. In the early 21st century, the CO_2 concentration exceeded 390 ppm. Temperature effects are also possible as a global increase in the temperature of surface air and the so called heat islands over large cities and industrial centers result in a decrease in both mean (global) and local (in cities) densities of oxygen. To sustain normal functions for humans and many animals the percentage of oxygen in the breathing environment must be within a small range. The Occupational Safety and Health Administration, OSHA, determined the optimal breathing range to be between 19.5 and 23.5% oxygen. 23.5% - maximum permissible oxygen level, 21% - percentage of oxygen found in normal air 19.5% - minimum permissible oxygen level.

Temperature: The temperature was fluctuated on working and non-working days in all the twelve sampling areas which are shown in fig 10.6. It was observed from the results that temperature was found to be in the limits. The variation in surface temperature controls the atmospheric convection[25]. This in turn affects the concentration of pollutants.

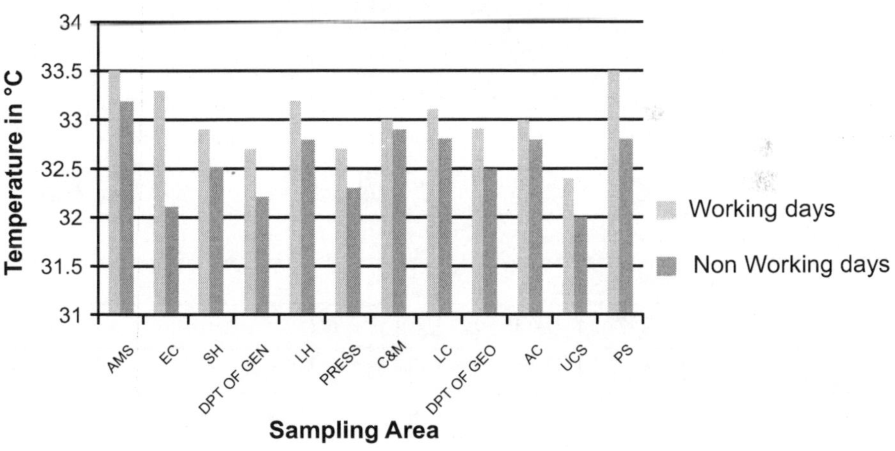

Fig. 10.6: Temperature on working and non-working days

Correlation analysis for air quality and noise level: The correlation coefficient for the systematic calculation between air quality and noise variables indicates indirect means for air quality monitoring. The degree of association that exists between two variables was measured by correlation coefficient, one taken as dependent variable (Chatterjee 2010). The greater the value of regression coefficient, the better and more useful the regression variables (Patil and Patil 2011). In the present study, the numerical values of correlation coefficient for the air and noise quality parameters were studied. It was revealed that highly positive correlation was observed between CO_2 and CO (0.6469), noise and CO(0.8845) on working days ,whereas on non-working days noise and CO(0.7828),temperature and CO(0.9075),temperature and noise (0.8282),which is depicted in table 10.3 and 10.4. Since the correlation coefficient gives the interrelationship between the parameters, correlation coefficients were calculated .A statistical analysis technique has been proven, to be a very useful tool for monitoring air pollutants concentration and noise level correlation for the present study. It can be concluded that most of the parameters are more or less correlated with each other.

Table 10.3: Working days average correlation for different intervals (Morning, afternoon and evening) for various parameters

	CO	*CO_2*	*O_2*	*Noise*	*Temperature*
CO	1				
CO_2	0.64692	1			
O_2	-0.46828	-0.59724	1		
Noise	0.884553	0.443014	0.35547	1	
Temperature	0.559545	0.480013	0.25214	0.417389	1

Table 10.4: Non-working days average correlation for different intervals (morning, afternoon and evening) for various parameters

	CO	*CO_2*	*O_2*	*Noise*	*Temperature*
CO	1				
CO_2	0.269814	1			
O_2	-0.13973	-0.00339	1		
Noise	0.782821	0.238459	- 0.04702	1	
Temperature	0.907537	0.180853	0.043581	0.828296	1

Conclusions

It is further recommended that the continuous monitoring need to be carried out to assess the pollutant levels concentration regularly in Osmania University campus to protect the staff and students from various health effects and improvement of the ambient air and noise quality levels by diverting the vehicles through by-lanes. The state government policies should accelerate the transition to a zero-emissions transportation system which includes setting targets for electric truck and mass transport adoption.

ACKNOWLEDGEMENT

The authors are thankful to Department of Environmental Science Osmania University for providing the facilities for research study.

REFERENCES

1. Ginzburga A.S., Vinogradovaa A.A., Fedorovaa E. I., Nikitichb E.V. and. Karpova A.V., Content of Oxygen in the Atmosphere over Large Cities and Respiratory Problems, Institute of Atmospheric Physics, *Atmospheric and Oceanic Physics*., 50(8), 782–792 (2014)
2. Mayer H., Air pollution in cities., *Atmospheric Environment*., (33), 4029-4037 (1999)
3. Central Pollution Control Board., Air Quality at Major Traffic Intersections of Delhi, Central Pollution Control Board, Ministry of Environment and Forests, Government of India, (1999)
4. Mondal R., Sen G.K., Chatterjee M., Sen B.K and Sen S.., Ground level concentration of nitrogen oxides (NOx) at some traffic intersection points in Calcutta, *Atmospheric Environment*., (34), 629-633. (2000)
5. Shyam Bihari Sharma, Suman Jain, Praveen Khirwadkar, Sunisha Kulkarni., The effects of air pollution on the environment and human health., *Indian Journal of Research in Pharmacy and Biotechnology*., 1(3)., 391-396 (2013)
6. Environmental Health Criteria (EHC 213, 2nd Edition) of the International Programme of Chemical Safety., World Health Organization United Nations Environment Programme, (1999)
7. Robin G., Sankaran S., A Study on Ambient Air Quality Monitoring In Chidambaram., *International Research Journal of Engineering and Technology*., (03), 2616-2619 (2016)
8. Fidell S, Barber D.S, Schultz T.J., Updating dosage–effect relationship for the prevalence of annoyance due to general transportation noise., *J Acoust Soc Am.,* (89), 221–233 (1991)
9. Fields J.M., Reactions to environmental noise in an ambient noise context in residential areas., *J Acoust Soc Am* (104), 2245–2260 (1998)
10. Miedema H.M.,VOS H., Noise sensitivity and reactions to noise and other environmental conditions., *J Acoust Soc Am*., 113(3), 1492-1504 (2003)
11. Michaud D.S, Keith S.E, McMurchy D., Noise annoyance in Canada., *Noise Health*, 7(27), 39–47 (2005)
12. Mehata K.V., Physicochemical characteristic and statistical study of ground water of some place of Vadgam taluka in Banaskantha district of Gujarat state (India)., *J Chem Pharm Res*., 2(4), 663-670 (2010)
13. Nair G.A., Bohjuari J.A., AlMariami M.A., Attia F.A., Ei-Toumi F.F., Ground water of North-East Libya., *J Environ Biol* (27), 695-700 (2006)

14. Nair G.A., Mohammad A.I., Fadiel M.M., Physico-Chemical Parameters And Correlation Coefficients Of ground water Of North-East Libya., *Pollut Res.*, 24(11), 1-6 (2005)
15. Kumar N., Sinha D.K., Drinking water quality management through Correlation Studies among Various Physicochemical Parameters a Case Study., *Int Environ Sci.*, 1(2), 253-259 (2010)
16. El-Sharkawy M.F., Alsubaie., A Study of environmental noise pollution in the university of dammam campus., *Saudi J Med Med* Sci., (2), 178-184 (2014)
17. Hunashala., Rajiv Patil., Yogesh., Assessment of Noise Pollution Indices in the City of Kolhapur India., *Procedia-Social and Behavioral Sciences.*, (37), 448-457 (2012)
18. Vinitha Pathak., Triathi B.D., Virendhra Mishra., Evaluation of traffic noise pollution and attitudes of exposed individuals in working place., *Atmospheric Environment.,* 42(16), 3892-3898 (2008)
19. Sharad Gokhale., Mukesh Khare., A hybrid model for predicting carbon monoxide from vehicular exhausts in urban environments., *Atmospheric Environment.,* 39(22), 4025-4040 (2005)
20. Kai Zhanga., Stuart Battermanb., Air pollution and health risks due to vehicle traffic., *Science Of The Total Environment.*, (15), 307-316 (2013)
21. Nagendra S., Khare M., Dirunal and seasonal variations of carbon monxide and nitrogen dioxide in Delhi city., *Int.J Environment and Pollution.*, 19 (1), 75-96 (2003)
22. Balashanmugam P., Ramanathan A.R., Nehrukumar V., Elango E., Ambient air quality studies on Cuddalore., *International Journal of Environmental Sciences.*, 2(3), 1302-1313 (2012)
23. Anjan Chatterjee., Page Widick., Rebecca Sternschein., William B., Smith., Ii Bianca Bromberger., The Assessment Of Art Attributes., *Empirical Studies Of The Arts.*, 28(2), 207-222 (2010)
24. Patil S.V., Patil C.D., Salunke B.K., Salunkhe R.B., Bathe G.A., Patil D.M., Studies on characterization of bioflocculant exopolysaccharide of Azotobacter indicus and its potential for wastewater treatment., *Appl Biochem Biotechnol.*, 163(4), 463-72 (2010)
25. Sonal Verma S., and Birva Desai., Effect of Meteorological Conditions on Air Pollution of Surat City, *J. Int. Environmental Application and Science.*, 3(5), 358-367 (2008)

Urban Environment and Spatial Science
Dr Mohd Akhter Ali, Dr. Kabir Mohan Sethy, Dr Muzafar Wani and M.Kamraju
Ane Books Pvt. Ltd. 2021, , ISBN : 978-93-90658-28-2, P.P. : 133 – 154

11

Climate Change and its Impact on Water- Comparative Study of two Panchayats: Bhaliadal of Ayurbhanj and Gupti of Kendrapada Districts in Odisha

Ms. Shakuntala Pratihary &
Prof Kabir Mohan Sethy

Climate change is the most important challenge of human civilization that is categorically felt since the beginning of present millennium. Repeated happening of catastrophic events across the globe is indicating towards the single connotation of climate change be it cloud bursting, flash flood, increased incidence of desertification, furious wild fire or repeated lightning strikes. The increased intensity and magnitude of these disastrous events have significant impact on the lives and livelihood of the people around the world. One prominent indicator of all these happenings is that the climate change that the humanity as a whole is facing today, is expressing itself via altering the water cycle in the atmosphere and distribution of water around different region. Raised temperature of earth's surface owing to global warming is having significant impact on the water cycle of the region hence alter the water distribution in an unpredictable manner. Most of the climate change impact is felt through water be it agricultural production, sea level rise, flash flood or hitting of cyclone.

Corresponding Author: Ms. Shakuntala Pratihary

Differential Impact of Global Warming on Water Cycle

Evaporation

Raised temperature of earth's surface creates warmer air, suitable condition to speed up evaporation from soil, plants and water bodies. The drier condition on the surface affects drinking water supplies for humans and animals along with difficulties for the plants to survive. The agriculture sector is most vulnerable to drier condition as small plant's stems and leaves dries up under hotter sun. Another side effect of high evaporation in coastal areas is that it leads to high humidity resulting in chocking of sweat gland of humans thus blocking the cooling effect of sweat during hot season. This increase sufferings and morbidity of coastal population.

Cloud Formation

Higher evaporation leads to cloud formation near earth's atmosphere. This process speeds up in the coastal areas having large number of water bodies. These clouds when collide with each other upon their movement creates lightning and thunder storm. Negatively charged particles suspended from sky near the atmosphere of earth get attracted towards the positively charged particles of earth. Result is lightning strikes on the ground. The increasing incidence of lightning in recent years is responsible for millions of life and property loss in earth. The lightning strikes are also responsible for increasing incidence of wild fire in many parts of world.

Precipitation

High evaporation owing to higher temperature results into higher precipitation in the form of rain, snow, thunder storm or frost in an unpredictable manner having significant impact on the life of people. Global warming has prominent impact on the weather pattern by affecting air temperature, water cycle, nature and types of precipitation in the region. Dry areas are becoming drier with more intense and prolonged droughts. It is also escalating conditions for wild fire, a serious threat to human kind as a society.

Another significant aspect is that global warming has affected the rainfall pattern of the wet region that has critically impacted on the rain fed agriculture. Along with this, irregularity in the rain fall hardens the soil surface and helps for quick run off of rain water. It peels out the rich nutrient of upper soil and fail to recharge the ground water table 11.1.

Surface Run off

Warmer and wetter air causing heavy precipitation often leads to flash floods. Catastrophic floods have serious repercussions causing damage to agriculture, property and lives. Heavy flow of water also stripe nutrients from soil and flush them into nearby water bodies along with other chemical fertilizer and pesticide residuals. Contamination of water bodies by chemical particles has significant impact on the aquatic life and life of people dependent on that water bodies.

Table 11.1: Impact of Rise in Temperature on Water Cycle

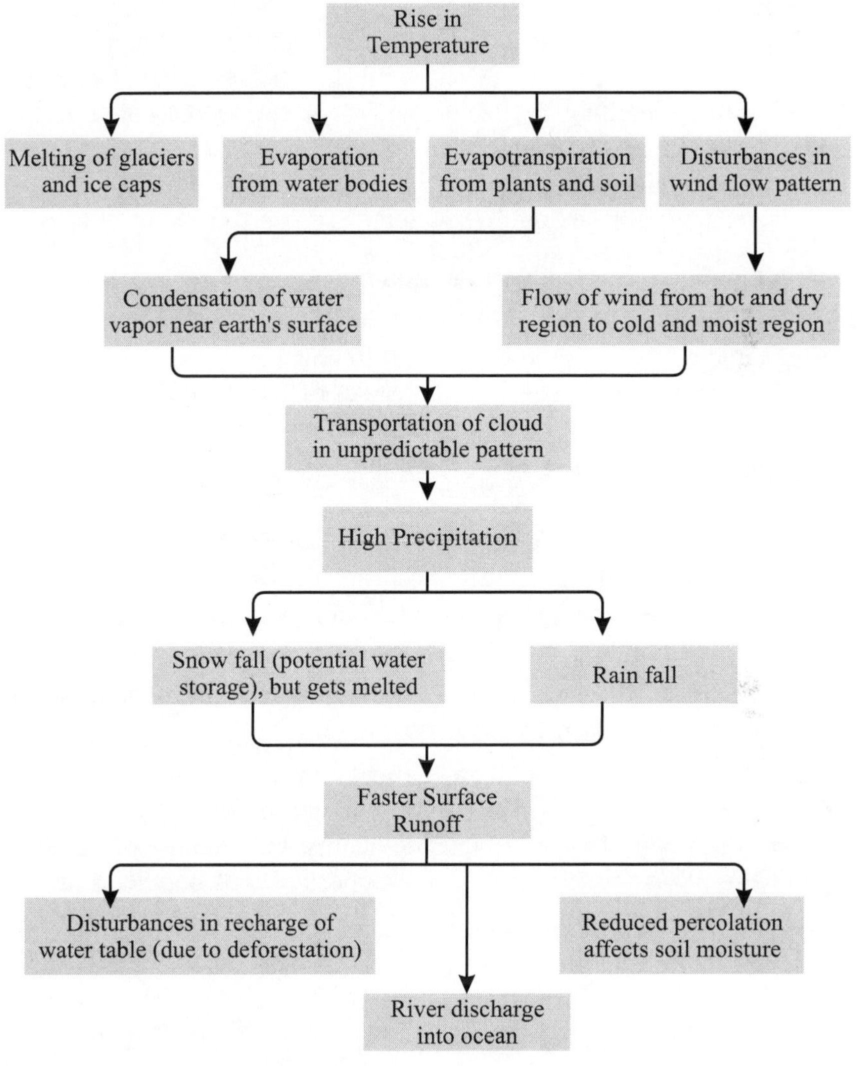

Oceans

Oceans are continually contaminated by the flash floods. Chemical particles enter in to the ocean world by the river channels and significantly affecting ocean life. Along with the pollution warm surface of ocean increase the acidity of ocean bed thus influencing the aquatic food chain. The raised surface temperature of ocean forces many sea animals to make pole ward movement further aggravating food web in the sea. The flow chart shows the flow of water which gets influenced by the rising temperature of the earth.

Further to this, the surface temperature of ocean has strong relation with the ocean current that ultimately affect the weather pattern in land mass. Study shows that higher ocean surface temperature alters the rainfall variable and makes weather less predictable. Along with this the sea level is continually rising owing to the melting of glaciers and ice-sheets in the pole due to rise in earth's temperature. Frequent formation of low pressure, storm surge and high intensity cyclone in recent years clearly indicates the co-relation between increased ocean temperature and formation of cyclonic pressure.

Impact of Changed Water Cycle on Humanity:

Water is the source of life on earth and it circulates in earth's atmosphere in a particular manner that has resulted in different pattern of life in different regions. Economic, social and cultural aspect of life draws its energy from the specific pattern of precipitation of that particular region. Climate change by impacting strongly on the water cycle and distribution affects the lives of people.

Following are the broad category through which climate change affects human life via impacting on the water cycle and distribution specifically of the poor and marginalized who depend on nature for their survival.

1. Changed precipitation pattern affects the availability of water in the region. Scarcity of water affects nutrition, health and hygiene of public and most importantly the peace of the region.
2. Agricultural production is severely affected. Water availability impacts on seeds germination, growth of plants, and maturation of fruits. Excessive water or scarcity of water affects the quality and quantity of agricultural production thus the income earning opportunity of people. Availability of water has strong impact on the ecology of region.Evidence shows that robust ecology boosts the agricultural production while weak one has negative impact.
3. Climate change is bringing sudden flash flood via torrential rain. Thatched house of the poor get destroyed along with all the belongings and saved crops. This has strong impact on the economic back bone of the family affecting food security and overall growth aspect.
4. Repeated flood contaminate the water source leading to water borne diseases and skin disease. Chances of infection increase many times.

Lack of resources and health security measures of the poor people cost them high due to these infectious diseases.

5. Raised temperature create moist climate conducive for vector born disease. Irregular precipitation along with hot and humid climate spread vector born disease like malaria, Chikungunya, dengue. Low level of awareness and resources increases the vulnerabilities of the poor people to these vector borne diseases that erode their single asset health and reduce the prospect to lead a good life in future.
6. Irregular rain and long spell of dry season creates scarcity of water. This affects food security of the region. Scarcity of water restricts healthy practices and hygienic habits thus increasing the risk of infectious diseases.

Water Stress Condition in Odisha Odisha is one of the most vulnerable states of India to natural disasters. Unique geo-climatic conditions of the state traditionally make the state vulnerable to disasters like flood, cyclone and drought. However in the recent years the intensity types and magnitude of disasters has increased many times. Alteration in water cycle owing to global warming has changed the climate of the state and subsequently the weather pattern. Now the state is experiencing long stretch of dry periods, absence of monsoon rain, unprecedented and unpredictable torrential rainfall leading to flash flood, urban flooding, repeated intense and higher magnitude storm surge, increased frequency of cyclone strike, heavy thunder storm and lightning strikes are some of the disasters that are creating havoc for the people of Odisha. Other disasters that has strong imprint on the lives and livelihood of the people of the state are sea-inundation and flooding of coastal habitation, increased salinity of soil and water bodies in the coastal areas due to frequent storm surge, reduced fertility of soil owing to long dry spell, unpredictable variation in temperature and precipitation infest agricultural crop with unknown pest and bugs and silent withdrawal of ecological services.

Unique geographical conditions of Odisha make the state vulnerable to various natural disasters. 480kmof long coast line of the state makes it prone to cyclones formed in Bay of Bengal. Even though the coast line is 17% of the total east coast of India the state has been affected by 35% of all the cyclone and severe cyclonic storm that have crossed the eastern coast. In recent years the frequency and magnitude of cyclone formation in the Bay of Bengal has increased many times. Last decade saw no major cyclonic formation in the east coast where as present decade witnessed six major cyclone of category four and above leaving aside numerous low pressures and storm surge. However the frequency of cyclone has gained momentum in the last three years owing to continuous rise in the sea water level and surface temperature.

Odisha is under tropical climatic zone and South West Monsoon, retreating North East Monsoon control the climate of the state. The monsoon rain used to cause flood in the major river channels of the state. However in recent years the change in monsoon wind pattern and resultant change in precipitation pattern is causing torrential rain within few hours. Result of such kind of rainfall is flashflood and urban flooding causing heavy loss of property and lives. It is also resulting in siltation at the river mouth that aggravate flood situation in main land leading to landslides and sufferings of people. Cloud burst and lightning strikes are the resultant impact of imbalance in the water cycles of the region. Lightning is emerging as a major killer in Odisha in recent years. In a conservative approach lightning strike is killing 350 individuals per year in the present decade.

Proneness to drought in Odisha has increased in recent years especially in western Odisha. Absence of monsoon rain, long dry spell and scanty rain fall is aggravating the water stress condition of western Odisha. Ground water level is continually dropping there due to insufficient recharge of water table that is creating a vicious circle of desertification process. Dropping down of ground water level is becoming fatal for green coverage and absence of strong root system of trees help the rain fall water to flow off the soil instead of getting into the soil. The vicious circle of desertification in western Odisha is creating millions of climate refugee who resort to migration as a survival strategy. The prolonged summer season with persistent heat wave and scanty water availability is increasing the morbidity of the humans and animals of the state.

The frequency and intensity of natural disasters has increased for the state especially in post-super cyclone years. Even though the geographical location of the state is making it vulnerable to natural calamities global warming induced climate change and extensive deforestation activities for the mining are accumulating forces that disturb the balance in water cycle of the region. The disturbance in the water cycle is affecting the precipitation and distribution of water that ultimately affects the wellbeing of the population of the state.

In this context two different Panchayats belonging to two different geographical locations are extensively studied to find out the ground reality of Odisha with regard to availability and accessibility of water. Bhaliadal in Mayurbhanj district is primarily a tribal Panchayat and Gupti in Kendrapara district is a coastal Panchayat. Both the Panchayats have different geographical terrain and are also exposed to different climate events.

KENDRAPADA DISTRICT

Kendrapada is a coastal district of Odisha where district's eastern boundary is bordered by Bay of Bengal. Mighty rivers along with their tributaries lie in this district along with numerous creeks. Water logging during rainy season is an age old problem of this district which is now added with sea water intrusion during high tide, frequent storms, low pressures and cyclone formed in the sea. This is taking heavy toll in terms of agricultural crop loss, contamination of water bodies and resultant health risk, increased salinity and loss of fertility of soil. The district has dearth of industrial units and infrastructure support system. Thus people of this district depend on agriculture and allied services for livelihood.

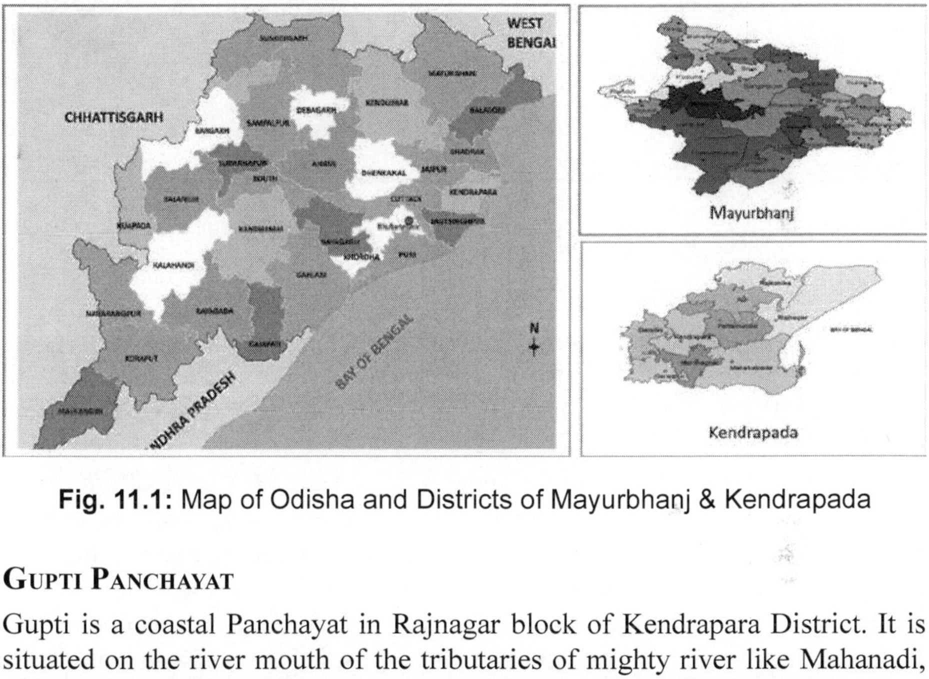

Fig. 11.1: Map of Odisha and Districts of Mayurbhanj & Kendrapada

Gupti Panchayat

Gupti is a coastal Panchayat in Rajnagar block of Kendrapara District. It is situated on the river mouth of the tributaries of mighty river like Mahanadi, Brahmani and Baitarani. There are 19 villages in this Panchayat. River and river based ecology is the prominent environment of this Panchayat. People are dependent on agriculture as a major livelihood option due to the absence of any industrial activity. However agriculture is rain fed in this Panchayat due to lack of irrigation facilities. Another feature of this Panchayat is that it comes under crocodile conservation programmes hence inland fishing is strictly prohibited. A particular class of the community does high sea contract fishing as bonded labor for certain period of time. Other than these two livelihood opportunities people of this Panchayat are either engaged as agricultural worker or daily laborer.

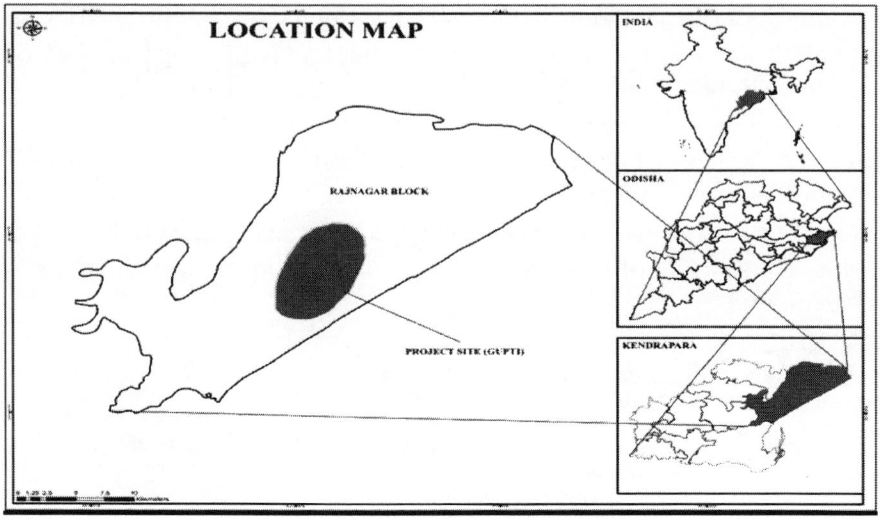

Fig. 11.2: Location Map of Gupti Panchayat

Mayurbhanj District

Mayurbhanj is the largest district of Odisha having huge tracts of lush green coverage. This district belongs to mountainous region and consists of rich iron ore and other important mining ore. Hence mining provides significant employment opportunity to the youths of this district. Other than mining activity people of this region are engaged in forestry and agriculture. More than 50% of the population of Mayurbhanj district are tribal people and depend on forest for their daily activity. In recent years owing to changes in water cycle due to rise in earth's temperature forest ecology is slowly and silently shrinking. Many eco-system services that used to harness the wellbeing and welfare of the tribal people are now vanishing. It is having significant impact on the income earning opportunity, food security of the local population. It is also impacting on the cultural entity of the tribal people and is affecting overall peace of the region. Dropping down of water table owing to mining activity and irregularities in monsoon wind pattern has great impact on agricultural production.

Agriculture and forestry are the age old livelihood engagement for the tribal people of this region. In the wake of rise in temperature, changes in precipitation pattern and absence of irrigation facilities, practicing agriculture is costing high for the farmers. Tribal of this district do organic farming in traditional manner that is highly sensitive to changes in weather pattern. Climate change in an unpredictable manner is creating huge loss that the farmers are unable to cope on their own.

Bhaliadal Panchayat

Bhaliadal Gram Panchayat of Mayurbhanj district comes under Thakurmunda Block is a forest dominated Panchayat and hence mostly inhabitated by the tribal population. This Panchayat consists of 6 villages out of which only 2 villages come under revenue village and rest are the declared forest village. This part of the forest area comes under Tiger Reserve Forest Area of Simlipal Bio Reserve National Park and hence construction activity in this Panchayat is strictly prohibitory.

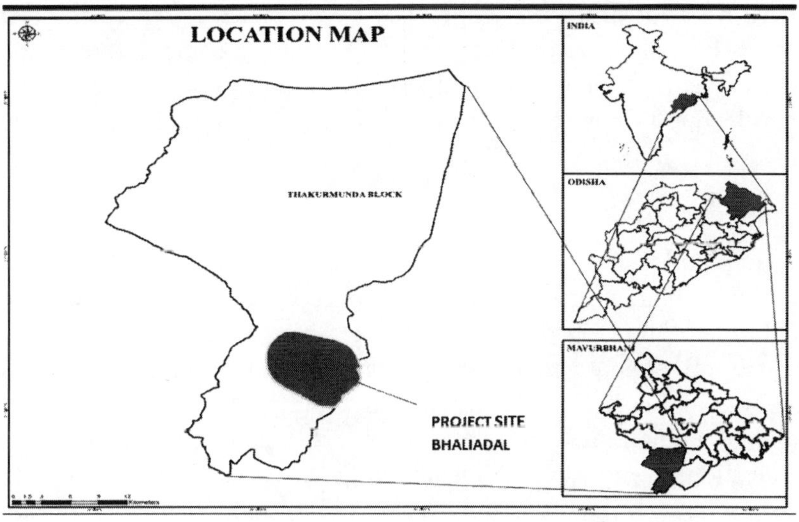

Fig. 11.3: Location Map of Bhaliadal Panchayat

However after Forest Reserve Act 2006, this Panchayat could witness some development initiatives in terms of establishment of primary and upper primary schools, SHGs, construction of forest roads, bore well. However looking at the number of households there is discrepancy between the number of population and availability of basic utility services.

The Gram Panchayat has no irrigation facilities and people are dependent on the nearby streams and community tube well for their daily requirements. The Panchayat has absence of any industrial base including small and cottage industries so the habitants depend on collection of non-timber-forest-products and agriculture for livelihood opportunity.

Objective of the Study:

The purpose of the study is to find out the differential impact of climate change on water availability and accessibility in different geographical location. Following are the objective of the study

- To find out different sources of water for different usage
- To find out water sources in different season
- To find out the distance of water sources in different season

The above objectives will help to find out to what degree the climate change is going to impact on water availability and accessibility at the ground level which has strong bearing on the welfare of population. For this purpose two Panchayat from Odisha were selected, one from coastal district having proximity with the Bay of Bengal and another from high land mountainous region with lots of green coverage. The two Panchayat represents different geographical locations, a perfect ground for making comparative analysis of climate change impact on water availability. In order to carry out this objective 200 sample questionnaires, 100 questionnaires from each Panchayat were administered.

Sample Selection

Sample population was collected from the two Panchayats of Gupti and Bhaliadal to conduct the survey of impact of climate change on water availability. For this purpose four village from Gupti Panchayat and six villages from Bhaliadal Panchayat were taken in to account.A total of hundred samples were collected from each Panchayat spreading over different village. The sample populations were interviewed with regard to prepared questioner. Some questions were asked to know the quantitative information and some were asked to ascertain the qualitative information from the respondent. Climate change is not proven fact at the grass root village level and most of the respondents are unaware about the term. Hence their experience with regard to change in temperature, rainfall pattern and increased frequency of disaster were taken into account as their testimony of climate change. However the respondent of the interview were majorly male, as social construct in this part of the world debar women population to participate in any kind of study or survey. Women are the primary stake holder in provisioning of water and food for the family. Their non-participation in the interview process couldn't shed light on the various issues of water stress condition and its impact on women health.

Source of Water

Water has multiple usages, at the house hold level and at the livelihood level. However both the studied Panchayat has no industry and the requirement of water for industry need is nil. On the other hand agriculture and allied sectors is the dominant employer in both the Panchayat and there is absence of any irrigation facilities. Agriculture is rain fed in both the area. So the questionnaire with regard to source of water is confined to house hold requirements. Again at the house hold level there is segregation of water source depending on the usage. As because availability of clean water as per need is a big question in both the region people have distributed their source of water as per their need. According to the questionnaire the need for water is divided into three categories, drinking and cooking need, bathing and washing purpose, and finally for the requirement of domestic animals like cattle.

Table 11.2 shows source of water for various household requirement in both the sample Panchayat in Summer Season. Gupti being a Coastal Panchayat seems to have a stable water source as close to 93% of the population depend on community tube well for drinking and washing need of water. Rest 7% of the population have own tube well to meet the above need of water. The cattle requirement of water in Gupti Panchayat is met from river water. Close to 95% of population in the Coastal Panchayat depend on river water for cattle need while 5% depend on community tube well for the same purpose. On the other hand availability of water is a critical aspect for the tribal people in Bhaliadal Panchayat. In summer season the water stress condition becomes acute in the tribal Panchayat. For this reason people of this Panchayat use multiple source of water for varieties of need.For drinking and cooking requirement 77% of total sample respondent in the tribal Panchayat depend on community tube well whereas 10% of the respondents depend on the Perennial stream. Out of the total respondents 5% of the population depends on community well and 3% each have their own well and own tube well while 2% uses pond water to satisfy the cooking and drinking need of water.

Table 11.2: Source of drinking, washing and cattle bathing water in summer season

District		*Kendrapara*						*Mayurbhanj*					
Block		*Rajnagar*						*Thakurmunda*					
Panchayat		*Gupti*						*Bhaliadal*					
Source of water		*Drinking*		*Washing*		*Cattle*		*Drinking*		*Washing*		*Cattle*	
	Sources	*No.*	*%*	*No.*	*%*	*No.*	*%*	*No.*	*%*	*No.*	*%*	*No.*	*%*
	Own well	0	0	0	0	0	0	3	3.2	0	0	0	0
	Community well	0	0	0	0	0	0	5	5.3	5	5.3	0	0
	Own tube well	7	7.1	7	7.1	0	0	3	3.2	1	1.1	1	1.1
	Community tube well	91	92.9	91	92.9	5	5.2	73	76.8	11	11.6	2	2.2
	River	0	0	0	0	92	94.8	0	0	1	1.1	1	1.1

District		***Kendrapara***						***Mayurbhanj***					
Block		***Rajnagar***						***Thakurmunda***					
Pan-chayat		***Gupti***						***Bhaliadal***					
Source of water		***Drinking***		***Washing***		***Cattle***		***Drinking***		***Washing***		***Cattle***	
	Sources	***No.***	***%***	***No.***	***%***	***No.***	***%***	***No.***	***%***	***No.***	***%***	***No.***	***%***
	Creek	0	0	0	0	0	0	0	0	0	0	0	0
	Pond	0	0	0	0	0	0	2	2.1	31	32.6	34	38.2
	Perennial stream	0	0	0	0	0	0	9	9.5	44	46.3	50	56.2
	Water Tank	0	0	0	0	0	0	0	0	2	2.1	1	1.1
	Mobile water tank	0	0	0	0	0	0	0	0	0	0	0	0
	Rain water harvesting	0	0	0	0	0	0	0	0	0	0	0	0
	Total	98	100	98	100	97	100	95	100	95	100	89	100

Natural supply of water is limited due to changes in precipitation pattern and insufficiency in recharging ground water level. Simultaneously Reserve Forest Act implemented for the Bhaliadal Panchayat restricts any construction activity including digging of tube well. So the people of the tribalPanchayat depend on various sources of water for their variety of need. In order to meet the need of water for washing and bathing 47% of the total respondent depend on the perennial stream and 33% of the respondent depend on the pond. Community tube well satisfies around 12% populations above need and 5% of the population depends on the community well. 2% of the total respondents said they depend on water tank and 1% use river water to meet the washing requirement of water. Multiple source ofwater for the same purpose indicates towards water stress condition in the region. It highlights not only on the availability of water but also on the accessibility and distance of water source that is adding to the physical burden. It is clear from Table-1 that in the tribal Panchayat domestic animal's requirement of water is met primarily from perennial stream and ponds. Table-1 data showing source of water for different house hold need in summer season is categorically expressed in Fig. 11.4.

Fig. 11.4 shows different sources of water and percentage of population dependent on these sources of water in summer season. It is evident from the figure that the coastal Panchayat is relatively stable with regard to the source of water because majority of population depend on the same source for the same need. On the other hand in the tribal sample Panchayat multiple water sources are used by different percentage of population to satisfy the same need.

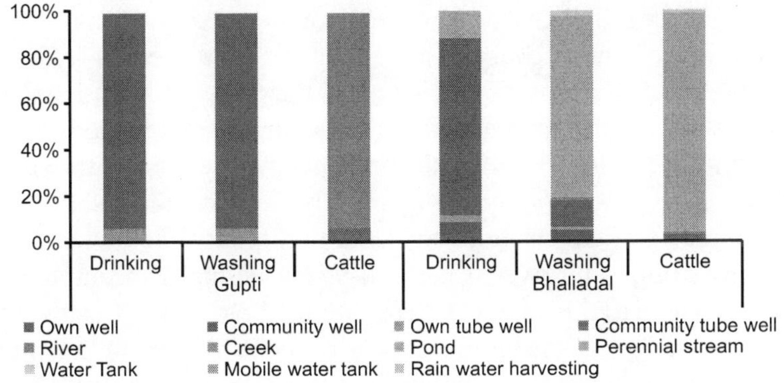

Fig. 11.4: Source of drinking, washing and cattle bathing water in summer season

Table 11.3: Source of drinking, washing and cattle bathing water in rainy season

District		*Kendrapara*						*Mayurbhanj*					
Block		*Rajnagar*						*Thakurmunda*					
Pan-chayat		*Gupti*						*Bhaliadal*					
Source of water		*Drinking*		*Washing*		*Cattle*		*Drinking*		*Washing*		*Cattle*	
	Sources	*No.*	*%*	*No.*	*%*	*No.*	*%*	*No.*	*%*	*No.*	*%*	*No.*	*%*
	Own well	0	0	0	0	0	0	3	3.1	0	0	0	0
	Commu-nity well	0	0	0	0	0	0	6	6.3	5	5.3	0	0
	Own tube well	7	7.1	7	7.1	0	0	3	3.1	1	1.1	1	1.1
	Commu-nity tube well	91	92.9	91	92.9	6	6.2	73	76	12	12.6	2	2.2
	River	0	0	0	0	91	93.8	0	0	0	0	0	0
	Creek	0	0	0	0	0	0	0	0	0	0	0	0
	Pond	0	0	0	0	0	0	2	2.1	30	31.6	34	38.2
	Perennial stream	0	0	0	0	0	0	9	9.4	45	47.4	51	57.3
	Water Tank	0	0	0	0	0	0	0	0	2	2.1	1	1.1
	Mobile water tank	0	0	0	0	0	0	0	0	0	0	0	0
	Rain water harvesting	0	0	0	0	0	0	0	0	0	0	0	0
	Total	98	100	98	100	97	100	96	100	95	100	89	100

Table 11.3 and Table 11.4 shows the source of water for various house hold requirement in rainy season and winter season respectively for both the studied Panchayat. By closely analyzing all the three tables it is evident that barring rainy season the source of water for summer season and winter season for various house hold need in both the Panchayat remain within a range of continuity. People of Gupti Panchayat majorly depend on two source of water, community tube well and river water. Community tube well water is used for human consumption and river water is used for animal consumption. On the other hand in Bhaliadal Panchayat across all the three major season of the year majority, close to 76% of the sample population depend on community tube well for drinking water requirement. Perennial stream satisfies around 10% sample population's drinking water requirement and close to 6% of the population depend on the community well for the same purpose. For the washing and bathing requirement of water close to 32% of the sample population depend on pond, close to 47% of the sample population depend on perennial streamand around 12% of the population depends on community tube well throughout the year. Few people depend on community well, own tube well, river and water tank for the same purpose. The domestic animal requirement of water is also met through various sources in the tribal Panchayat. However around 57% of the sample population depend on perennial stream and 38% depend on the pond for the above purpose. Very few number of people depend on own tube well, community tube well, river and water tank to satisfy domestic animal requirement of water.

Table 11.4: Source of drinking, washing and cattle bathing water in winter season

District		*Kendrapara*						*Mayurbhanj*					
Block		*Rajnagar*						*Thakurmunda*					
Panchayat		*Gupti*						*Bhaliadal*					
Source of water		*Drinking*		*Washing*		*Cattle*		*Drinking*		*Washing*		*Cattle*	
	Sources	*No.*	*%*	*No.*	*%*	*No.*	*%*	*No.*	*%*	*No.*	*%*	*No.*	*%*
	Own well	0	0	0	0	0	0	3	3.2	0	0	0	0
	Community well	0	0	0	0	0	0	5	5.3	5	5.3	0	0
	Own tube well	7	7.1	7	7.1	0	0	3	3.2	1	1.1	1	1.1
	Community tube well	91	92.9	91	92.9	5	5.3	73	76.8	12	12.6	2	2.2
	River	0	0	0	0	90	94.7	0	0	1	1.1	1	1.1

District		***Kendrapara***						***Mayurbhanj***					
Block		***Rajnagar***						***Thakurmunda***					
Pan-chayat		***Gupti***						***Bhaliadal***					
Source of water		***Drinking***		***Washing***		***Cattle***		***Drinking***		***Washing***		***Cattle***	
	Sources	***No.***	***%***	***No.***	***%***	***No.***	***%***	***No.***	***%***	***No.***	***%***	***No.***	***%***
	Creek	0	0	0	0	0	0	0	0	0	0	0	0
	Pond	0	0	0	0	0	0	2	2.1	30	31.6	34	38.2
	Perennial stream	0	0	0	0	0	0	9	9.5	44	46.3	50	56.2
	Water Tank	0	0	0	0	0	0	0	0	2	2.1	1	1.1
	Mobile water tank	0	0	0	0	0	0	0	0	0	0	0	0
	Rain water harvesting	0	0	0	0	0	0	0	0	0	0	0	0
	Total	98	100	98	100	95	100	95	100	95	100	89	100

Analysis of Table 11.2, Table 11.3, and Table 11.4 signifies to the fact that people of both the Panchayat treat ground water to be the safest of all the available sources for which they use it to satisfy drinking and cooking requirement of water. It further highlights to the fact that even though people treat ground water to be the safest of all, they do nothing to conserve and preserve ground water level to satisfy future requirement. Ground water table is also vital for the sustenance of ecology. In the event of disturbance in precipitation pattern it has become more important to take note of recharging of ground water table to avoid onslaught of the process of desertification. However people of both the Panchayat are unaware about the issue and rely on the extraction aspect of ground water for the present requirement ignoring the future requirement. None of the respondent in both the Panchayat interviewed is doing anything regarding rain water harvesting or ground water recharging issue. It can be said that both the two above concept are alien to the respondent's knowledge system and need policy makers active intervention to bring in these concept in day to day practice to avoid water stress condition in Odishain the event of climate change circumstances.

Fig. 5 and Fig. 6 shows source of water for different household need in both the Panchayat in rainy season and winter season respectively. It is evident from both the figure including Figure-1 that in Gupti Panchayat around same percentage of population use the same source of water for the same need across all the seasons. It highlights to the fact the water is sufficiently available in Gupti Panchayat as per people's need. Another point to be focused is that in this Panchayat people are solely dependent on the ground water source for human consumption. This fact highlights to the vulnerability aspect of Gupti Panchayat. Being a coastal Panchayat Gupti remains vulnerable to multiple natural disasters like flood, storm surge, saline water incursion through creeks and ferocious impact of cyclone. All these events contaminate surface water bodies and make it unfit for human consumption. Hence without having any option for the source of water people of this Panchayat rely on the ground water either in the form of community tube well or own tube well. However communities are needed to be sensitized with regard to the recharging of ground water by arresting the surface run-off of rain water. In this way the water table of the area can be managed along with fulfilling people's requirement.

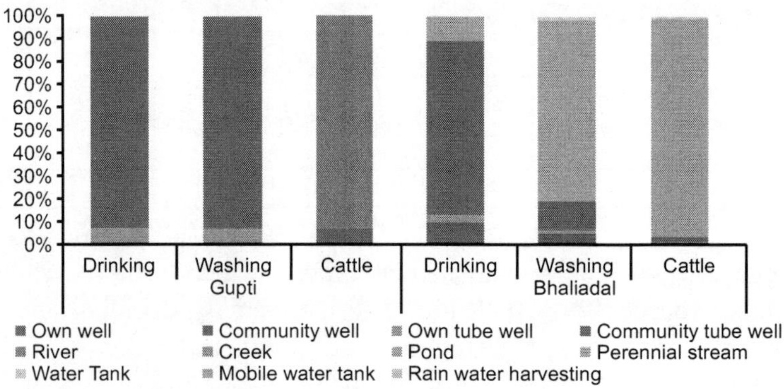

Fig. 11.5: Source of drinking, washing and cattle bathing water in rainy season

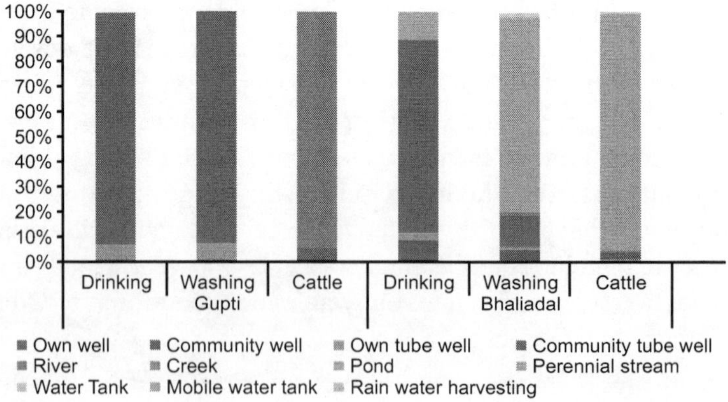

Fig. 11.6: Source of drinking, washing and cattle bathing water in winter season

Fig. 11.4, Fig. 11.5 and Fig. 11.6 shows the source of water for house hold consumption need in summer season, rainy season and winter season respectively in both the studied Panchayat. It is evident from the analysis of the above figure that in the tribal Panchayat people rely on multiple sources of water for multiple functioning. Even for human consumption need depending on the categories of requirement the source of water varies. When it comes to drinking and cooking requirement majority of people depend on ground water in various format like community tube well, own tube well, community well and own well. However there are some people who cannot access the wells and depend on perennial stream and ponds for the same purpose. Tribal habitation is sparsely populated with scattered house hold across an area unlike row wise settlement in coastal habitation. So distance is a major factor in deciding welfare of tribal people when it comes to access of source of water.

The above figures shows that in the tribal Panchayat around 80% of the sample population use surface water for washing and bathing need, less dependency on the ground water reserve. In case of domestic animals requirement people of Bhaliadal Panchayat solely depend on surface water source leaving aside merely 3% of the sample population who use ground water for the same purpose. Water bodies in the tribal Panchayat are less prone to contamination unlike its counterpart in Gupti Panchayat. So the usability aspect of surface water is higher in Bhaliadal Panchayat than Gupti. However during the data collection procedure elderly respondents of the tribal Panchayat shared their experience about the past years when water stress condition was not an issue back then the way it is now felt. Mayurbhanj being a mining dominated district is experiencing large scale deforestation activity, a prominent bottleneck in the ground water recharging issue. Added to the loss of network of root system change in the precipitation pattern is affecting the availability of water as per people's need. So in order to satisfy their varieties of need people travel long distance in this Panchayat as shown in Table-4

Distance of Water Source

Table 11.5 shows distance of water source for various house hold need in both the studied Panchayat. In Bhaliadal Panchayat around 19% of the sample population cover a distance of 100-250mtr for the drinking water requirement, around 18% of the population cover the same distance range to satisfy washing and bathing water need and 5.8% of the population trade the same distance for the domestic animals water requirement. Around 73% of the population travel the distance of 250-500mtr to collect drinking water while close to 47% cover the same distance for washing and bathing need of water and around 44% of the population cover the same range of distance for domestic animal water requirement. Around 7% of the sample population covers the distance range of 500mte-1km to meet drinking water requirement, 33% of the population do the same for washing and bathing need of water and 45% of the people travel the distance to satisfy domestic animals water requirement. Distance of water source always highlights on the physical burden in fetching water. Generally women are responsible for bringing water for household consumption. Longer the distance higher is the physical strain. However in this tribal Panchayat women are not allowed to participate in any formal interview so their ordeal couldn't be properly covered in this research paper.

Table 11.5: Distance of Drinking, Washing and Cattle Bathing Water

District		*Kendrapara*						*Mayurbhanj*					
Block		*Rajnagar*						*Thakurmunda*					
Pan-chayat		*Gupti*						*Bhaliadal*					
Dis-tance of water		*Drinking*		*Washing*		*Cattle*		*Drinking*		*Washing*		*Cattle*	
	Dis-tance	*No.*	*%*	*No.*	*%*	*No.*	*%*	*No.*	*%*	*No.*	*%*	*No.*	*%*
	Within house	0	0.0	0	0.0	0	0.0	0	0	0	0.0	0	0.0
	Less than 100 meter	0	0.0	0	0.0	0	0.0	0	0	0	0.0	0	0.0
	100-250 meter	92	94.8	92	94.8	11	12.2	18	18.9	16	17.4	5	5.8
	250-500 meter	2	2.1	2	2.1	1	1.1	69	72.6	43	46.7	38	44.2
	500 mtr-1 km	3	3.1	3	3.1	78	86.7	7	7.4	30	32.6	39	45.3
	1-2 km	0	0.0	0	0.0	0	0.0	1	1.1	1	1.1	2	2.3
	more than 2 km	0	0.0	0	0.0	0	0.0	0	0	2	2.2	2	2.3
	Total	97	100	97	100	90	100	95	100	92	100	86	100
		Drinking				*Washing*				*Cattle*			
		□□=115.599				□□=115.877				□□=54.920			
		p=0.000				p=0.000				p=0.000			

Fig. 11.7 shows the distance of water source for various house hold requirement in both the Panchayat. It is evident from the figure that in the coastal Panchayat fetching water is less tiresome than the tribal Panchayat

for the entire house hold requirement. In Gupti Panchayat around 95% of the total respondents cover a distance range of 100-250mtr to get water for human consumption need. Close to 2% of the total respondent cover the distance range of 250-500mtr and 3% travel the distance range of 500mtr-1km to satisfy human need of water. On the other hand to meet the domestic animal need of water 12% of the population cover the distance range of 100-250mtr while 88% of the respondent travel the distance of 500-1km range.

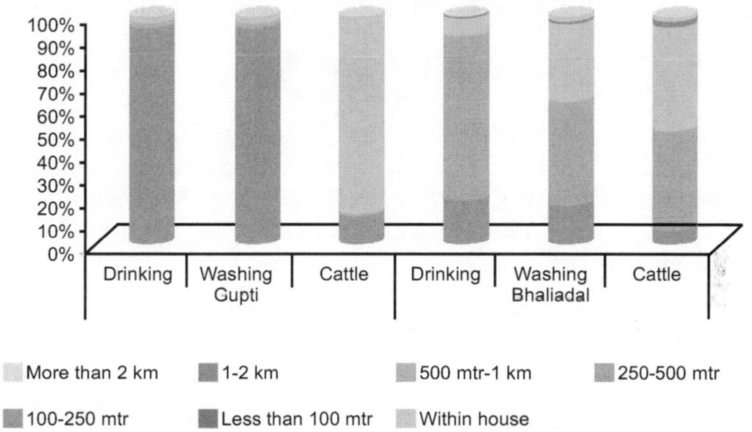

Fig. 11.7: Distance of drinking, washing and cattle bathing water

The analysis of the source of water and the distance of water in both the Panchayat it is evident that in the coastal Panchayat majority people use less of surface water for human consumption requirement and more of ground water that lies within a range of 100-250mtr. On the other hand for the animal requirement of water they depend on the river water that lies within a distance range of 500mtr-1km. In Bhaliadal Panchayat majority people use ground water for drinking and cooking purpose but for the other two requirement of water the tribal population depend on the surface water that is available in ponds and perennial streams and lies within a range of 250-500 meter and 500 meter to one kilometer.

Conclusion

The study shows that the water cycle is getting impacted badly in both the locations. In the coastal Panchayat surface water is getting contaminated by saline water incursion and in the tribal Panchayat ground water level is depleting. This is having impact on the availability as well as the quality of water. The change in the precipitation pattern is having direct influence on the surface runoff of rain water and adversely impacting the recharge of water. This calls for immediate attention of the policy makers to come up with watershed projects which can help to recharge water. This can only happen with the active engagement of the community members. The most interesting finding shows that the water conserved by the community may not use the same water but will help others to use that water. This calls for each and every community members to actively participate in water conservation so that there is inter-dependence amongst the communities and we survive as one family on this earth.

Bibliography

1. Amin, F.M., The Impact of Participatory Capacity And Vulnerability Assessment In Improving Livelihood : A Comparison Participating and Non-Participating Communities in WAJIR County, A Research Project ,November 2015, College of Humanities And Social Science Faculty of Arts Department Of Sociology And Social Work, Nairobi
2. Biodiversity and Climate Change, Convention On Biological Diversity, International Day For Biological Diversity, 2007,UNEP

   Centre for Environment and Development (cDAR), 2015
3. Cyclone Fani DAMAGE, LOSS AND NEEDS ASSESSMENT, 2019, done by Government of Odisha in collaboration with United Nation India, Asian Development Bank and The world Bank
4. Depth & Severity of Poverty In Rural Orissa: A District Level Estimation, Directorate Of Economics & Statistics, Odisha, 2017
5. Development Polices And Rural Poverty In Orissa: Macro Analysis And Case Studies- A Study by Vasundhara, Supported by Planning Commission, Government of India, 2005
6. District Disaster Management Plan, Kendrapara District, Odisha 2015, OSDMA
7. District Human Development Report, Mayurbhanj, 2011, Poverty and Human Development Monitoring Agency, Planning and Coordination Department, Government of Odisha
8. District Irrigation Plan Of Kendrapara (Odisha), Pradhan Mantri Krishi SinchayeeYojana (PMKSY), March 2016, District Level Implementation Committee, Kendrapara, Odisha
9. District Irrigation Plan Of Mayurbhanj (Odisha), Pradhan Mantri Krishi Sinchayee Yojana (PMKSY), March 2016, District Level Implementation Committee, Mayurbhanj, Odisha
10. District Statistical Hand Book, Kendrapara, 2011, Directorate of Economics and Statistics, Odisha

11. District Statistical Hand Book, Mayurbhanj, 2015, Directorate of Economics and Statistics, Odisha
12. Eco system and Human Well –being- A Report Of The Conceptual Framework Working Group of Millennium Ecosystem Assessment, Island Press, 2009
13. Ecosystem and Human Well Being : Synthesis Report, Millennium Ecosystem Assessment, 2005, Island Press, Washington DC
14. Gopalakrishnan, R., M. Jayaraman, G. Bala, and N. H. Rabindranath. 2011. Climate Change and Indian Forest. Current Science (Bangalore) 101(3): 348-55. Government of India. 2014. Economic Survey, 2014.
15. Guhathakurta, P., &Rajeevan, M. (2008). Trends in Rainfall Pattern over India. International Journal of Climatology, 28(11), 1453-1469
16. Hanley, N., Shogren, J.F., White, B.,- Introduction To Environmental Economics, Oxford University press Inc. New York, 2001
17. Hedger, M., Singh, A., and Reddy, M., Building Climate Resilience At State Level: Disaster Risk Management And Rural Livelihood in Orissa, Strengthening Climate resilience Discussion Paper 5, September 2010, Strengthening Climate Resilience Institute of Development studies, University of Sussex, UK
18. Manas Jena-Inclusive Development Of Odisha Prospect And Challenges, Auroshree Publication, Bhubaneswar, 2015
19. Mishra, P.K., Socio Economic Impact of Climate Change In Odisha : Issues, Challenges And Policy Options, Journal of Climate Change, Vol.3, No. 1 (2017), pp. 93-107, DOI 10.3233/ JCC- 170009
20. Mohanty, B.,- Tribal Population Of Mayurbhanj, IOSR Journal Of Humanities And Social Science, Vol. 22, Issue 1, Ver.5 (January 2017), pp. 57-60
21. Nanda Ambika, Patra Sudhakar,- Climate Change, Agriculture And Environment, SSDN Publishers And Distributers, New Delhi, 2019
22. Odisha Climate Change Action Plan (For the Period 2018-23) Phase-II, 2018, Forest & Environment Department, Government of Odisha
23. Odisha Climate Change Action Plan2010-2015, 2010, Forest & Environment Department, Government of Odisha
24. Odisha Economic Survey 2017-18, Planning and Convergence Department, Government of Odisha
25. Orissa Human Development Report 2004, Planning and Coordination Department, Government of Orissa
26. *Proceedings Of The* Odisha Environment Congress 2015, 22nd-24thDecember 2015, Focal Theme- Environment: Health & Nutrition,
27. Progress Report on Implementation of Odisha Climate Change Action Plan, 2015, Climate Change Cell, Forest and Environment Department, Government of Odisha

28. Samling, C.L., Das, S., Hazara, S., - Migration In the Indian Bengal Delta And The Mahanadi Delta: A Review of Literature, Working Paper, Collaborative Adaptation Research Institute In Africa And Asia (CARIAA)
29. Sangram, K.P.- Climate Change And Climate Induced Disasters In Odisha, Eastern India: Impact, Adaptation, And Future Policy Implication, International Journal Of Humanities And Social Science Invention, Volume-5 , Issue-8, August-2016, pp60-63, www.ijhssi.org
30. Steinback, D., Kaur, N., Manuel, C., Saigal, S., Agrawal, A., Panjiyar, A. and Barnwal, A., Building Resilience To Climate Change: MGNREGS, Drought and Flooding in Odisha, IIED Issue Paper, November 2017, IIED London

Urban Environment and Spatial Science
Dr Mohd Akhter Ali, Dr. Kabir Mohan Sethy, Dr Muzafar Wani and M.Kamraju
Ane Books Pvt. Ltd. 2021, , ISBN : 978-93-90658-28-2, P.P. : 155 – 161

12

Transformation of Transboundary River Padma (Ganges)

Shaik Riyaz Basha, Dr.B.Laxamiah
[1]*Ph.D Scholar, OU.*
[2]*Senior ICSSR fellow, OU*

Abstract

India and Bangladesh are the land of Rivers. By which india consists of nearly 400 and Bangladesh 700 Rivers. Apart from that these countries having the two of the world's biggest rivers the Ganges and the Brahmaputra. with 54 transboundary rivers. The Padma is one of the major transboundary waterways which streams from India (as Ganges) to Bangladesh. The Padma River morphologically highly dynamic in nature. The Ganges-Padma River System is one of the three significant river Systems of the Bangladesh. The ganges and therefore the padma are the most fundamental channels of this river system with a braided channel and meanderings. Researchers have noticed a rise within the river's sinuosity and braiding. During the last 240 years the morphology of Padma River has been heavily affected by natural events in the fluvial system. The river's curves became most extreme, since 1967, in excess of 66,000 hectares are lost, roughly the Chicago city. From the last 30 years (1998-2018), the researchers calculated on its transforming in size, shape, and place. since from 1988 till now through the Landsat Satellite Images of NASA earths Observatory. Which are applied to realize the specified result to the study scope was to estimate the both erosion and deposition land covers, to see the movements, shape, depth, width and overall appearance of the Padma river.

Keywords: Padma River, Ganges-Padma River System, Transboundary Rivers, Ganges-Brahmaputra-Meghna Basin.

Corresponding Author: Shaik Riyaz Basha

Introduction

Both India and Bangladesh are the land of Rivers. By which India consists of nearly 400 and Bangladesh 700 Rivers (1). Apart from that these countries having the two of the world's biggest rivers the Ganges and the Brahmaputra with 54 transboundary rivers. Which comes under the worlds populated Basin known as Ganges-Brahmaputra-Meghna Basin (2). Bangladesh is one among the riverine countries within the world with quite 7% of its lands, occupied by the rivers (3). The Padma is one among the main transboundary rivers which flows from India (as Ganges) to Bangladesh (Fig. 12.1). It forms in India at the junction of the rivers Ganges and Jamuna, at that point converges with the Meghna River and at last join into the Bay of Bengal. The Padma River morphologically highly dynamic (4). From past 30 years the Scientist have been measuring the differences in its shape, depth, width and overall appearance through the Satellite images by using GIS and RS Technological tools. Finally, an Observation is made by Researchers on its transforming in size, shape and location since from 1988 till now (5).

Study Area

Ganges River is one of the largest river systems of the world and a major river flowing through India and Bangladesh (Fig. 12.1). It rises within the Gangotri glacier (Himalayas) near Gaumukh nearly 3,900 m within the Uttarkashi district of Uttarakhand. Here, it's referred to as the Bhagirathi. At Devprayag, the Bhagirathi meets the Alaknanda. hereafter it's referred as the Ganga(6). From thier the river continually flows in a southeasterly direction across India and crosses the western border of Bangladesh. In Bangladesh the Ganges is popularly referred to as the River Padma from its place of passage at Durlabhpur and Manakosa unions of Nawabganj,shibganj upazila area. The Study area (Fig-3) river Padma is situated with in the Bangladesh, which is almost 120 km long and its width varies from 4-8 km (8). River Padma is downstream of the ganges, more specifically, the combined flow of the ganges and jamuna after their conversion at goalandaghat. The study area padma river which lies between 23°50′–23°13′N latitude and 49°43′–90°39′E longitude, and it passes through the Chandpur, Shariatpur, Madaripur, Faridpur, Rajbari, Munshiganj, Dhaka, Manikganj and pabna districts (Fig. 12.3) (8). The yearly normal release is about 35,000 m3s−1 and with the average width of 10.3km and therefore velocity is starting from 4 to 5 m s−1, with varying depth from 20 - 21 m (9-10). The Ganges-Padma River System (Fig. 12.2) one among the three significant river systems of the Bangladesh. The ganges and the padma are the important channels of this river system. The ganges and therefore the padma are the most fundamental channels of this river system with a braided channel and meanderings. Additionally, the greater part of the other significant distributaries also follows sinuous course.

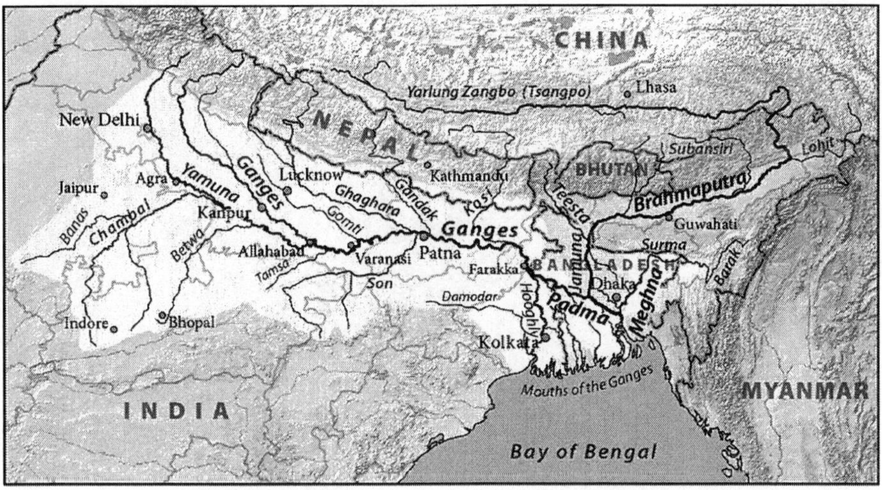

Fig. 12.1: The major rivers that flow into the Bay of Bengal, including Ganges and Padma

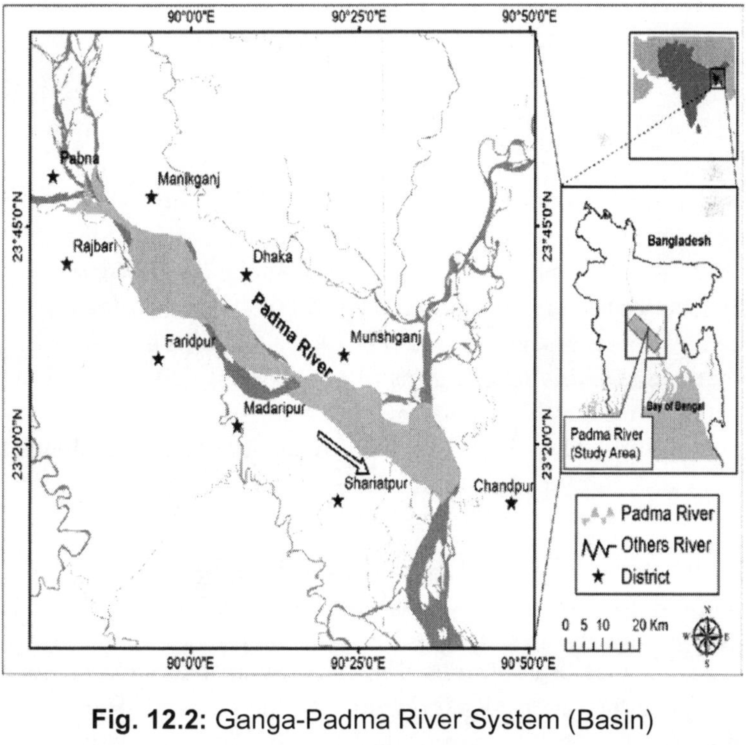

Fig. 12.2: Ganga-Padma River System (Basin)

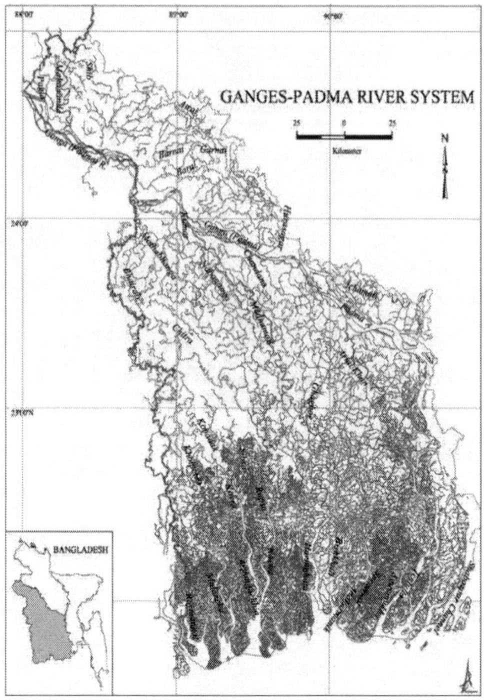

Fig. 12.3: Study Area Padma River

Morphological Trends of River Padma

During the last 240 years the morphology of Padma River has been heavily affected by natural events in the fluvial system (7). The river streams bends turned out to extreme from 1995-1996. The curvatures began to create in 1992, and started to decrease in 2002, and has since vanished. Since 1967, in excess of 66,000 hectares are lost, roughly the Chicago city (5). Various lives, houses and farms have been lost or uprooted in recent years as a result of riverbank erosion that can swallow huge lumps of the shore. The most erosion patterns have two major reasons. Primarily the river Padma is a free-streaming natural waterway with little bank safety, aside from some irregular sandbags to guard settlements. secondly rapid erosion in the bank sits due to an enormous sand bed (5).

From the past 30 years (Fig. 12.4), Researchers have watched a rise within the river's sinuosity and braiding. Furthermore, a constant dynamism on its transforming in size, shape and place. The Padma River liable into meanderings because of enormous Sinuosity. Such river streams develop due to stream erodes the outer edges, broadening the channel. The stream on the internal edge has less energy, permitting huge sediments to be deposited across the river. Few times the meandering river streams leave scars where the water once streamed, as you can see in the 2014 of Harirampur region (Fig 12.4). Due to high amount of sediment of the river carries, there is a lot of sediment, they will in general heap up in places and redirect the water stream, made the braided waterway regions at a few spots.

The Padma is in constant transition between a single thread meandering pattern and multi-channel braiding. In the Cource of recent years, the river has transformed from a moderately narrow, straight line into meanders to braided Cource and recent times its again back to straight. Within the following image (Fig. 12.4), the most recognizable change occurs upstream close to the Harirampur upazila area, where encountered the foremost erosion. Because of further downstream, meanders eroded the land close to Char Janajat. These satellite images show the progressions to the shape and width of the river Padma since 1988 to 2018 (Fig. 12.4).

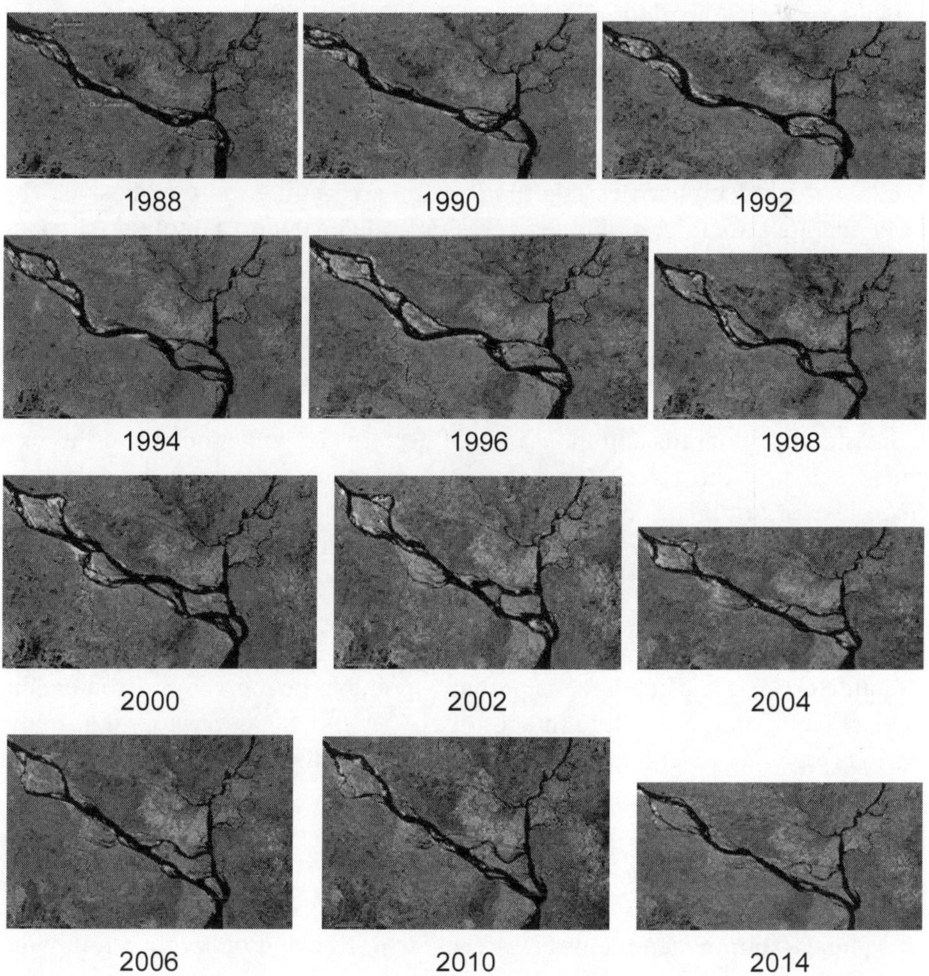

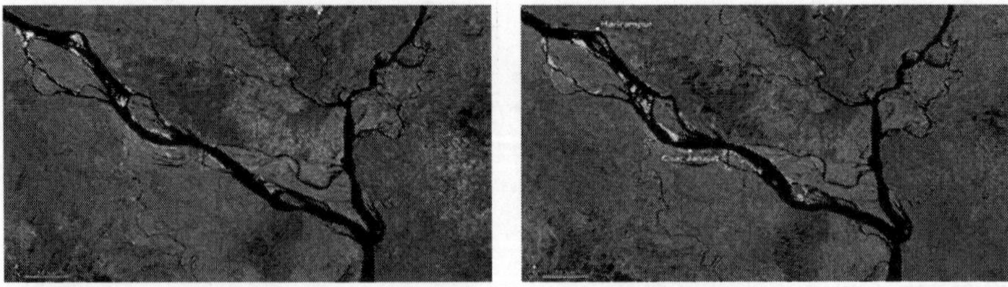

2016 2018

Fig. 12.4: Padma river Morphological Satellite Images of past 30 years

Methodology

The Image Data for this Study were acquired from the Official website of NASA - Earth Observatory which were the Landsat Satellites. These Satellite Images are the Collections of Landsat 7 and Landsat 8, which incorporates the mixture of shortwave infrared, close to infrared, and visible light to feature contrasts among land and water. All these Satellite picture data by NASA were procured in dry seasons of January and February at Bangladesh. Which helps to Understand and monitor the Erosion-accretion of the Padma River Banks. which demonstrates that the streams are getting more extensive. The river channels are migrating due to erosion and deposition activities. All maps and statistical data have been considered in this study are collected from the various secondary sources like Books, journals and Articles of several Authors and research Scholars through the Internet Sources.

Conclusion

Consistently, hundreds and thousands of hectares of land eroded and fall into the streams of the river. Bringing about significant arrangement and thus huge loss of terrains (lands) and shows the prospective scenario of the river Padma. Over the past few years (Fig. 12.5) of great observation of Scientist and Researchers, today it is easily studied and trackable the patterns and trends of the river Padma by using the Landsat satellite picture from the period 1998. Examination of multi-date satellite information has demonstrated that in future erosion and accretion is probably going to be more within the Padma stream. The Landsat Satellite Images of NASA earths Observatory during the period (Fig. 12.5) were applied to realize the specified result to research area to estimate both eroded and deposited land covers, to picture the movements, width, depth, shape, and overall presence of the channels of the Padma river.

Past few years, there is a decrease rates of Padma river erosion, sinuosity and braiding. Erosion slowed due to the meandering curves, vanished because of sedimentation, when the water streams over the land rather than following the curve of the river. But it doesn't mean the region is free from erosion. Any disturbance within the environment such as floods, avalanches and construction could impact the morphology of the river.

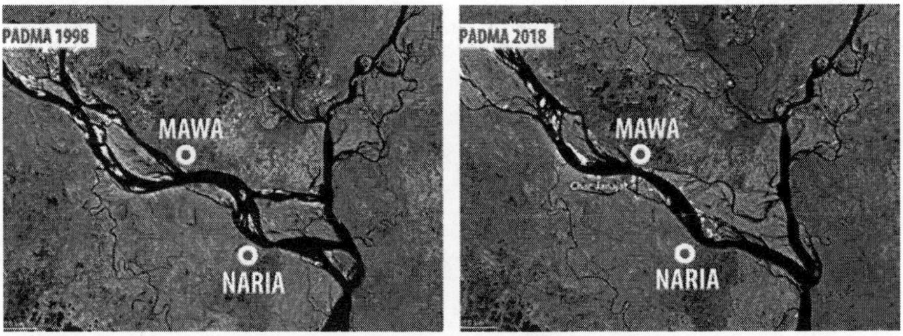

Fig. 12.5: Study Area Padma River

Reference

1. wikiepedia.org
2. https://www.futuredirections.org.au/wp-content/uploads/2016/05/Maddy-FW-India-Bangladesh-and-the-Farakka-Barrage.pdf
3. Hossain M.M., Baki A.B.M., Ahmad S.S., 2008. The Flood Problem and Mitigation Methods in Bangladesh. 4th International Symposium on Flood Defense: Managing Flood Risk, Reliability and Vulnerability. Toronto, Ontario, Canada.
4. Yeasmin A., 2011. Changing trends of channel pattern of the Ganges–Padma River. International Journal of Geomatics and Geosciences 2: 669–675.
5. https://earthobservatory.nasa.gov/world-of-change/PadmaRiver
6. Chapter No-3 Darinage sysytem, India Phisical environment,Class 11 Geography, NCERT
7. Shajahan, Amreen & Reja, Md Yousuf. (2012). Riverbank Erosion and Sustainable Planning Guidelines for Bangladesh with Emphasis on Padma River. Journal of Habitat Engineering and Design. 4. 145-156.
8. Chowdhury M.H., 2003. Padma River. In: Banglapedia the National Encyclopedia of Bangladesh. Bangladesh Asiatic Society. Dhaka.
9. CEGIS [Center for Environmental and Geographic Information Services], 2010. Long-term Erosion Process of the Padma River. Prepared for Jamuna-Meghna River Erosion Mitigation Project. Bangladesh Water Development Board. Dhaka.
10. ADB [Asian Development Bank], 2010. Padma Multipurpose Bridge Project: Environmental Assessment Report. Project Number: 35049. Asian Development Bank. Dhaka, Bangladesh. Online: www.adb.org/sites/default/files/project-document/63200/35049-01-ban-eia.pdf (accessed 20 July 2017).

Urban Environment and Spatial Science
Dr Mohd Akhter Ali, Dr. Kabir Mohan Sethy, Dr Muzafar Wani and M.Kamraju
Ane Books Pvt. Ltd. 2021, , ISBN : 978-93-90658-28-2, P.P. : 163 – 174

13

Developmental Planning for the Slums in Srinagar City

Sameer Fayaz*, G. M. Rather, M. Sultan Bhat
Deptt. of Geography and Regional Development University of Kashmir
**Corresponding author E-Mail ID: bhatsameer3384@gmail.com.*

Abstract

Prevailing evidence has portrayed that slums do not accommodate all the urban poor, nor are all slum dwellers always poor. However, in general terms, slums are the expression of poverty, group inequality and social exclusion (Slums of the World-2003). Slums are distributed throughout the Srinagar city. Clustering was done to study the physical attributes of slums in Srinagar city. These clusters show inequality in various aspects like housing conditions, age of slums, drainage facililities. The quality of housing conditions increases from core to periphery while as the urban amenities decreases from core to periphery. Some clusters need much improvement than other, for this composite score technique was done for prioritization. The present study lays emphasis on suggesting the suitable measures for improvement of Socio-Economic well being of slum dwellers in the Srinagar city.

Key Words: Slums, Clustering, Urban amenities, Composite Score, Prioritization

Introduction

Slums are manifestation of urban poverty (Bunch, 1986).Poor health is one of the essential by-products of defective or deteriorated housing (Smith, 1966). However, due to rising population, especially in urban populations, the number of slum dwellers is rising. One billion people worldwide live in slums and the figure will likely grow to 2 billion by 2030 (United Nations, 2003). Housing as a unit of environment has profound influence on the health, social

Corresponding Author: Sameer Fayaz

behaviour, satisfaction and general welfare of the community (Omole, 2010). Bad sanitation and inaccessibility to water is the root cause of health hazards specific to urban slums (Bagheri, Kahkesh and Nikbakhesh 2011). Slums are the expression of poverty, group inequality and social exclusion (Slums of the World-2003).Urban poverty is the result of lack of basic urban services and migration (Parveen, 2005). Anuradha (2006) revealed that very low quality of life exists in the slum. The housing, nutrition, literacy and medicinal facilities are poor and suggests slum improvement programme by giving them proper nutrition, education and to check infant mortality. Slums play an essential role in a city life. As a place of residence for low cost labour, they keep the wheels of the city moving in many different ways. As a first stopping point for immigrants, they provide the affordable housing that enables them to save for their future absorption. Slums play a significant role in producing the services and commercial activities that the formal sector fails to provide through the mobilization of local enterprises and industry (Slum of the World, 2003). Many governments around the world have attempted to solve the problems of slums by clearing away old decrepit housing and replacing it with modern housing with much better sanitation (Mandal, 1998).

Study Area

The present study has been carried out in the Srinagar city. Latitudinal extent of the city is 33°53′49′′ - 34°17′14′′N latitudes and 74°36′16′′ - 75°01′26′′E longitudes and encompasses an area of 278.1 km².

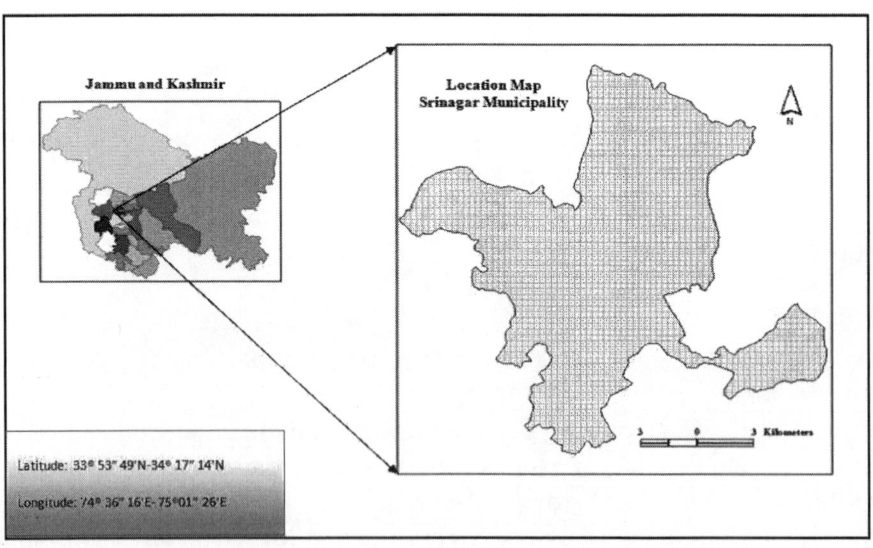

Fig 13.1

Objectives

1. To identify the areas of slum population in Srinagar city.
2. To suggest the suitable measures for improvement of Socio-Economic well being of slum dwellers in the city.

Data Base and Methodology

The Survey of India toposheets (1971) on scale 1:50000 (J/12, J/16 and K/13) were used in the present study to generate various data layers such as slum distribution map with commercial areas, industrial areas. Drainage and water bodies map, road map were also generated etc. These toposheets were also used to delineate the study area. This study relied more on primary sources of data and partly on secondary data. Primary data has been generated through sample survey with the help of structured questionnaires/ schedules, interviews, observations etc. The data pertaining to various socio-economic and demographic variables of slum areas have been collected from various departments. The data on population and its various attributes was obtained from Census Department; data regarding the rehabilated Dal dwellers in various parts of Srinagar city have been collected from Srinagar Municipal Corporation (SMC), Town Planning Organization (TPO), Srinagar Development Authority (SDA) and J & K Housing Board Srinagar.

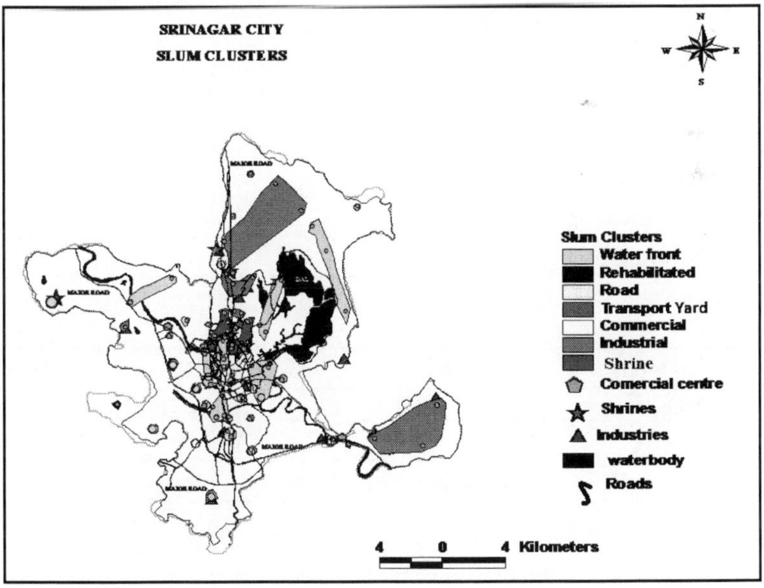

Fig. 13.2*

**Source:* Based on SMC data, 2011

The SOI toposheets (1971) on scale 1:50000 (J/12, J/16 and K/13) were geometrically registered through polyconic projection technique in compatible format for subsequent analysis in ERDAS 9.0. Further, the satellite image of the study area was registered and rectified with reference to already geo-referenced 1:50000 scale topographic maps of the same area. Further, the area of interest from the already geo-referenced SOI topographic maps was clipped out by the technique of Subsetto facilitate a perfect mosaic in GIS. Subsequently, the data regarding slums of the study area was processed in ArcView 3.2a for the preparation of various thematic maps.

Table 13.1: Slum Clusters in Srinagar City based on population Size - 2011*

Slum Clusters	*Slum Locations*	*Ward*	*Slum Clusters*	*Slum Locations*	*Ward*
Water Front Cluster	Drugjan	Dalgate	Road Cluster	Ahmad nagar	Ahmad Nagar
	Kursoo	Raj Bagh		Bonamsar	Dalgate
	Buchwara	Dalgate		Barthana	Parimpora
	Rambagh	Mehjoor Nagar		Chanapora	Chanapora
	Baghat	Baghat-I-Barzulla		Narakura	Khumani Chowk
	Maloora	Malroo		Mehjoor nagar	Mehjoor Nagar
	Sangam	Palpora		Natipora	Natipora
	Lachmanpora	Allochi Bagh		Tarabal	Tarabal
	Qamarwari	Qamarwari		Suzat	Lawaypora
	Nawabazar	Nawab Bazar		Saidapora	Alesteng
	Hassanabad	Hassanabad		Basurbagh	New Theed
	Jogi lanker	Jogi Lanker		Rambagh	Rawalpora
	Nundresh colony	Nundreshi Colony		Mahrajpora	S. D Colony
	Guzarbal	Chattabal		Iddgah	Iddgah
	Karfali Mohalla	Syed Ali Akbar		Sweeper colony	Mehjoor Nagar
	Sutra shah	Shaheed Gunj	Commercial Cluster	Batamallo	Batamallo
	Achan	Palpora		Gowkadal	Lal Chowk

Slum Clusters	*Slum Locations*	*Ward*	*Slum Clusters*	*Slum Locations*	*Ward*
	Chunt kul	Barbarshah		Amira Kadal	Lal Chowk
	Hazratbal	Hazratbal		Ganpatyar	Ganpatyar
	Manzgam	Nishat		Shaheed gung	Shaheed Gunj
	Bongam	Harwan		Sutra shah	Karan Nagar
	Tailbal	Tailbal		Anchar	Soura
	Jamal Atta	Aali Kadal		Solina	Jawahar Nagar
	Iqra colony	Allochi Bagh		Safa Kadal	Safa Kadal
	Baranpather	Magarmal Bagh		Barbarshah	Barbar Shah
	Qalamdan Pora	Islamyarbal		Bhagwan-pora	Barbar Shah
Indus-trial Cluster	Khonmoh	Khonmoh		Gonikhan	Wazir Bagh
	Zainakoot	Zainakoot	Shrine Cluster	Arm masid	Khawja Bazaar
	Zewen	Panthachowk		Sazgaripora	Kawadara
	Rangreth	Humhama		Jamia Masjid	Jamia Masjid
	Bota Kadal	Madeen Sahib		Mahraj gunj	Mahraj Gunj
	Tibetan colony	Makdoom Sahib		Zindshah Sahab	Zind Shah Sahib
	Old Buchpora	Buchpora		Vichernag	Nowshera.
	Botshah Mohalla	Lal Bazar		Malik Angan	Bana Mohalla
	Mandibal	Nowshera		Khan kai Mohalla	Khan Kai Mohalla
	Mughal Mohalla	Umer Colony		Akilmir	Akilmir
	Goosoo	Alesteng		Makdoom Sahab	Makdoom Sahib

Slum Clusters	*Slum Locations*	*Ward*	*Slum Clusters*	*Slum Locations*	*Ward*
	Bakur	Alesteng		Alamgari bazar	Zadibal
	Zoonimar	Zoonimar	Transport Yard Cluster	Dobi Mohalla	Batamallo
	Balahama	Khonmoh		Pantha-chowk	Pantha Chowk
			Rehabilitat-ed Cluster	Boat man colony	Bemina
				Dal colony	Bemina
				Samurbugh	Pantha Chowk

***Source:** Based on data obtained from SMC-2011

Though the slum population of the city is distributed among the different wards, their spatial distribution pattern is the outcome of geographical and economic factors. The identification of slums was done on the basis of parameters used by Srinagar Municipal Corporation and Town Planning Organization of Kashmir. The slums have been classified in the following clusters based on geographical and economic factors 1. Water Front Cluster 2. Rehabilitated Cluster 3. Road Cluster 4. Transport Yard Cluster 5. Commercial Cluster 6. Industrial Cluster 7. Shrine Cluster.Random sample survey was used for data collection and the questionnaire/schedule was the main tool. A sample size of 2 percent of the households was selected for the sample survey. Household survey of 374 sample households was carried out to study the physical ecology and socio-economic characteristics of different slums in Srinagar city. Pilot survey / personal observation and personal interview were the techniques of data collection. Statistical techniques like correlation and chi-square test were employed to explore the relationship and association between physical parameters.

Slums in Srinagar City

Slums in Srinagar City are to be identified on the basis of total living conditions. Slums are generally characterized by overcrowded Kuchha buildings, dilapidated structures with unhygienic living conditions, inadequate basic amenities, poor layout, accessibility and poor ventilation. For the purposes of study, slums in Srinagar have been divided in two categories viz Kuchha-Pucca areas and "Khoperi and Pahari" (tented/small illegal structures) settlements.

Barring a few good localities most of the old residential areas in the inner city and traditional urban villages have slum conditions.

Srinagar City, the largest urban centre in the hierarchy of urban settlement system of J&K State is growing at a rapid pace. It is likely to continue to be the apex urban centre and centre of administration, business, technology, information and a major tourist centre. With the up gradation of Airport into International Airport, Srinagar is likely going to be a global city and radical changes are expected to take place with respect to tourism, trade and commerce, level of infrastructure etc., which is likely to make city development more challenging in nature (Bhat, 2008).

Government Schemes for Improvement of Slums in Srinagar City

Under Jawahar lal Nehru National Urban Renewal Mission (JNNURM), the goal was to provide affordable housing with quality living environment with special emphasis on provision of housing for houseless and urban poor. Greater stress has been madc on provision of basic service and amenities including up gradation of lanes and drains, sewage disposal, solid waste management, provision of parks, play fields, street lighting, community halls, community latrines slaughter houses and up gradation and development of link roads. Provision of these facilities is likely to improve the living environment in these slum areas. In addition to the up gradation and environmental improvement of slums provision for housing for the urban poor including economically weaker sections (EWS) and low income group (LIG) economic categories is also to be made and a number of housing colonies are proposed to be taken up at Sumerbug and Rakhi-Shalina, Noorbagh, Wanganpora Iddgah and resettlement of urban poor housing scheme for slum dwellers of Dal. These schemes are expected to provide affordable developed land and housing to the urban poor of Srinagar and improve their living conditions and is shown in table In the absence of developed/affordable land and clear policy to address their problems, the urban poor in Srinagar suffer from many inadequacies in terms of access to the basic services and socio-economic needs. It is, therefore, imperative that articulated policies and programmes are to be charted for the slum communities and urban poor of the city, both in terms of infrastructure and basic services and socio-economic development. Most of these people live in informal housing sector or in the core of the city where dilapidation, congestion, lack of services and facilities is a prevalent problem (Town Planning Organization Srinagar, 2006). Prioritization of slum clusters for the provision of basic facilities in slums of Srinagar city has been done on the basis of composite score in order to highlight the clusters having bad housing, improper sanitation and low education and income.

Composite Scorefor Prioritization for Slums in Srinagar City

To find out the priority clusters, the variables used were housing, disposal system, street lights, education and income. In order to identify gaps in the provision of different facilities in the slums of Srinagar city, a composite score has been worked out. The individual scores of various facilities have been aggregated in order to derive the composite score of each cluster. The variable having percentage between 0-10 percent were assigned as score 1. The variables having percentage between 10-20 percent were assigned as score 2. Similarly the variables having percentage between 90-100 percent were assigned as score 10. The clusters having highest score are considered as lower in facility and the clusters having lowest score are considered as higher in facility. This methodology for prioritization was used by Jennifer (Jennifer, 2005). Rehabilitated cluster has the highest composite score of 44, water front has the score of 29, industrial cluster has the composite score of 28, Shrine cluster shows the composite score of 24, road cluster has the composite score of 20, commercial cluster has the composite score of 19 and lowest composite score is found in Transport yard cluster

The composite Score was divided into four categories, very high priority, high priority, medium priority and low priority and treated in a GIS environment to get the prioritization map and are briefly described as under;

Very High Priority Zone

Very high priority zone comprises of rehabilitated cluster with slum areas of Boat Man colony, Dal Colony, Samurbugh housing colony. In this priority zone all the variables like housing, disposal type, street lights, education and income are dilapidated, inadequate and improper and absent. That is why this zone is the very high priority zone.

High Priority Zone

This priority zone comprises of Water front with slum areas of Drugjan, Kursoo, Buchwara, Rambagh, Baghat, Maloora, Sangam, Lachmanpora, Qamarwari, Nawabazar, Hassanabad, Jogilanker Rangparistan, Nundresh colony, Guzarbal Chattabal, Syed ali Akbar, Sutra shah, Achan, Chunt Kul, Hazratbal, Manzgam, Bongam, Tailbal, Ali Kadal, Alochibagh, Baranpather, Islamyarbal and Industrial cluster with slum areas of Khonmoh, Zainakoot, Zewan, Rangreth, Botakadal Madeen sahib, Tibetan colony, Old Buchpora, Botshah Mohalla, Mandibal, Mughal Mohalla, Gasoo, Bakur, Zoonimar and Balahama. This zone has bad housing and disposal system. The other three variables like education, street lights and income are found in good percentage but the housing (73.83 %) is dilapidated and also disposal type (65.42 %) is inadequate. There is need for renewal, renovation and proper establishment of disposal system.

Only 22 percent housing is dilapidated in industrial cluster of this zone but disposal system (64.81 %) is inadequate, street lights (80 %) are quite improper. The education and income are below 50 percent.

Medium Priority Zone

This priority zone comprises Shrine with slum areas Arm Masjid Khoja bazar, Sazgaripora, Kawadara, Jamia Masjid, Mahrajgunj, Zindshah Sahab, Vichernag, Malik Angan, Khankai Mohalla, Akilmir, Makdoom Sahab and Alamgari Bazar Zadibal and Road cluster comprises of slum areas Ahmad nagar, Bonamsar, Barthana, Chanapora, Narakura, Mehjoor nagar, Natipora, Tarabal, Suzat, Saidapora, Basurbagh, Rawalpora, Mahrajpora, Iddgah, Sweeper colony.

Though the housing is dilapidated (70.73 %) in this zone but the street lights, disposal type, education and income is quite showing good percentage. The housing and street lights are good in this zone. Also income is moderate but the disposal is overcoming these variables.

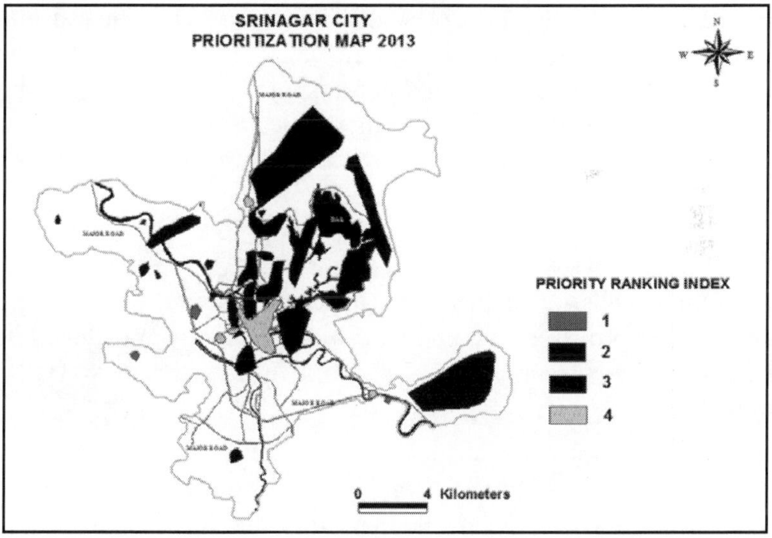

Fig. 13.3*

**Source:* Based on SMC data

Low Priority Zone

This priority zone comprises of Transport yard cluster with slum areas Dhobi Mohalla, Panthachowk and Commercial cluster with slum areas of this cluster

Batamaloo, Maisuma Gowkadal, Amirakadal, Ganpatyar, Shaheed Gung, Karanagar, Soura, Solina, Safakadal, Barbarshah, Bhagwanpora and Gonikhan. The housing is dilapidated in this zone (82 %). The variables like disposal type, street lights, education and income overcome the housing variable. The same pattern is found in commercial cluster as found in Transport yard cluster as shown in table 13.2.

Conclusion

The present research was carried out in the Srinagar city with the main objective of analyzing the inequalities in slums of Srinagar city. The study reveals that slums are not evenly distributed among different wards of the city which leads to various problems like inequality in standards of life and deterioration of city environment. The analysis indicates that there is a lack of basic facilities among different clusters. Some clusters are more developed in terms of a particular facility while others lag far behind the mean level of development of the city in terms of that facility.To identify gaps in the provision of different facilities in the slums of Srinagar city, a composite score has been worked out. The composite Score was divided into four categories, very high priority, high priority, medium priority and low priority. Very high priority zone comprises of rehabilitated cluster. High priority zone comprises of water front cluster and industrial cluster. Medium priority zone comprises shrine cluster and road cluster. Low priority zone comprises of transport yard clusterand commercial cluster. In the absence of proper planning that leads to further deterioration in the living environment of the city. Therefore, community approach is needed for ensuring the reduction in slum conditions.

Suggestions

Slum upgrading consists of physical, social, economic, organizational and environmental improvements undertaken cooperatively and locally among citizens, community groups, businesses and local authorities (Hall, 1975). Actions include:

1. Installing or improving basic infrastructure – for example, sanitation/ waste collection in industrial and road cluster, rehabilitation in water front cluster, commercial cluster, sewerage and flood prevention in water front clusters, electricity, security lighting and public parks in industrial, rehabilitated and road clusters. Constructing or rehabilitating community facilities in road, rehabilitated and industrial clusters.
2. The housing in industrial and road cluster is proper but these lack drainage and basic facilities. So the need is to provide drainage and general facilities in these slum clusters.

Table 13.2: Composite Score of Different Variables in Slum Clusters of Srinagar City*

Variables	***Housing***	***Score***	***Disposal type***	***Score***	***Street light***	***Score***	***Education***	***Score***	***Income***	***Score***	***Composite Score***
Condition	***Dilapidated***		***Inadequate***		***Improper***		***Illiterate***		***Low***		
Water front Cluster	73.83	8	65.42	7	37.00	4	37.00	4	57.00	6	29
Rehabilated Cluster	76.92	8	100.00	10	100.00	10	75.00	8	77.00	8	44
Road Cluster	22.00	3	35.53	4	21.00	3	47.00	5	45.00	5	20
Transport yard Cluster	75.00	8	0.00	1	0.00	1	46.00	5	25.00	3	18
Commer-cial Cluster	87.32	9	0.00	1	0.00	1	41.00	5	23.00	3	19
Industrial Cluster	22.22	3	64.81	7	80.00	8	47.00	5	44.00	5	28
Shrine Cluster	70.73	8	32.00	4	0.00	1	47.00	5	56.00	6	24

****Source:*** Based on Sample Survey 2013-14

3. In rehabilitated, water front and Shrine cluster, self employment and government funded schemes should be implemented in these slum areas.
4. Though commercial and Transport yard cluster are falling in low priority zone but the housing is dilapidated in these clusters. So the immediate need of the hour is rehabilitation, renewal and renovation.

Reference

1. Anuradha, S (2006), *Quality of Life of Slum Dwellers: A case study of Bindtoli, Patna West, Annals,* NAGI Vol 26, pp. 72-86.
2. Bagheri, M; Kahkesh, F.H and Nikbakhesh, B (2011), Monitoring the situation of slum dwellers, Face of urban poverty the case of Mallashieh-Iran. *American Journal of Scientific Research*, Issue 22 (2011) pp.101-109.
3. Bhat, M.S (2008), *Urban System in Himalayas*. Dilpreet Publishing House New Delhi.
4. Bunch, M J (1996), Physical Ecology of Slums in Madras, Indian Geographical Journal, Vol. 71(1), 1996.
5. Chandramouli, S (2003), Slums in Chennai-A Profile in Martin J Bunch, V Suresh and Kumaran T, eds; *Proceedings of the Third International Conference on Environment and Health Chennai India*, Department of Geography, University of Madras and Faculty of Environmental Studies, York University, pp. 82-88.
6. Fayaz, S (2014), *Physical Ecology and Socio-Economic Characteristics of Slums in Srinagar City*, Un Published M.Phil Dissertation, University of Kashmir.
7. Hall, P (1975), *Problems in Modern Geography.* David and Charles Publications London, pp. 43-44.
8. Jennifer, B (2005), *the effect of Socio-economic Status on Academic Achievement*, Ph.D Thesis Bachelor of Arts, Wichita State University.
9. Mandal, R.B (1998), *Urban Geography*, Rawat Publications Jaipur, Pp.459-461.
10. Master Plan 2000-2021, Srinagar Metropolitan Area, Srinagar Development.
11. Omole, F.K (2010), *An Assessment of Housing Conditions and Socio-economic Life Styles of Slum dwellers in Akure-Nigeria*, Contemporary Management Research, vol. 6.
12. Praveen, S (2005), *Changing Face and Challenges in urbanization- A case Study of Uttar Pradesh,* concept Publishing Co. New Delhi, pp.62.
13. Smith, E.B (1966), *Health Hazards of the Slums*, Journal of the National Medical Association, Vol. 59, No. 2.
14. Town planning Organization Kashmir (2006), City Development Plan for Srinagar City.
15. UN□HABITAT (2003), *The Challenge of Slums, Global Report on Human Settlements 2003*, United Nations Human Settlements Programme London, Earth scan. University Press, New Delhi.

Urban Environment and Spatial Science
Dr Mohd Akhter Ali, Dr. Kabir Mohan Sethy, Dr Muzafar Wani and M.Kamraju
Ane Books Pvt. Ltd. 2021, , ISBN : 978-93-90658-28-2, P.P. : 175 – 182

14

Informal Settlements and its Challenges in Kabul City-Afghanistan

Fidel Rahmati, Prof. AV Shashikala
[1]*Ph.D. Research Scholar, Senior Fellow ICSSR*
Department of Geography, Osmania University
Hyderabad, Telangana-500007
rahmatifidel@gmail.com, avshashikala@gmail.com
[2]*Senior Fellow ICSSR, Department of Geography,*
Osmania University, Hyderabad, Telangana-500007
rahmatifidel@gmail.com, avshashikala@gmail.com

Abstract

Urbanization, migration, and lack of proper response by local authorities to the high demand for housing after 2001 are the three main factors for rapid informal settlement in Kabul city of Afghanistan. Most of the returnees from the neighboring countries such as Iran and Pakistan during the Karzia government period settled in the periphery of Kabul city without any proper urban infrastructure, proper access to facilities, streets, and freshwater. Almost 69% of the city population lives in informal sector settlements which have been led to so many challenges. In this paper, the main focus is on informal settlement and the main challenges in Kabul city. For analyzing the data, secondary data has been collected from various sources like books, Center for Statistic Organization of Afghanistan, Journals, authentic internet websites, and libraries. The main outcome of the paper will be useful for the researchers and academicians related to urban development and planning, security, and environmental studies.

Kew Words: Informal settlement, Kabul City, Challenges, Planning, Environment.

Corresponding Author: Fidel Rahmati

Introduction

The informal settlement is also called unauthorized housings, are those where housing are built in violation to the master plan in Kabul City. Informal settlements are mostly the feature of developing countries and Kabul city is no exception. In case of Afghanistan apart from urbanization process, rapid population growth, returning of migrants are considered as one of the factors in increasing slums in the Kabul city. At the same time low capacity and resources for implementing government policies led to growing slums in the periphery of the main city.

Study Area

Kabul is the capital and largest city of Afghanistan located in the eastern part of the country with estimated population of 4.222 million.

Kabul city is consist of 22 districts playing as the mosaic for all major ethnic groups of Afghanistan which serves as the center of political, economic and cultural. Kabul has the 75th ranking of the largest city in the world.

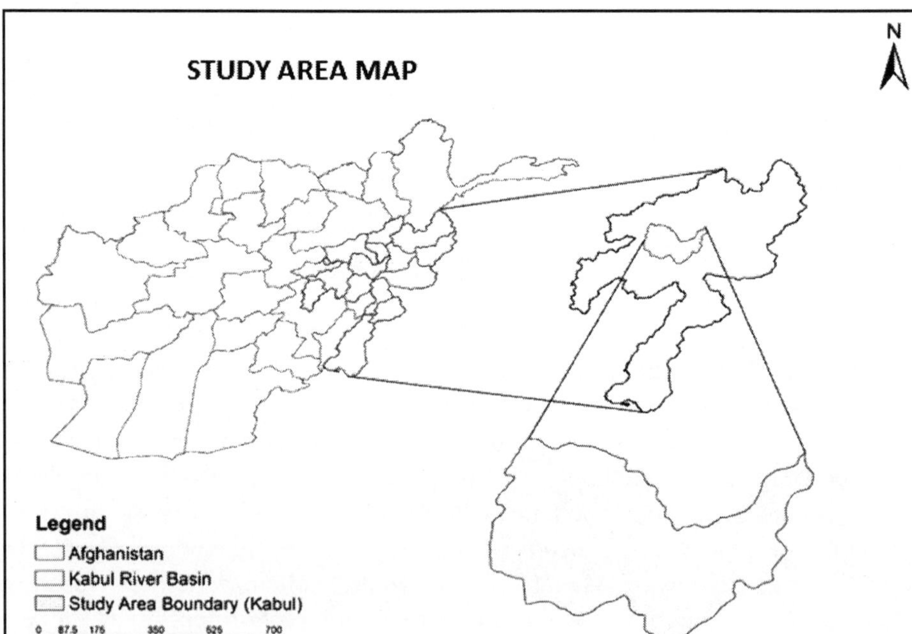

Fig. 14.1

Source: Fidel.et.al. 2020.

Afghanistan is with an estimated population of 38,935,009 as of July 2020 based on the latest explanation of United Nation data, so, Afghanistan population is equivalent to 0.5 percentage total world population which come under the rank of 37 in the world. The population density in Afghanistan is 60 per $Km^{2.}$ The urban population make 25.4 percent which make 9, 904, 33 people in 2020. The average age in Afghanistan is 18.4 years (Rahmati, F. et.al, 2020).

Objective

The major objective of this research is to study the informal settlements and its main challenges in Kabul City.

Methodology

We have mostly used secondary data to study the main research topic. Data were collected through government reports, books, and journals. The Statistic data collected from different sources like, internet authentic sources, unpublished literatures.

Brief Literature Review

In order to develop and direct the overall research to its main objective it is very much essential to analyze the existing literature of the related topic. Hereby, we have been gone through the most relevant literatures.

Rahmati, F. et.al (2020) in their paper titled "A Study on Urban Growth and Its Impact on Kabul City, Afghanistan" states that the quality of urban environment depends on the quality of infrastructure and their appropriate management. Utility services like sanitation, sewerage, drainage, drinking water supply, waste management, electricity, gas and fuel for cooking are inevitable physical infrastructure for maintaining the urban environmental quality. But urbanization in Kabul City was not happen in a normal norm and manner which indeed has certain limitations and barriers with haphazard growth of informal sectors. Decades of war, migration from inside and outside the countries to Kabul City, low capacity and resources for implementation of government policies and the average annual population growth by 3.076 % after the year 2000 are among the major factors for outbreak of informal settlements in Kabul City.

Rezayee. Et.al. (2019), in his paper "Built Environment Problems in Informal Settlement: Evidence from District 13 of the Kabul City, Afghanistan". Mentions that approximately 69% of people live in informal settlements in Kabul City which has a huge negative impact on health and happiness of the residents due social and environmental problems caused by these settlements.

The research has been done in one of the Kabul District (13 District of Kabul City). In this area of Kabul informal residents live without proper living facilities such as; drainage system and sewage system, lack of open space, greenery and recreation, lack of proper and standard streets. In addition to that, shortage of pedestrian, absence of water supply system, nonexistence of proper solid waste management, lack of access to proper healthcare system are considered as the challenges created by informal settlement in the study area.

Nazire, H. et.al. (2016) "Effects of Informal Settlement Upgrading in Kabul City, Afghanistan: A Case Study of Afshar Area". Argues that post-Taliban rapid migration, urbanization, land grabbing and limited government capacity to respond to these demand on time and sufficiently are factors caused urban informality in the capital city of Kabul. Though there were some upgrading programs by collaboration of international agencies and government which merely focused on physical improvement rather than an integrating one which is a recent innovation in neighboring countries.

The upgrading need to cover all dimensions of informal residents such as: social, economic, ecological, institutional and spatial. Taking these point in view help not only promote social and spatial development, but also helps in promoting peace and security.

Fazli, M (2016), "Factors behind the Growth of Informal Settlements in Kabul". States that, the prime factors contributing informal settlements in Kabul are insecurity, political changes, getting a better life, job and education.

Gebremedhin, Y (2005), "Preliminary Assessment of Informal Settlements in Kabul City". Argues that there is no coherent and clear policy on urban land management and the previous Master Plan cannot be responsive to the existing reality and challenges. A part from this, even having a good Master plan without security, stability, rule of law, and willpower for reform, it will not be possible to implement the Master Plan or upgrade in such a way that ensure sustainability in the long run.

Informal Settlements

There is no crystal and clear definition for informal settlement. The UN-Habitat define the informal settlement in two different ways. Firstly, the areas in which residents grab the land without any proper legal claim and construct groups of housing units. Secondly, construction of housing in areas which does not match with the current planning proposed by the local government.

The above definition shows that the informal settlements lack the two main elements which are crucial for formal settlements; "legal claim and planning/ regulation".

Informal Settlements Challenges

Since informal settlements are not proper housing in proper areas so, mostly faced different challenges. These housing and settlements can be available in any countries but most of the time it's the attributes of developing countries. The attributes of informal settlements are low quality housing, lack of basic services and infrastructure, absence or shortage of recreation and greenery areas, facing environmental threating and health issues, insecurity and prone to crimes.

The informal settlements are mostly isolated from social, spatial and economic zone of urban environment. These settlements are prone to different manmade and natural disasters due to its unsuitable areas such as steep slopes, landslides, near to river and prone to flooding which make it difficult for government authorities for providing services such as waste management or garbage collection and firefighting services.

Moreover, the informal settlers suffering from low education and literacy rate which shows absence of proper schools and classes, hospitals, unemployment, cleanliness, proper streets and pavement, potable water and etc.

Factors Behind Growth of Informal Settlements in Kabul City

In 1925 Kabul had a population around 90,000 and the basic present structure of Kabul city was established in the 1940's and 1950's. By 1962 Kabul became the largest city of Afghanistan with its population reaching 380,000. The first Master Plan of Kabul city prepared during 1962-1964 by Afghan experts and Russian for 800,000 residents.

But, unfortunately due to the political turmoil and unstable situation in Afghanistan from 1970's onward the first, second and third Master Plan implementation was stopped. This scenario and conflicts in Afghanistan led to the displacement and migration to Kabul city.

Table 14.1: Past Master Plans of Kabul City*

Master Plans of Kabul City-Afghanistan	*Approved Year*	*Horizon Year*	*Planned Population (Million)*	*Covered Area (km^2)*
First Master Plan	1962	1987	0.8	237.80
Second Master Plan	1970	1995	1.4	299.00
Third Master Plan	1978	2002	2.0	323.30

****Source:*** UN-HABITAT-2001.

Fig. 14.2

Fig. 14.2: Informal Settlements of Kabul, Source: Gregory Maasen/ Alamy, https://www.alamy.com/stock-photo-informal-settlements-in-kabul-afghanistan-174950735.html. Retrieved-2020.

Especially after 2001, almost three millions refugees return back to the county form neighboring countries which most of them reside in the capital city of Kabul. A part from that, the population growth with an average annual population by 3.076 % after the year 2000 which led to the fastest growth of urbanization in Kabul, lack of government abilities and proper response/ policies to deal with this haphazard, are among the major factors for outbreak of informal settlements in Kabul City.

Conclusion and Recommendations

Kabul is the Capital city of Afghanistan with the residents of almost 4.22 million. Due to political turmoil in the country the Kabul master Plans did not implement properly and led to the unprecedented informal settlements. Though the government of Afghanistan with the support of international organization conducted the upgrading of the informal settlements in the study area which was not implemented properly due to several constrains. The informal settlements needs an urgent improvement in social, economic and spatial arena of their residency. The following points are recommended to be carried out in order to reform the challenges of informal settlements in Kabul city:

1. In order to provide proper services to the Informal settlements, upgrading of the informal settlement of Kabul city is a must through Kabul Municipality.
2. Allocation of proper budget for government employees for providing them housing and flats.

3. Developing highways for connectivity of New and Old city of Kabul in order to reduce the traffic congestion.
4. Kabul population is more than 4 Million so, it will be difficult for the current Municipality authority to management the city's affairs. Therefore, it will be better to divide the Kabul City Municipality management for New and Old Kabul city separately in or der to improve the quality and quantity of services in the city.
5. Lack of infrastructures are the main challenges in the city, it is better for local government to focus on main infrastructure which is needed for a big city like Kabul.
6. Drainage system, sewage and waste management recycling and banning plastics use in the Kabul city can improve the environmental quality of the urban area and decrease the air pollution.
7. Providing proper potable water for informal settlements, Underground water management system, policies, and preventing measures for Kabul residents from digging deep water well/ bore well can sustain and safeguard the precious underground water in the city.

ACKNOWLEDGMENT

I am also thankful to Mr. M.Kamraju Student, Osmania University, Hyderabad, Telangana.

REFERENCE

1. Rahmati, Fidel, et.al. "A STUDY ON URBAN GROWTH AND ITS IMPACT ON KABUL CITY, AFGHANISTAN."2020.
2. REZAYEE, MAQSOOD, SITI HAJAR MISNAN, and GABRIEL HOH TECK LING. "BUILT ENVIRONMENT PROBLEMS IN INFORMAL SETTLEMENT: EVIDENCE FROM DISTRICT 13 OF THE KABUL CITY, AFGHANISTAN." *Journal of Sustainability Science and Management* 14, no. 6 (2019): 143-163.
3. Nazire, Haroon, Michihiro Kita, Seth Asare Okyere, and Shigeki Matsubara. "Effects of informal settlement upgrading in Kabul City, Afghanistan: A case study of Afshar area." *Current Urban Studies* 4, no. 04 (2016): 476.
4. Fazli, Mirwais. "Factors behind the Growth of Informal Settlements in Kabul." In *the 6th Annual Conference on Architecture and Urbanism*, pp. 81-86. 2016.
5. Gebremedhin, Yohannes. "Preliminary assessment of informal settlements in Kabul city." *USAID–Land Titling and Economic Restructuring in Afghanistan* (2005).
6. World Bank Report. (2010). Kabul Urban Reconstruction Project (Kurp), Urban Upgrading for unplanned Area, Kabul, Afghanistan.

7. Bertaud, Alain. (2005), Urban Land Management in Afghanistan, Kabul Urban Development Current City Structure, Kabul, Afghanistan.
8. Oliphant, Wesley. (2009), Afghanistan from Within: A look at Afghanistan's Urbanization Across its Provinces, California, and USA.
9. Kammeier, H. Detlef And Issa, Zabihullah.(2017), Urban Governance in Afghanistan: Assessing the new Urban Development Program and its Implementation, Kabul.
10. Nemat, A. Khaliq. (2008), Challenges and Policies for Environmentally Sustainable Transport System of Afghanistan, Singapore.
11. Hernandez, Andre and Gebremedhin, Yahannes. (2007), Formalizing Urban Development; Challenges in Afghanistan, Kabul, Afghanistan.
12. Yachiyo, Engineering Co. (2011), Kabul City Master Plan Project Report, Kabul Afghanistan.
13. Mumtaz, Babar and Noschis. (2004), Development of Kabul, Reconstruction and Planning Issues, Switzer land.
14. EST. (2009), Urban Transportation and Environment Challenges in the City of Kabul, Afghanistan, Seoul, Korea.
15. Calogero, Pietro. (2011), Planning Kabul: The Policies of Urbanization in Afghanistan, Calfornia, USA.
16. MoADA. (2015), State of Afghan Cities, Kabul Municipality, Kabul, Afghanistan.

Urban Environment and Spatial Science

Dr Mohd Akhter Ali, Dr. Kabir Mohan Sethy, Dr Muzafar Wani and M.Kamraju

Ane Books Pvt. Ltd. 2021, , ISBN : 978-93-90658-28-2, P.P. : 183 – 194

15

Trace Metals in Fruits

Syeda Azeem Unnisa, B. Kiran, Aaron Jasper Molgeri

[1]*Department of Environmental Science*
University college of Science,
Osmania University, Hyderabad, India
Email:syeda_30@yahoo.co.in

[2]*Department of Environmental Science*
Department of Botany
University college of Science,
Osmania University, Hyderabad, India
Email:syeda_30@yahoo.co.in

[3]*Department of Environmental Science,*
University college of Science,
Osmania University, Hyderabad, India
Email:syeda_30@yahoo.co.in

Abstract

The present study was undertaken to know the status of heavy metal concentration in fruits from various markets of Hyderabad. Twelve fruit samples in duplicate namely Apple (Green), Apple (Red), Banana, Grapes, Guava, Mousambi (*Citrus limetta*), Orange, Papaya, Pineapple, Pomegranate, Sapodilla, Tomato were collected in the 2019. The samples were detected for ten trace metals namely As, Cd, Pb, Cr, Co, Hg, Ni, Zn, Mo and Se by using Inductively Coupled Plasma Mass Spectrometry (ICP-MS). Arsenic and mercury were below detectable levels in all fruits, whereas Cd content was detected only in Apple (Red) 0.42mg/kg, Guava 0.01mg/kg , Orange 0.01mg/kg and Pine apple 0.02mg/kg. The chromium content ranged between 0.02-0.18 mg/kg. The cobalt content was not detected in Apple (green), Mosambi, Orange, and Sapota and the other fruits ranged between 0.01-2.64 mg/kg. The Nickel content ranged between 0.01-36.89 mg/kg. The Lead content was not detected in Apple (green), Guava, Mosambi, Orange, Papaya and Sapota.

Corresponding Author: Syeda Azeem Unnisa

The remaining fruits were observed to have the lead content ranged between 0.01-0.56 mg/kg. The zinc content ranged between 0.30-2.51 mg/kg. The Molybdenum content ranged between 0.01 to 8.43 mg/kg which was detected in some fruits namely, apple (green), apple red, mosambi, orange, papaya, sapota and tomato. The Selenium content ranged between 0.01 – 0.13mg/kg. The heavy metal concentration in fruits at daily intake passes health risk issues.

Keywords: trace metals; Fruits; Toxicity; Contamination; ICPMS

INTRODUCTION

Health risk from food contamination is a major issue worldwide. The high demand of food during the last few decades has raised questions about food safety which has increased research in the field of risk associated with consumption of food which can be contaminated by pesticides, heavy metals and/or toxins (D'Mello, 2003). Heavy metals are one of the important contaminants of food supply chain and can cause harm to humans, animals and the environment (Zaidi et al., 2005). This issue is becoming more common worldwide and especially in developing countries. Heavy metals are mostly non-biodegradable, with long biological half-lives and bioaccumulate in the different body organs and lead to unwanted side effects (Jarup, 2003; Sathawara et al., 2004).

Fruits are fortified with vitamins, minerals, and fibres and contain useful antioxidants. Consuming heavy metal contaminated fruits is a threat to human health that ultimately leads to harmful diseases. Bioaccumulation of heavy metals in the food chain through contamination of water, soil and air is of great concern (Lokeshwari, 2006). Cr, Ni and Pb concentrations in the soils of Jagiroad paper mill area, Assam , India, mainly originated from paper mill effluent and soil Cd was associated with natural concentration (Reza *et al.,*2013). Elements such as lead (Pb), cadmium (Cd), mercury (Hg), chromium (Cr) and arsenic (As) get accumulated into fruits and other farm produces through these water sources (Anjali *et.al* 2016). It is well known that plants take up metals by absorbing them from contaminated soils as well as from deposits on parts of the plants exposed to the air from polluted environments (Chojnacha *et al.,*2005; Khairiah *et al.,*2004). The term heavy metal chiefly arose with discussions of pollutants discharged to the environment in the form of air, water or soil contaminants, while many heavy metals have considerable toxicity, others are considered not deemed to possess significant toxic properties, and, in fact, several of these elements including zinc, iron, copper, chromium and cobalt are necessary for metabolic function for a large class of organisms (Hogan 2011). Heavy metals, in general, are not biodegradable, have long biological half lives and have the potential for accumulation in the different body organs leading to unwanted side effects (Jarup 2003; Sathawara *et al.,*2004;Arora *et* *al.* 2008) . It is encouraged to take more vegetables and fruits in our diet, as they are a good source of vitamins, minerals, fiber (Chojnacha *et al.*,2005; Khairiah *et al.*,2004). High level of heavy metals in the environment has created a certain fear in people questioning the presence of heavy metal residues in daily food. Consumers are scared and alarmed about their food safety (Jorhem and Sundstroem, 1993; Pennington et al., 1995a,b; Milacic and Kralj, 2003; Saracoglu et al., 2004).

The increasing trends in food contamination in urban areas are largely attributed to the polluted environment in urban agriculture, contaminated food transport and supply chains, poor market sanitary conditions, and the use of contaminated or waste water for irrigation purposes hence the objective of this study is to study the heavy metal concentration in the fruits from Hyderabad markets. Keeping in view the potential toxicity, persistent nature and accumulative behaviour it is necessary to test and analyze food items such as vegetables, fruits and meat to ensure that the levels of these contaminants meet the agreed standard requirements. This study therefore presents data on the level of heavy metals in selected fruits.

Materials and Methods

Study Area

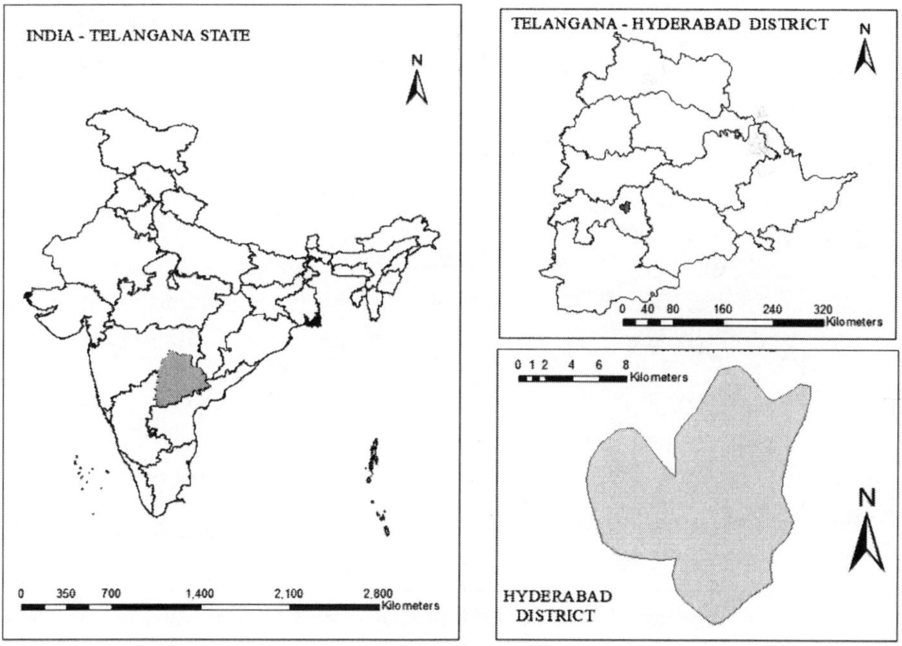

Fig. 15.1

Table 15.1: Details of fruit samples collected for study

S.No	*Fruit Name*	*Scientific Name*	*Quantity (kg)*
1.	Apple (Green)	*Malus pumila*	One
2.	Apple (red)	*Malus pumila*	One
3.	Banana	*Musa paradisiacal*	One
4.	Grapes	*Vitis vinifera*	One
5.	Guava	*Psidium gujava*	One
6.	Sweet Lemon (Mausambi)	*Citrus limetta*	One
7.	Orange	*Citrus reticulate*	One
8.	Papaya	*Carica papaya*	One
9.	Pineapple	*Ananas comosus*	One
10.	Pomegranate	*Punica granatum*	One
11.	Sapodilla	*Manilkara zapota*	One
12.	Tomato	*Solanum lycopersicum*	One

Hyderabad is the capital and largest city of the Indian state of Telangana. Occupying 650 square kilometres (250 sq mi) along the banks of the Musi River, located on the Deccan Plateau in the northern part of South India. At an average altitude of 542 metres (1,778 ft), much of Hyderabad is situated on hilly terrain around artificial lakes. Hyderabad City has a population of about 6.9 million, with about 9.7 million in Hyderabad Metropolitan Region, making it the fourth-most populous city and sixth-most populous urban agglomeration in India.

Sampling

Samples were collected from different markets of Hyderabad during 2019. 1 Kg of each fruit (Apple (Green), Apple (Red), Banana, Grapes, Guava, Sweet Lemon, Orange, Papaya, Pineapple, Pomegranate, Sapota, Tomato) was collected from each market and was analyzed for heavy metals after pre-treatment with nitric acid and microwave digestion.

Heavy Metal Analysis

All chemicals used were analytical grade. Ultra-pure water was obtained from a Millipore water system (Millipore), Ultra-pure Nitric acid (HNO_3, Merck) was used to digest the samples. Stock standard solutions of arsenic, cadmium, nickel and lead concentration containing 10 µg/mL in 2% HNO_3 was prepared. The certified reference materials (CRM) were procured from National Institute of Standard Technology (NIST-8436) and European Commission (EC-804) and used for method validation.

Dried and sliced fruit samples were grounded into powder using a mortar and pestle. Microwave digestion system (CEM-MARS-USA) was used to digest homogenized fruit samples (between 0.5 and 1.5 g) and were placed in Teflon digestion vessel with 3 ml of ultra-pure HNO_3 and 1 ml of Hydrogen Peroxide (H_2O_2). Sealed containers were placed in a microwave oven and heated according to the digestion program (program : Power 1600W (100%), Ramp time 15 minutes, Temperature 200° C, Hold time 15minutes and cooling time 15minutes). After digestion, sample solutions after cooled down to room temperature were transferred in to acid cleaned 25ml standard volumetric flasks and made up to 25 ml with double distilled water and prepared under the same conditions as the calibration standards in 6% (v/v) HNO_3. Blank digestion was carried out similarly. Nickel, Arsenic Cadmium, Lead, Chromium, Cobalt, Mercury, Nickel and Zinc in fruits were determined using ICP-MS (PerkinElmer Élan 9000- USA). Certified Reference Material samples were procured from NIST and EC and used for method standardization, standard graphs were drawn.

Table 15.2: Permissible limits of heavy metals in edible fruits expressed in mg/kg

Element	*Recommended max. Level mg/kg or µg/g (dry weight)*	*Reference*
Cadmium	0.2	WHO/FAO (2011)
Lead	1.5	WHO/FAO (2011)
Zinc	150	Anon (1987)
Chromium	2.3	WHO/FAO (2001)
Cobalt*	50	Pendias & Pendias, (1992)
Nickel*	67	Wieght (1991)

Results and Discussion

The heavy metals affect the nutritive values of fruits and vegetables and also have deterious effect on human beings by consuming these food items. National and international regulations on food quality have lowered the maximum permissible levels of toxic metals in human food. Hence, an increasingly important aspect of food quality should be to control the concentrations of trace metals in food.

The range of heavy metals (As, Cd, Cr, Co, Hg, Ni, Mo, Pb and Zn) found in fruits was analysed by using ICP-MS. The results showed that As and Hg was not detected in the fruit samples. Almost all fruit samples are within the limits except for Apple where cadmium is found. In the present study, almost all concentrations of the analyzed heavy metals in the fruits studied were within the maximum permissible limits as reported by Zhen (2008)9[9], Xiao *et al.* (2010) and Sheng *et al.* (2014) in China, Orisakwe *et al.* (2012) in Nigeria, Türkdoğan *et al.* (2002) in Turkey, Roba *et al.* (2016) in Romania and Khan *et al.* (2013) in Pakistan.

Cadmium content was not detected in most of the fruits except for Apple (red) 0.42mg/kg, Guava 0.01mg/kg, Orange 0.01mg/kg and Pine apple 0.02mg/kg which is shown in fig. 15.2. All the fruits are within the permissible limits except apple (red) i.e., more than 0.2 mg/kg prescribed by WHO/FAO (2011). The highest content was found in Apple(red) and lowest in Orange and Guava. Similar results were also found by Wodaje Addis Tegegne (2017).

The chromium content was detected in all the fruits which ranged between 0.02 to 0.18 mg/kg which were below the permissible limits (2.3 mg/kg) prescribed by WHO/FAO (2011). The highest content was observed in Banana and lowest in Apple(green) which is shown is fig. 15.4. Similar results were also reported by Wodaje Addis Tegegne (2017).

The cobalt content was not detected in some of the fruits like Apple (green), Mosambi, Orange, and Sapota and the other fruits ranged between 0.01 to 2.64 mg/kg which is shown in fig. 15.5. The highest content found in apple (red) which was below the permissible limits (50 mg/kg) prescribed by Pendias and Pendias (1992). The highest content was observed in apple (red) and lowest in banana, grapes, orange and papaya.

The Nickel content in the fruits ranged between 0.01to 36.89 mg/kg which is depicted in fig. 15.6. Highest content was detected in Apple (red) of 36.89 mg/kg. The content was below the permissible levels (67 mg/kg) prescribed by Wieght (1991) The highest content was observed in apple(red) and lowest in orange and mosambi.

The Lead content was not detected in some fruits like Apple (green), Guava, Mosambi, Orange, Papaya and Sapota. The remaining fruits were observed to have the lead content ranged between 0.01 to 0.56 mg/kg and the highest content was found in Apple (red) which is shown in fig. 15.3. The levels are below the permissible limits (1.5 mg/kg) prescribed WHO/FAO 2011. The highest content was observed in apple (red) and lowest in grapes. Lead in fruits might be a consequence of road traffic and lead emission from petrol vehicles (Zhen 2008; Cherfi *et al.* 2014)

The zinc content was detected in almost all the samples except in Tomato which is shown in fig. 15.7. The zinc content in the fruit samples ranged between 0.30 to 2.51 mg/kg which was below the permissible limits (150 mg/kg) prescribed by Anon (1987). Similar results were also reported by Wodaje

Addis Tegegne (2017). The highest content was observed in guava and lowest in orange.

The Molybdenum content ranged between 0.01 to 8.43 mg/kg which was detected only in some fruits namely, apple (green), apple red, mosambi, orange, papaya, sapota and tomato depicted in fig. 15.8. Acute exposure to Mo has been linked to diarrhoea, anaemia and gout. Pneumoconiosis has also been associated with Mo-induced copper deficiency (Expert Group on Vitamins and Minerals, 2003, WHO, 2011a).

The Selenium content ranged between 0.01 – 0.13mg/kg which is shown in fig. 15.9. Several studies demonstrated that low Se as an efficacious anti carcinogen whereas high Se can induce carcinogenesis, cytotoxicity and genotoxicity. (Selvaraj, 2012; Selvaraj et al., 2013).

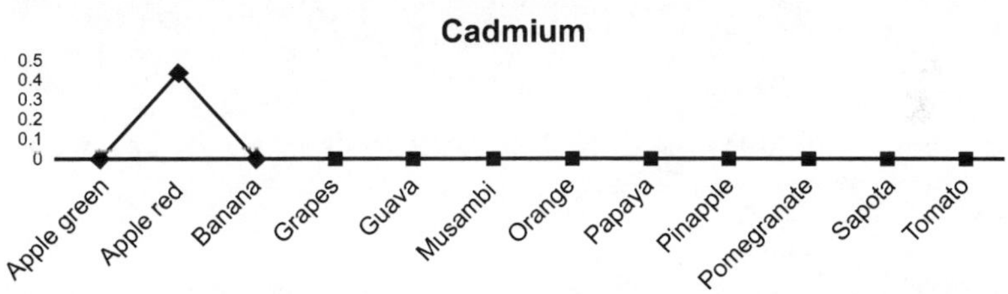

Fig. 15.2: Concentration of Cd in various fruits (mg/kg – dry weight)

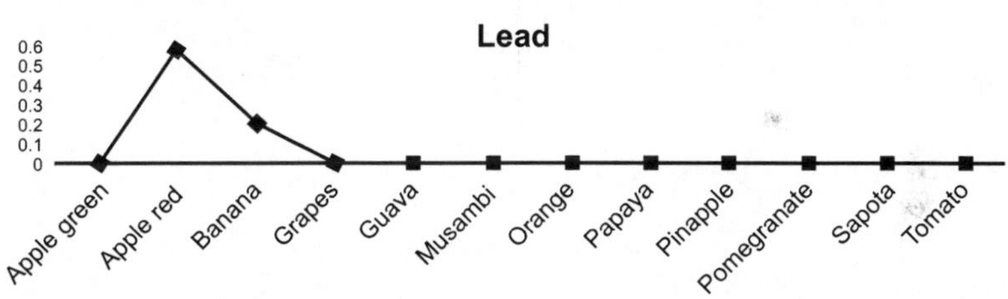

Fig. 15.3: Concentration of Pb in various fruits (mg/kg – dry weight)

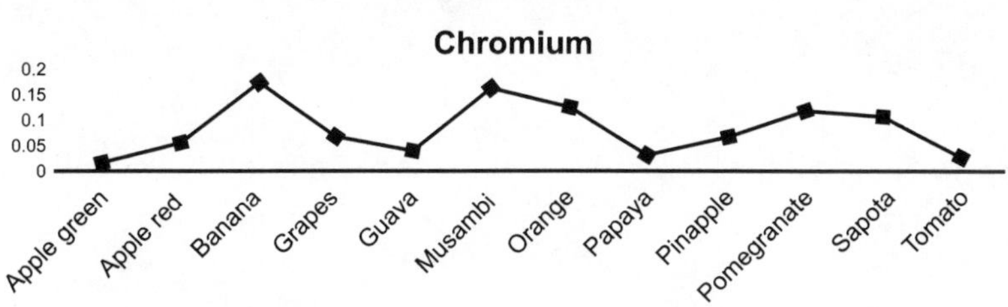

Fig. 15.4: Concentration of Cr invarious fruits (mg/kg–dryweight)

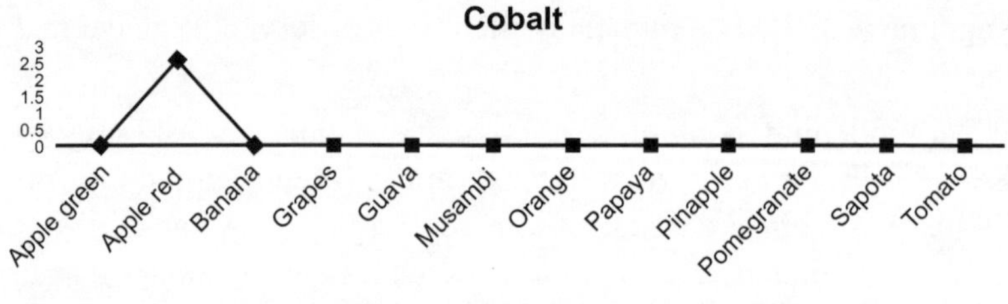

Fig. 15.5: Concentration of Co in various fruits (mg/kg – dry weight)

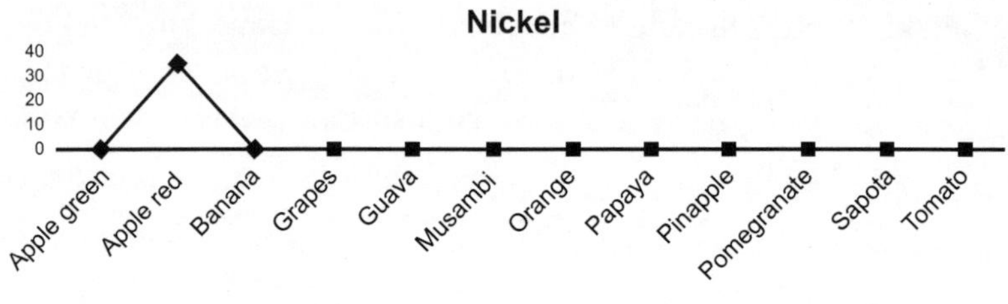

Fig. 15.6: Concentration of Ni in various fruits (mg/kg – dry weight)

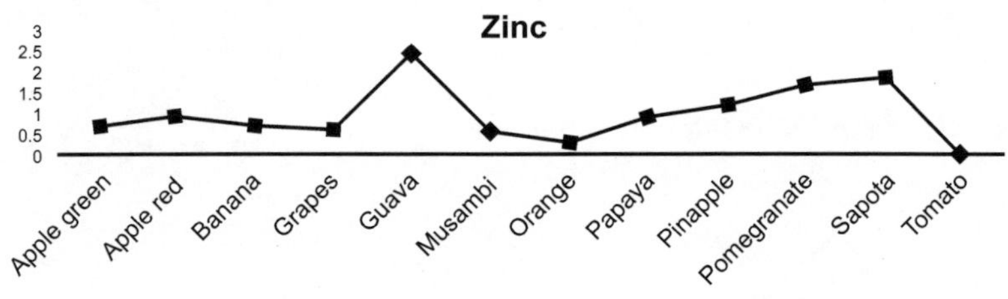

Fig. 15.7: Concentration of Zn in various fruits (mg/kg – dry weight)

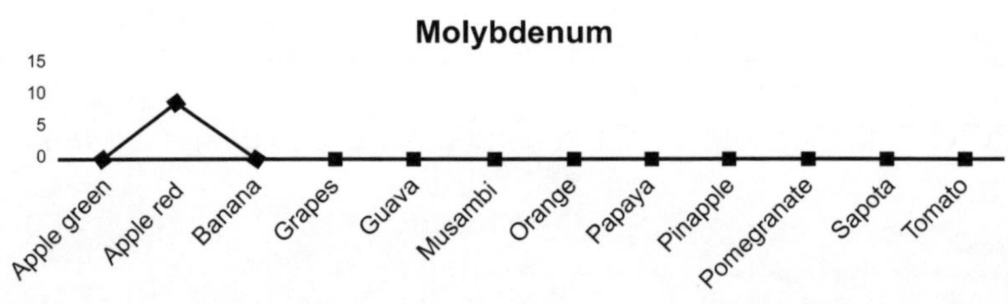

Fig. 15.8: Concentration of Mo in various fruits (mg/kg – dry weight)

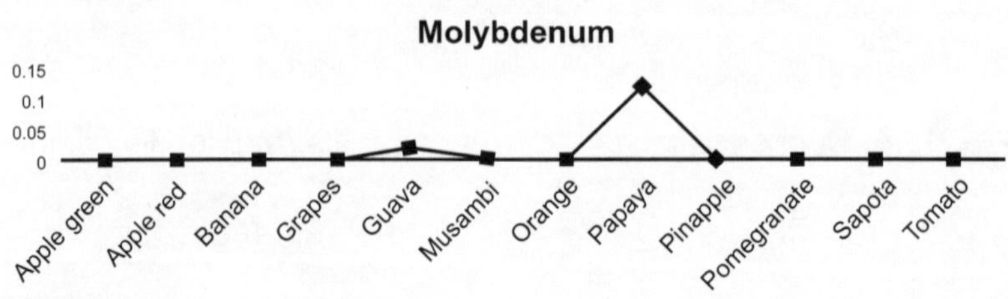

Fig. 15.9: Concentration of Se in various fruits (mg/kg – dry weight)

Arsenic (As) and lead (Pb) have been used in pesticides such as calcium arsenate, lead arsenate, and copper arsenate when applied to orchard crops such as apples and peaches Arsenic (As) very slowly leached through soils and Lead (Pb) is immobile (Veneman et al., 1983; Hood,2006). Heavy metals are found in many fertilizers and in some pesticides, added as micro nutritional or pest control components. However they can be present as naturally occurring contaminants or from fertilizer products manufactured from waste materials. Heavy metals may be of particular concern in tree fruit production because of the importance of foliar sprays, which deposit fertilizer and pesticide residues directly onto fruit. Currently heavy metals and nutrient management include natural enrichment of Cd and As by using P fertilizers, anthropogenic heavy metal contamination of Zn fertilizers, Cu and As contamination of soil resulting from pesticide application. The heavy metal contents of some orchard soils may be high enough to cause adverse effects in people, plants and the environment. (Peryea, 2001). Chromium is known to be a toxic metal that can cause serve damage to plants and animals. Oxidative stress induced by chromium initiates the degradation of photosynthetic pigments causing decline in growth (Peralta et al., 2001) In tomato (Lycopersicon esculentum) chromium toxicity results decrease in the plant nutrient acquisition (Moral et al.,1995; Moral et al., 1996). Nickel is an essential nutrient for plants. However, the amount of Ni required for normal growth of plants is very low. (Izosimova ,2005). However, Ni^{+2} concentration is increasing in certain areas by human activities such as mining works, emission of smelters, burning of coal and oil, sewage, phosphate fertilizers and pesticides (Gimeno et al.,1996).

Conclusion

The present study reveals that heavy metals such as cadmium, lead, chromium, cobalt, nickel and zinc were observed in fruit samples which are prescribed by the WHO in 2011.However it was observed that cadmium content in apple (red) exceeded the limit. This is an important indication as human health is directly affected by ingestion of fruits. The bio-monitoring of trace elements in fleshy fruits needs to be continuously monitored because these are the nutrient rich source of food for humans for all ages. The concentration of heavy metals in fruits indicated that they are contaminated from different sources and if regularly consumed from the same place the chances of bioaccumulation in human body may result in toxicity. The study concludes that regular survey for heavy metals concentration in fruits should be done in order to evaluate health risk exist to protect the end user and assure food safety.

Reference

1. Anjali Verma, Priyanka Sharma, Namita Dhusia, Nandkishor More., 2016. Determination of heavy metal content in fruits and fruits juices consume in urban areas of Lucknow, India. International Journal of Food Science and Nutrition. 1(5),44-50.
2. Anon, B., 1987. Food Standards Code 2987. Autralian Government. Public Service, Canberra.
3. Arora M, Kiran B, Rani S, Rani A, Kaur B, Mittal N. 2008. Heavy metal accumulation in vegetables irrigated with water from different sources. *Food Chemistry*, 111, 811–815.
4. Cherfi A, Abdoun S, Gaci O. 2014. Food survey: levels and potential health risks of chromium, lead, zinc and copper content in fruits and vegetables consumed in Algeria. *Foodand Chemical Toxicology*, 70, 48–53.
5. Chojnacha, K., Chojnacki,A., Gorecka, H. and Gorecki, H., 2005. Bioavailability of heavy metals from polluted soils to plants. Science Total Environment. 337(1-3), 175-182.
6. Expert Group on Vitamins and Minerals, 2003 Expert Group on Vitamins and Minerals**Risk Assessment: Molybdenum** (2003)
7. Gimeno-Garcia E, Andreu V, Boluda R (1996) Heavy metals incidence in the application of inorganic fertilizers and pesticides to rice farming soils. Environmental Pollution. 92:19–25.
8. Hogan, C.,2011. Heavy metal. Ed. Emily Monosson. Encyclopedia of Earth, NCSE, Washington DC Retrieved from http://editors.eol.org/eoearth/wiki/Heavy_metal . [Accesed 2 June, 2019].
9. Hood,E. 2006. The apple bites back: claiming old orchards for residential development," Environmental Health Perspectives. 114: 471–A476.
10. Izosimova A (2005) Modelling the interaction between calcium and nickel in the soil-plant system. FAL Agric Res Special issue 288:99.
11. Jarup, L., 2003. Hazards of heavy metal contamination. British Medical Bulletin. 68, 167-182.
12. Joint FAO/WHO Food Standards Program. 2001.. Twenty-fourth Session, Geneva, July 2-7, 2001.
13. Joint FAO/WHO Food Standards Program. 2011. Fifth Session,The Hague, March 21 – 25, 2011.
14. Khairiah, J., Zalifah, M.K., Yin, Y.H., Aminah, A., 2004. The uptake of heavy metals by fruit type vegetables grown in selected agricultural areas. Pakistan Journal of Biological Sciences 7(8), 1438-1442.
15. Khan K, Lu Y L, Khan H, Ishtiaq M. Khan S, Waqas M, Wei L, Wang T Y. 2013. Heavy metals in agricultural soils and crops and their health risks in Swat District, northern Pakistan. *Food and Chemical Toxicology*, 58, 449–458.

16. Lokeshwari, H, G.T. Chandrappa, 2006. Impact of Heavy Metal Contamination ofBellandur Lake on Soil and Cultivated Vegetation. Current Science, 91(5), 622 –627.
17. Moral,R., Gomez, I., Pedreno, J.N and Mataix,J .1995 "Effects of chromium on the nutrient element content and morphology of tomato," Journal of Plant Nutrition, vol. 18, no. 4, pp. 815–822.
18. Moral,R., Gomez, I., Pedreno, J.N and Mataix,J. 1996 "Absorption of Cr and effects on micronutrient content in tomato plant (Lycopersicun esculentum M.)," Agrochimicals, vol. 40, no. 2-3, pp. 132–138.
19. Orisakwe O E, Nduka J K, Amadi C N, Dike D O, Bede O. 2012. Heavy metals health risk assessment for population via consumption of food crops and fruits in Owerri, South Eastern, Nigeria. *Chemistry Central Journal*, 6, 77.
20. Pendias, A.K. and Pendias, H. 1992. Trace Elements in Soils and Plants. Boca Roton, CRC Press, pp. 271-276.
21. Peralta JR, Gardea Torresdey JL, Tiemann KJ, Gomez E, Arteaga S, Rascon E (2001)Uptakeandeffectsoffiveheavymetalsonseedgerminationandplantgrowth in alfalfa (Medicago sativa) L. B. *Environmental Contamination* and *Toxicology* 66:727–734.
22. Peryea, F. J. (2001). Heavy metal contamination in deciduous tree fruit orchards: implications for mineral nutrient management. *Acta Horticulturae,* 564, 31–39.
23. Reza, S.K., Baruah, U., Sarkar, D., 2013. Hazard assessment of heavy metal contamination by the paper industry, north-eastern India. Internal Journal of Environmental Studies 70(1), 23-32.
24. Roba C, Roşu C, Piştea I, Ozunu A, Baciu C. 2016. Heavy metal content in vegetables and fruits cultivated in Baia Mare mining area (Romania) and health risk assessment. Environmental Science and Pollution Research, 23,6062–6073.
25. Sathawara, N.G., Parikh, D.J., Agarwal, Y.K., 2004. Essential heavy metals in environmental samples from western India. Bulletin of Environmental Contamination and Toxicology 73, 756-761.
26. Selvaraj V, Tomblin J, Yeager Armistead M, Murray E. Selenium (sodium selenite) causes cytotoxicity and apoptotic mediated cell death in PLHC-1 fish cell line through DNA and mitochondrial membrane potential damage. Ecotoxicology and Environmental Safety 2013;87: 80–83.
27. Selvaraj V. Yeager□Armstead M, Murray E. Protective and antioxidant role of selenium on arsenic trioxide-induced oxidative stress and genotoxicity in the fish hepatoma cell line PLHC□1. Environ Toxicol Chem 2012; 31:2861–9.
28. Sheng D, Zhu L B, Wang D. 2014. Heavy metal pollution and health risk alert evaluation of fruits in Bengbu city, Anhui Province. *Journal of Southwest University for Nationalities* (Natural Science Edition), 40, 837–842. (in Chinese)

29. Türkdoğan M K, Kilicel F, Kara K, Tuncer I, Uygan I. 2002. Heavy metals in soil, vegetables and fruits in the endemic upper gastrointestinal cancer region of Turkey. *EnvironmentalToxicology and Pharmacology*, 13, 175–179.

30. Veneman, L.M., Murray, J.R and Baker, J.H. 1983. Spatial distribution of pesticide residues in a former apple orchard. Journal of Environmental Quality. 12(1): 101–104.

31. WHO 2011a, WHO Molybdenum in Drinking Water: Background Document for Development of WHO Guidelines for Drinking-water Quality (WHO/SDE/WSH/03.04/11/Rev/1) World Health Organization, Geneva, Switzerland (2011).

32. Wieght., 1991. quoted from Kaid, A.S., 2007. Studies on the Heavy Metals in Water, Soil and Plant in Colar District, unpublished M.Sc thesis, Bangalore University, Bangalore.

33. Wodaje Addis Tegegne., 2017. Analysis of Heavy Metal Levels in Some Edible Fruits from Selected Markets in Ethiopia. Journal of Modern Chemistry & Chemical Technology. 6(1), 236-238.

34. Xiao Z L, Cong Q, Qu J. 2010. Assessment of heavy metal pollution in orchard soil and its affections to fruit quality around molybdenum mining area. *Science Technology and Engineering*, 10, 5831–5834.

35. Zhen H. 2008. Pollution characteristics of heavy metal in grains and fruits at both sides of Shenyang-Dalian expressway. *Journal of Meteorology and Environment*, 24, 1–5.

Urban Environment and Spatial Science
Dr Mohd Akhter Ali, Dr. Kabir Mohan Sethy, Dr Muzafar Wani and M.Kamraju
Ane Books Pvt. Ltd. 2021, , ISBN : 978-93-90658-28-2, P.P. : 195 – 204

16

Geopolitical Issues of Kabul River A Case Study of Af-Pak

Fidel Rahmati, Prof. AV Shashikala
[1]*Ph.D. Research Scholar,*
Department of Geography,
Osmania University Hyderabad, Telangana-500007
rahmatifidel@gmail.com, avshashikala@gmail.com
[2]*Senior Fellow ICSSR*
Department of Geography,
Osmania University, Hyderabad, Telangana-500007
rahmatifidel@gmail.com, avshashikala@gmail.com

Abstract

Water is a vital element for the survival of societies, the water crisis in the 21st century has made it even more important. Therefore, the 21st century is famous as century of thirst. Water can also play an important factor in shaping conflict or cooperation between countries while crossing the international borders. Afghanistan's water resources are made up of five large basins with a total surface water content of 5 billion cubic meters annually. Since 2001, with the new government in Afghanistan; food security, employment, potable water supply and electricity generation are among the strategic priorities for Afghanistan. Therefore, Afghanistan's economic development plans have raised serious concerns with neighboring countries especially Pakistan. This research paper is basically qualitative in nature and based on secondary data in which; books, published research studies, newspaper articles, seminar and conference papers, publication of national and international journals, magazines and documents available in the internet, government policies and plans has been used. The main objective of this paper to study the Geopolitical issues of Kabul River between Afghanistan and Pakistan. The paper will be helpful

Corresponding Author: Fidel Rahmati

in showing some likely policies for cooperation between both the countries to ensure sustainable ecosystem, rather than a kind of conflict mentality on Kabul River.

Keywords: Afghanistan, Pakistan, Sustainability, Geopolitics, Conflict Management.

Introduction

Afghanistan is one of the countries with surplus water resources, but despite the fact, still there is less progress in developing, and utilizing of the water bodies of the country. According numerous international organizations and United Nations prediction, in the near future, much of the world's contest will be on fresh water resources. Afghanistan has five major water basins with surface water of 57 BCM per year. Afghanistan's status as upstream riparian country has turned it into a rich source of water for neighboring countries such as Iran, Turkmenistan, Pakistan, Tajikistan and Uzbekistan. In spite of surplus water bodies of Afghanistan, the investment and study on water sector has suffered from severe shortcomings.

The lack of technical knowledge in this area has been one of the relatively serious obstacles to the sustainable development and management of the rivers in the country, and this dilemma has affected the understanding of water's driving role in economic growth. On the one hand, the politicization of water resources has made the issue of transboundary waters bodies of Afghanistan one of the most sensitive issues between Afghanistan and its neighbors (especially Pakistan which is the focus of this paper), and on the other hand, due to four decades of conflict, Afghanistan has not been well developed, and its important water bodies infrastructure has been destroyed.

Till now there is no meaningful agreement between Afghanistan and Pakistan on utilizing of the water resource.

Unfortunately the Kabul River basin, has been subjected to highest controversy between AF-PAK. Both countries have been working directly and indirectly to find common ground but their efforts so far have been failed. Distrust, cross-border terrorism and long-standing rivalry over the Duran Line between the two countries are some of the reasons which were not able to reach a water treaty to address cross-border water issues.

Almost population of Eastern provinces of Afghanistan utilize somehow from the Kabul River apart from 4 million population of Kabul Capital City of Afghanistan. This river basin is very significant for Afghanistan because, one third of the population of the country live in the Kabul flood plains. Meanwhile, Majority of the Khaiber Pashtun Khawa population live in the Kabul River basin and depends on its water and more than two million residents of Peshawar directly depend on Kabul River.

As the water use demand Increases for both the countries in coming decades and as the climate change led to drought and a decrease in the amount of annual precipitation, therefore, there will be a huge stress on Kabul river water which indeed add to the unrest in the region. In a broad sense, water security considers as one of the national security element. Therefore, it is very much needed to have a common understanding and agreement between the two countries in order to maintain the water security and cooperation in the region.

Objectives

The objective of this paper is to delineate the Geopolitical issues of Kabul River between Afghanistan and Pakistan

Data and Material

This paper is written based on the secondary data such as books, published papers, newspaper articles, national and international journals, government documents and policies. The interpretation of the data was carried out keeping in mind the overall perspective of the research study.

Study Area

Kabul is the capital and largest city of Afghanistan located in the eastern part of the country with estimated population of 4.222 million. Kabul city is consist of 22 districts playing as the mosaic for all major ethnic groups of Afghanistan which serves as the center of political, economic and cultural. Kabul has the 75th ranking of the largest city in the world.

Analysis

Kabul River Basin

Water is measured as source of power, shortage of water is a very serious and strategic issue which will affect the economic and social development of nations.

Therefore, lack of water weakened the national power. Major sources of water in Afghanistan are natural glaciers and rain –covered mountains.

Total amount of annual rainfall in the country is 163 BCM in which 57 billion cubic meters of surface water, 18 billion cubic meters of groundwater and the remain of them vapored or partially absorbed by living things or soil. Out of 57 billion cubic meters of surface water, only 17 billion cubic meters are used and the rest are out of reach and out of 18 billion cubic meters of groundwater in Afghanistan only 3 billion cubic meters are used annually.

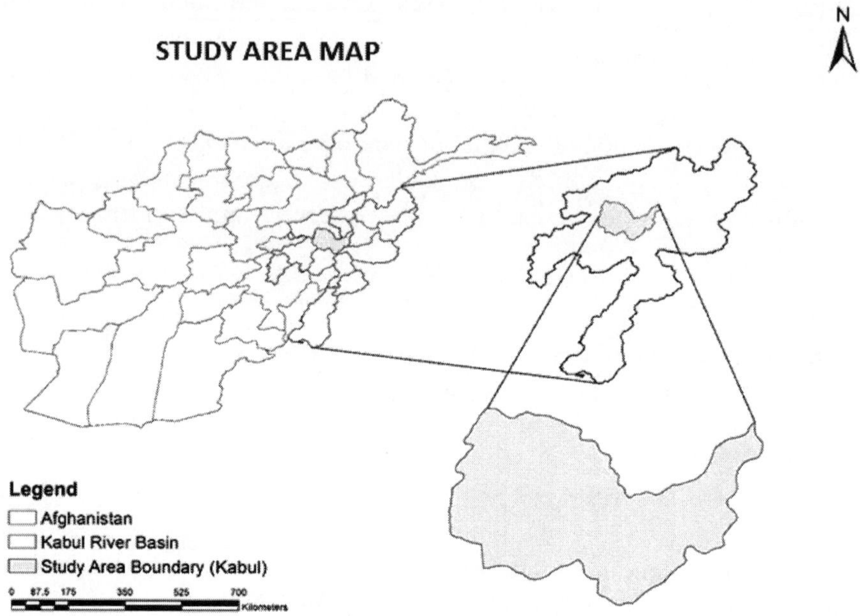

Fig. 16.1

Source: Fidel Rahmati. et.al. retrieved-2020.

There are five major river basin in Afghanistan out of which four of them are transboundary river such as Amudarya, Harirood –Murghab, Helmand, kabul (Indus) and one national river which is Northern river basin.

The Kabul River and its tributaries originates from the southern slopes of the Hindukush and the central Mountains and flows into the Pakistan Sindh over distance, that is why it's called the Sindh or Indus basin. The River has 700 Km length, 560 Km in Afghanistan. After crossing Kabul city, it irrigates much of the eastern Afghanistan and has many branches. Logar River in Pol-e-Charkhi area, Panjshir River near Surubi, Alishing and Alinagar river near Daronta and Kunar river in northeast of Jalalabad city and others joins Kabul river to make huge water river. This is the only river that after crossing Peshawar joins to the Sindh River. In fact Kabul River with its small and large tributaries, is the only river in the country that after joining Sindh of Pakistan, flows to the Indian Ocean. The Kabul River covers an area of 76908 Sq.Km, which makes 11.91% of Afghanistan's catchment.

As per the report, Afghanistan has the capacity of generating 23,000 Megawatts of hydroelectric energy from its rivers including Kabul River which has the capacity of producing 3,100 Megawatts of electricity.

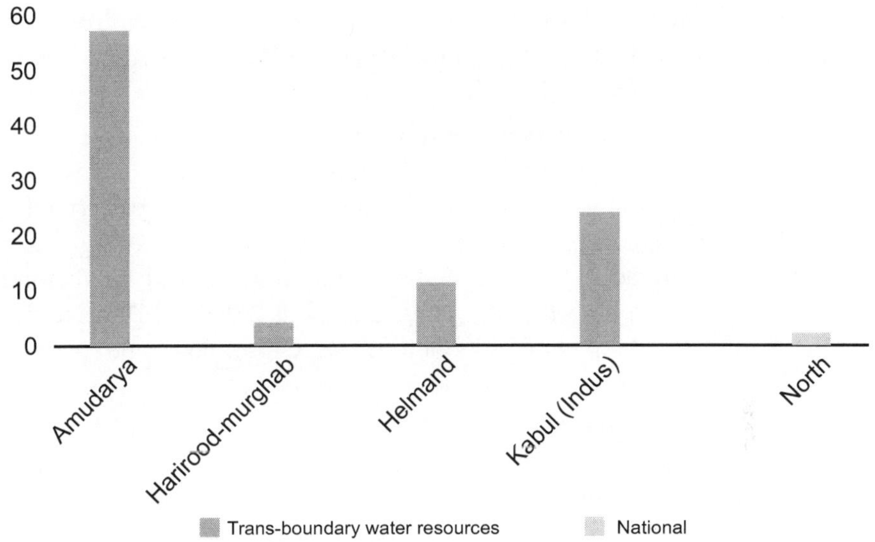

Fig. 16.2: Illustrate the porportion of total river flow and its volume (Source: Arezzo, 2015).

The river system irrigates 300,000 hectares of land in Kabul River Basin. According to United Nations Food and Agriculture Organization and ground water studies, Afghanistan has 95 billion cubic meters of water available in the country which includes 84 billion cubic meters of surface water (88 percent) and 11 billion cubic meters of ground water (12 percent).

Due to lack of capacity and infrastructure, Afghanistan is only utilizing less than 25% of its surface water resources and less than one third of its groundwater, therefore, shares 90% of its water resources with its neighbors.

Table 16.1: Afghanistan's Major Rivers and Its Catchment*

No	*Catchment Name*	*Area (%)*	*Volume (%)*
1	Amu	14	57
2	Harirood- Mur	12	4
3	Hilmand	41	11
4	Kabul	11	24
5	North	11	2

***Sources:** Arezzo, 2016.*

Cross-Border Disputes

Kabul River Basin management is one of the controversial point between Afghanistan and Pakistan. Each of these two countries has their own plans and priorities for managing of the crises which can be originates from water resources through; mismanagement, population growth, dependency on Kabul river water, water quantity and its effect on agriculture.

Afghanistan has the lowest water storage and capacity in the region, so Afghanistan government needs to somehow management it is water resources. A part from existing major hydro-powers dams in Kabul river basin namely; Mahipar, Naghlu, Sarobi I and Sarobi II, In the recent years Afghanistan government has planned to build 12 dams on Kabul River with total storage capacity of 4.7 million acre feet of water and about 2,092.5 MW electricity capacity with the total budget of $6.847 billion which is going to be sponsored by World Bank and India.

The government argues that, the water capacity has not been used during the last four decades as a result, river water freely flow to the neighboring countries without any restriction. The reasons behind that, were four decades of conflict and instability in the country. These issues prevented the previous governments from planning, implementing any developmental projects on its own water river. Moreover, during those decades of instability and unrest in Afghanistan, the technical capacity was not capable of implementing such projects. Though, Pakistan benefits form water flow coming from Afghanistan. Pakistan provides no financial support for flow control structures or management of the river, even though it has significantly increased its water use form the Indus River during the last four decades. Currently both the countries feel a high water demand than before. Therefore, due to this uncooperative stance from Pakistan, Afghanistan has also been reluctant to share river flow data with Pakistan.

Unfortunately, cross-border terrorism, security challenges in Afghanistan and Pakistan and border disputes created an environment in which both the countries could not cooperate, initiate, dialogue on the current water demand and related issues. Such behavior from both sides has a long negative impact on both societies which they live in the Kabul River Basin. In addition to that, without any meaningful cooperation of both the countries, there will be political, economic, and societal damage for both the countries or even led to a conflict. Collaboration is possible, when both the countries have political willpower for resolving all disputes related to the water for a sustainable ecosystem in the region.

AF-PAK Water Conflict

Water has been considered as one of the significant diplomatic tools. Afghanistan has surplus water resources which shares with neighboring countries. Therefore, the water conflict has been one of the major serious challenges in Afghanistan.

According to United Nations there are ten countries facing severe water scarcity, Pakistan is one among them but at the same time Afghanistan is also facing several challenges due to an increased demand for water, drought and less capacity to use its water bodies. According to statistics collected in the 1950s, the discharge capacity of the Kabul River Basin to Pakistan is about 21 billion cubic meters but Afghanistan uses about 4 cubic meters of its own water, the rest flows to Pakistan.

Taken in to account the current situation of Afghanistan, the interfering policies of neighboring countries are undeniable. There have been several border disputes over transboundary waters between Afghanistan and neighboring countries in the past. It is said that one of the factor for security deterioration in the Kunar Province of Afghanistan is water issue between both the countries. In 2009, Iran's intervention to stop construction of the Salma Dam in Herat Province was confirmed by the security forces of Afghanistan.

At the same time, Pakistan reacted against construction of 12 hydroelectric power dam in 2010. In 2011, the disputes arose over Helmand trans-boundary water between Afghanistan and Iran. In fact Pakistan believes that their interest will be jeopardized by constructing of these dams and hydroelectric power generation in Afghanistan. In recent years, Afghanistan was not able to use its water due to political instability in the country.

Most likely, water issues with neighboring countries has been considered as one of the factor of prolonging conflict in Afghanistan, so developing a regional water policy would be a better way for Afghanistan to become self-sufficient in water and energy.

Suggestions

Afghanistan and Pakistan have no agreement as a joint water management mechanism on the Kabul River. Distrust, cross-border terrorism and long-standing rivalry over the Durand Line between the two countries are considered as the reasons behind absence of a water treaty to address cross-border water issues. However, this does not mean that there can never be a mechanism for cooperation. In fact, the documentary treaty between Pakistan and India is a perfect example of cooperation between the two countries that have no common aspirations, but have created an important mechanism to address common water security challenges. India and Pakistan have established professional bodies dealing with water issues at national level Afghanistan also needs to build the capacity to institutionalize its efforts to contain water and provide informed policy options. Third-party involvement such as the World Bank is another good policy which can help improve some international concerns that Afghanistan does not want to work with its neighbors on water issues because it fears lack of knowledge of hydrological and conflict resolution over cross-border waters in the country. Establishing a joint commission or working group between the two countries could be a starting point for more peaceful resolution of the related issues. The joint commission can be a trusted third party such as the World Bank or any other reputable body for generating hydroelectric power for the common consumption of the two countries provided by, to maintain national interests of Afghanistan.

Conclusion

Firstly, Afghanistan needs to develop and invest on capacity building in water resources of the country and research institutes in order to carry out some extensive research on the water resources so that the country can take advantage of its water which has been given to it.

Secondly, Regional geopolitics and economic instability has added to the complexity of trans-boundary water management in the study area. But at the same time, if shared water bodies are properly managed, can be a beginning point for improving and enhancing cooperation between the two countries.

Thirdly, peaceful and friendly negotiations are a much better and more possible way to achieve beneficial results. Given the fact that there is no bilateral treaty to facilitate the "fair and equitable" allocation of water between Afghanistan and other beneficiaries. May be treaties and policies related to cross-border water resources, defend Afghanistan's balanced rights against its powerful neighbors, which will encourage Afghanistan for enriching their potential resources in a better manner.

Therefore, if Afghanistan is willing to provide enough and sustainable hydroelectric power and provide basic livelihoods for its people by investing in water resources while at the same time establishing peaceful relations with its neighbors, it must act in accordance with international legal norms and laws.

Acknowledgment

I am very thankful to Nizammuddin Sir, librarian, Department of Geography, Osmania University for his valuable suggestions regarding the study. I am also grateful to Dr. Mohd. Akhter Ali and M.Kamraju for their valuable suggestions and comments.

Reference

1. *Afghanistan, ministary of energy and water. Warer issues. Kabul: ministry of energy and water of Afghanistan. 2015.*
2. *Allan, A. water security policies and global system for water-scarce regions. World bank-2001.*
3. *Arezzo, Abdulghafour.2016. water crisis and silent deplomacy. Tajekistan: Embassy of Kabul in Tajekistan. 2016.*
4. *Azimi, Mohammad Azim. 2017. An Introduction to Afghanistan National Security, Geography and Environment. Kabul: Negar.*
5. *Dooran, Research Center. 2017. Journal for Afghanistan Waters Studies. Kabul: Doran.*
6. *McChrystal, Gen Stanley. "The Politics of Water Security in the Kabul River Basin." Atlantic Monthly (2010).*
7. *Dooran, Research Center. 2017. Journal for Afghanistan Waters Studies. Kabul: Doran.*
8. *Shredor, J, and J Ahmadzai. 2016. Transboundary Water Resources in Afghanistan (Climate Change and land-use implication). Cambridge: Elsevier.*
9. *Qureshi, Asad Sarwari,. 2002. Water Resource Management in Afghanistan the Issues and Options. Pakistan: Islamabad.*
10. *Yousaf, Suliman. "KABUL RIVER AND PAK-AFGHAN RELATIONS." (P. Abeygunawardena,Technical Assistance to the Islamic Republic of Afghanistan for Preparing the Small to Medium- Sized Hydropower Development Project, (AsianDevelopment Bank (ADB) October 2005)- retrieved, 2020.*
11. *Water Management, Livestock and the Opium Economy. How the Water Flows: A Topology of Irrigation Systems in Afghanistan, (Afghanistan Research and Evaluation Unit Issue Paper Series on June 2008).*
12. *Panikkar, Bindu, Asim Zia, Susan Sgorbati, Michael Cohen, Muhamad Abed, Muhammad Fayyad, Nadia Hashimi et al. "Transboundary Water Governance in the Kabul River Basin: Implementing Environmental and Public Diplomacy between Pakistan and Afghanistan." Complexity, Governance & Networks 5, no. 1 (2019): 101-120.*
13. *Gitanjali Bakshi and Sahiba Trivedi, The Indus Equation: Indian Support for Afghan Dams on the Kabul River,*
14. *(Strategic Foresight Group, 2011), available at* www.strategicforesight.com. *(Yousaf, Suliman. "KABUL RIVER AND PAK-AFGHAN RELATIONS."), retrieved-2020.*

15. *McChrystal, Gen Stanley. "The Politics of Water Security in the Kabul River Basin." Atlantic Monthly (2010), retrieved-2020.*
16. *Shredor, J, and J Ahmadzai. 2016. Transboundary Water Resources in Afghanistan (Climate Change and land-use implication). Cambridge: Elsevier, retrieved-2020.*
17. *Najib Agha Fahim, Interviewed by Afghan Paper on 2015 " water as an opportunity or Challenge",* http://afghanpaper.com/nbody.php?id=93671, *retrieved-2020.*
18. *Pashwak Afghan News Agency, 2016-retrieved, 2020.*
19. *Shredor, J, and J Ahmadzai. 2016. Transboundary Water Resources in Afghanistan (Climate Change and land-use implication). Cambridge: Elsevier*
20. *An introductiion to Afghanistan's national power. Kabul: Univerity of Afghanistan. Geographical fundamental of Afghanistan economy. Kabul: Khurasan. 2012.*
21. *Rahmati, Fidel.* "A Study on Urban Growth And Its Impact on Kabul City, Afghanistan." *International Journal on Advance Research and Innovative Ideas In Education (Ijariie) 6, No. 4 (2020): 280–84.*
22. *Rahmati, Fidel; Ali, Mohd. Akhter; Kamraju, M..* "A Study on Strategic Location of Siliguri Corridor and Its Issues." *International Journal of All Research Education and Scientific Methods (IJARESM) 8, no. 7 (2020): 5–9.*
23. *Rahmati, Fidel, Mohd Akhter Ali, and M Kamraju.* "A Study on India -China Current Geopolitical Issues and Implications." *International Journal of Scientific Research in Engineering and Management (IJSREM) 4, no. 6 (2020): 1–10.*

Urban Environment and Spatial Science
Dr Mohd Akhter Ali, Dr. Kabir Mohan Sethy, Dr Muzafar Wani and M.Kamraju
Ane Books Pvt. Ltd. 2021, , ISBN : 978-93-90658-28-2, P.P. : 205 – 217

17

Urban Expansion in the Northern Territories of Himalayan Region- India

Manzoor A.Wani
Bashir A. Lone,
Ishtiaq A. Mayer
manzoorwani8559@gmail.com

Abstract

The study envisaged the expansion of urbanization with spatio-temporal analysis during three decades (1901-2011) in the northern territories of Himalayan region of India. The study appraises the impact of different socio-economic determinants on urban expansion at district level by retrieving Census data of India from 1981-2011. The coefficient of correlation and regression analysis have been used to find out the association between urban growth expansion and different socio-economic variables. In the study a continuous growth of urban expansion is seen in all districts at creeping rate due to limited and diversification of resources. High urban expansion is seen in the district Srinagar (summer capital) with 98 % and Jammu district (winter capital) with 50 % total urban population. Extreme rural-urban disparities, push-pull factors (rural-urban) and improved economic conditions in rural areas resulted in the mass migration towards established urban centres, which resulted in the urban explosion in Class I towns followed by Class IV, CLASS 11, CLASS 111, CLASS V, and CLASS V1 Towns respectively. The study will be benefited to the administration, planners and policy makers to formulate and execute plans to reduce and curtail the flow of migration towards two primate city by initiating infrastructural developmental approach at other sub-urban areas.

Key Words: Population, Disparities, Migration, Urban expansion, Urbanisation

Corresponding Author: Manzoor A.Wani

INTRODUCTION

Urbanization has emerged as one of the potent global environmental change in the recent years has impacted mountainous environment especially in developing regions where process of urbanization following unsystematic, unplanned and irrational (Prakesh et al, 2018). With continuous growth of population, and era of industrialization, process of urbanization is on the high especially in favourable planes compared to hilly terrain of the Himalayan (Peeyush et al, 2014). In simple terminology urbanization is the process by which rural population gets transformed into urban population through improved socio-economic reforms (Baghat 1992). Urbanisation is a limited process of a cycle through which a region by transforming from agrarian to industrial society and from traditional society to modern society (Davis 1965). Historical evidence suggests that urbanization process is continuous and universal phenomena and will occur through the passage of time (Kundu 2003). Urbanization is a specific process of reconstruction through spatio-temporal framework that can be operationalized in the space through spatial arrangement of population settlement in a hierarchical system of varying size (Raza 1991). Urban expansion is simply a concentration of different with functionally integrated specialization and advanced technology (Kundu 2011). High level of urbanization is seen in the developed countries with some reached at the final stage and are experiencing stinted growth due to host of factors (Brockerhoff 1999). The onset of modern and universal process of urbanization is relatively a recent phenomenon and is closely related with economic and industrial revolution (United Nation 1996 & 2010).

Developing countries had experienced the process of urbanization in the middle of 20th century (Hussain 2000). Government of India announced that from the total population of 121 crore Indians, 83.3 crore live in rural areas while 37.7 crore resides in the urban areas, country with a total of 11976 towns as per 2011 Census and has increased for the first time since independence, the absolute increase in urban population more than in rural areas (Mohan et al, 1982). Urbanization and urban area a process and fact respectively, they are not confined to the city alone, though they tend to find their origin in the city (Mohan et al, 1982).

The history of urbanization in Jammu and Kashmir State is quite as old as towns and urban places like Pandrethan, Naranag, Awantipora flourished during the ancient period. During the medieval period, urbanization was associated with the seats of administration, capitals and trading centers. During the period of Sikhs and subsequently, after the arrival of English people, the rate of urbanization accelerated (Sidiqque 1998). The subsistence nature of urbanization in Jammu and Kashmir forces the rural migration to urban areas (Srinagar and Jammu) for want of employment and avail other facilities and not for the urban environment (Zutshi 1986). Srinagar city being the largest urban center in the Himalayan region is growing at an alarming rate in terms of size and areal extent (Nissar et al, 2015).

In spite of some of the glaring evils of urbanization and industrialization we should not revert to the primitive methods of production. What is needed is the greater attention should be paid to human values and human welfare than the material gains.

Data Base and Methodology

Study Area

The present study focuses on erstwhile State of Jammu, Kashmir and Ladakh. The state with recent bifurcation constitutes two separate Union territories i.e. Jammu Kashmir with (legislative assembly), and eastern Ladakh division without assembly. The area is surrounded from all sides by highly rugged snow –capped mountains. With unique geographical personality area experience huge diversities in socio-cultural, economic and political environment. The total area of the state is 22.2 lacs km2 and is presently distributed between India, Pakistan and China. The region with 125.4 lacs of population with approximately 98 per cent of the total population residing in the union territory of JK and remaining 2 % of the population in Ladakh region. Area wise Ladakh shares maximum area (70 %), and 30 % of the total area is shared by Jammu and Kashmir divisions respectively. Figure I show the location map of the study area. Keeping the above figures of land- population distribution in the area and discrete geo-physical environment area is of high importance to appraise the urban growth expansion at inter-district level. Figure I show the district map of the study area.

Data collection

Urban demographic data was collected from J&K Census Department from 1981-2011to undertand the demographic and geo-spatial dimensions of urbanization in the State an inter-district analysis. With insurgence of political turmoil in 1991census enumeration was not carried in the State nor any related field survey were conducted during this period. Different demographic indicators were taken to assess the relationship with urban expansions which includes:

- Percentage of total urban population
- Urban decadal growth rate

- Socio-economic variables such as urban population distribution, sex ratio, literacy rate, occupational structure (non-agriculture workers).
- Classification of towns on the basis of population size and number of towns.

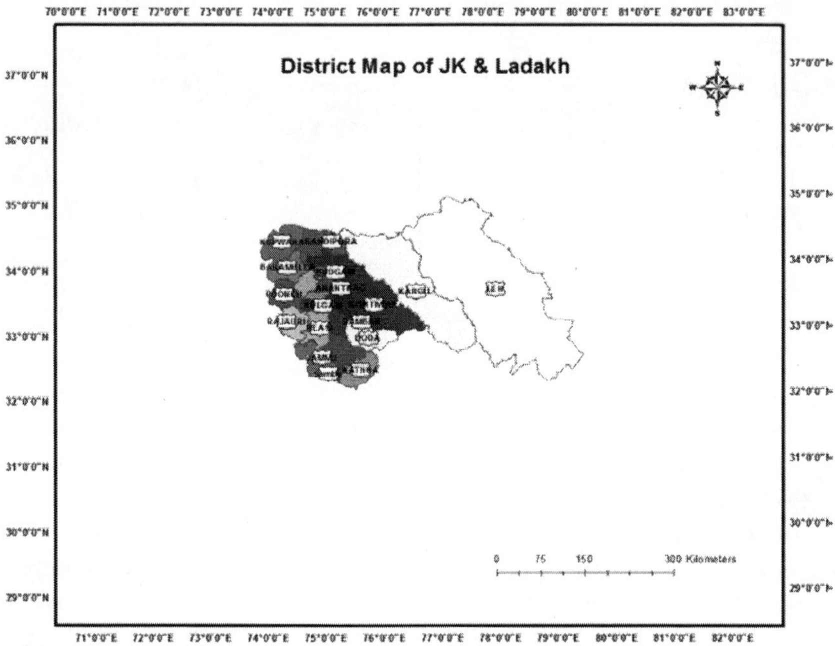

Fig. 17.1: Map of the location area

Source: Generated using J&K district boundary.

Statistical Techniques

Association of urban expansion with different demographic indicators were processed and analysed by adopting average mean, standard deviation, coefficient of variation (CV) were used to measure the dispersion of different indicators. Average percentage method was adopted to describe the whole group of data by taking value of one. Relationship of urbanization with different demographic indicators was assessed through coefficient of correlation by taking population as a dependent variable. Causal effect relationship between different demographic determinants and urban expansion was carried through regression analysis. Regression analysis technique involves finding causal-effect relationship of dependent variable, Y, (urban population) on different independent variables like literacy, population growth, nonagricultural workers, density of roads, density of towns etc. the equation: $Y = a + bX$.

Results

Level of Urbanization

State of Jammu and Kashmir has seen a sharp rise rise in the urban expansion i.e. State witnessed overall increased growth of 269 percent as compared to national urban expansion of 247.7 percent from 1901-2011. Continuous urban expansion is seen in the region. Since 1961 urban expansion has gained momentum with improved economic conditions, lack of basic amenities in the rural areas, and more political insecurity in rural areas has resulted in the mass migration from rural-urban mostly towards three nodal regions (Srinagar, Jammu and Kargil). From 1901-201, urban expansion has seen an increasing trend (+269 %) in the study area which is 22% more from national average as shown in the table 17.1. Only three districts (Srinagar, Jammu, & Leh) has shown major take-off in the urbanization growth i.e. between 20% -30% in Leh and >30% in Jammu and Srinagar during 2011, these three districts acts as nodal regions of their respective divisions i.e. Ladakh, Jammu, and Kashmir divisions. < 10% of progression is seen in the level of urban expansion in the districts Kupwara, Poonch, Rajouri, Doda, Kragil, Ramban, Reasi, Shopian and Kishtwar in 2011 census. These regions are characterized with backward socio-economic along with poor infrastructure and impeded accessibility and connectivity to nodal regions. Table 17.2 below shows the take-off level of urbanisation district wise.

Table 17.1: Comparative analysis of Urban expansion (1901-2011)*

Census Years	*India*	*Jammu and Kashmir*
1901	10.85	7.42
1911	10.29	11.71
1921	11.18	11.04
1931	11.99	15.39
1941	13.86	13.12
1951	17.29	14.05
1961	19.97	16.16
1971	19.91	18.59
1981	23.24	21.05
1991	25.71	NA
2001	27.78	24.8
2011	37.7	27.38
Change %	247.46	269

Source: Census of India

Table 17.2: District wise take-off stage in the levels of Urbanization 1981-2011*

% age of level	*Districts (1981)*	*Districts (2011)*
<10%	Kupwara, Udhampur, Pulwama, Kargil, Doda, Rajouri and Poonch	Kupwara, Poonch, Rajouri, Doda, Kargil, Shopian, Ramban, Reasi and Kishtwar
10-20%	Leh, Baramullah, Anantnag, Kathua, and Budgam	Pulwama, Budgam, Kathua, Anantnag, Udhampur, Baramullah, Kulgam, Bandipora, Ganderbal and Samba
20-30%	Jammu	Leh
> 30%	Srinagar	Srinagar and Jammu

Sources: Census of India, J&K Series, 1981 and 2011

Spatio-Temporal Analysis of Urban Expansion from 1981-2011

With inter- district regional disparities in terms of basic socio-cultural and economic perspectives such as connectivity, education infrastructure, health infrastructure and socio-economic insecurity people tend to migrate selective urban centres which resulted in the urban expansion in few districts of the region such as Srinagar, Jammu, Leh, Udhampur , while as rest of districts of the region i.e. Baramulla, Kupwara, Budgam, Doda, Kragil, Kathua, Pulwama, Poonch and Rajouri where perpetual backwardness in terms of socio-economic and other infrastructural development are lagging to the larger extent has seen a slow rise in the urban expansion during the last three decades (1981-2011). With uneven distribution of resource allocation two nodal regions (Srinagar & Jammu) have witnessed extensive care from administrative bodies that simultaneously, affecting the growth of other periphery regions. The result of uneven approach at inter-district level can be seen with the extensive urban expansion in two nodal regions of the area, with Srinagar (98%) of urban population and Jammu 50 % of urban population with low percentage of urban population in other remaining districts of the region in 2011 census conducted by govt. of India. Badgam district proximity to the Srinagar district showed decreasing urban population as compared to other districts of the region which shows increasing rate in the urban expansion from 1981-2011 (Table 17.3). Deceasing rate of urban population in the district of Badgam is prime concern to the urban local bodies with deteriorating air quality standards mainly due extensive brick manufacturing units emits huge amount of black carbon and other harmful pollutants forces people migrate to other. Spatio-temporal change in the urban expansion (1981-2011) at inter-district level is seen in the fig. 17.2.

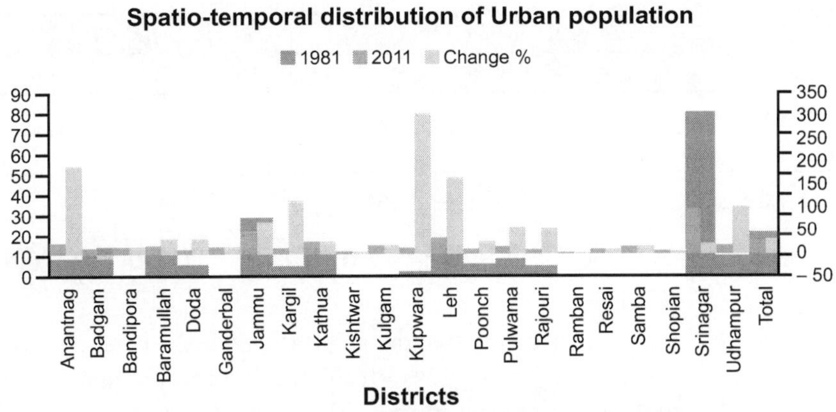

Fig. 17.2: Spatio-temporal distribution of urban population (1981-2011)

Table 17.3: Spatio-temporal analysis of urban expansion (1981-2011)*

Districts	*1981*	*2011*	*Change %*
Anantnag	8.98	26.22	192
Badgam	14.13	12.99	-8.06
Bandipora	0	16.66	16.66
Baramullah	13.49	18.1	34.17
Doda	5.92	7.97	34.62
Ganderbal	0	15.81	15.81
Jammu	29.64	50	68.69
Kargil	5.34	11.6	117.22
Kathua	11.38	14.55	27.85
Kishtwar	0	6.44	6.44
Kulgam	0	18.99	18.99
Kupwara	2.95	12.03	307.79
Leh	12.75	34.21	168.31
Poonch	6.32	8.1	28.16
Pulwama	8.98	14.35	59.79
Rajouri	5.23	8.14	55.64
Ramban	0	4.16	4.16
Reasi	0	8.57	8.57
Samba	0	16.81	16.81
Shopian	0	6.14	6.14

Districts	*1981*	*2011*	*Change %*
Srinagar	80.5	98.6	22.48
Udhampur	9.53	19.49	104.51
Total	21.05	27.38	30.07

****Sources:*** Census of India, J&K Series, and 2011

Spatial Distribution of Urban Population by Size & Class of Town (1981-2011).

With respect to population size only two districts fall in Class I category having urban population >1 lac sharing 49.72 % of the total urban population in the region (2011 census), with decreasing rate (-22.57 %) from 1981-2011. The decreasing rate in the growth of urbanization can emphasized due to the creation of 8 new districts in 2007 and migration from urban to other urban centers due to prevailing political turmoil during the last decade mostly experienced in the entire region of the Kashmir valley. Due to spike in the economic conditions due to direct improved connectivity and accessibility, trade links with two nodal regions (Jammu & Srinagar) resulted in the emergence of 6 towns in the class (II) category having total population between 50K- 1lac in 2011. Stunning growth is seen in other urban class categories. With the shift of towns to Class II category due to improved economic stability and development of connectivity and accessibility with nodal regions, decline in the number of town were seen in the classes II & V. Class IV sharing 6.96 % of the total urban population constitutes the highest number of towns in the region mainly with the creation of new districts. The distribution of urban population, shift in the number of towns (1981-2011), %age of urban population in different classes is shown in the table 17.4.

Table 17.4: Distribution of Urban Population by Size/ Class of Towns (1981-2011)*

Class	*Population range*	*No. of Towns 1981*	*No. of Towns 2011*	*Surplus & deficit 1981-2011*	*%age Urban Population 1981*	*%age Urban Population 2011*	*%age change urban population 1981-2011*
I	>1 lac	02	2	0	64.22	49.72	-22.57
II	50K - 99,999	0	06	5	0	11.9	11.9
III	20K - 49,999	05	07	2	11.75	8.63	-26.55

Class	*Population range*	*No. of Towns 1981*	*No. of Towns 2011*	*Surplus & deficit 1981-2011*	*%age Urban Population 1981*	*%age Urban Population 2011*	*%age change urban population 1981-2011*
IV	10K -19,999	07	33	26	6.96	21.10	203.16
V	5K -9999	20	24	1	11.60	5.2	-55.17
VI	<5K	24	28	1	5.47	2.73	-50.09
	All Classes	58	100	35	100	100	+5.42

Sources: Census of India, J&K Series, 2011

Association of Socio-Economic Determinates with Urbanization

Socio-economic variables (population, literacy rate, sex ratio and occupational pattern) have a significant impact on the growth of urbanization. With mass migration from rural to urban areas and from smaller towns to urban cities, has retarded the growth of smaller urban centres in the study area. As region is presently having only two town in the Class I category with total urban population >1 lac. With this unevenness in the distribution of urban population in the study area, we gauged differentiation of different socio-economic variables on the urbanization at inter- district level by adopting coefficient of variation technique (CV). In the study, variation in the distribution of urban population 104.6 %, followed by non-agriculture workers 37.2 %, while as least coefficient of variation were seen in the literacy rate 13.63 %. Table 17.5 shows the coefficient of variation (CV) of different socio-economic variables with their association on urbanization.

Table 17.5: Coefficient of variation of different determinants of urbanization*

S. No.	*District*	*Urban Population (%age) 2011*	*Literacy 2011 % age*	*Sex Ratio 2011*	*Non agriculture workers (%age) 2011*
1	Anantnag	26.22	59.97	902	98.14
2	Baramula	18.1	66.82	783	54
3	Budgam	12.99	58.60	791	55
4	Doda	7.97	75.04	795	31
5	Jammu	50	80.03	856	68
6	Kargil	11.6	75.52	621	49
7	Kupwara	12.03	62.0	685	37

S. No.	*District*	*Urban Population (%age) 2011*	*Literacy 2011 % age*	*Sex Ratio 2011*	*Non agriculture workers (%age) 2011*
8	Kathua	14.55	73.09	890	43
9	Leh	34.21	80.97	494	58
10	Pulwama	14.35	60.23	789	44
11	Poonch	8.1	78.13	745	30
12	Rajouri	8.14	82.0	511	29
13	Srinagar	98.60	60.73	899	99.4
14	Udhampur	19.5	88	695	36
15	Bandipora	16.66	57.82	845	39.45
16	Shopian	6.14	68.72	756	37.84
17	Kulgam	18.99	57.02	917	39.85
18	Ganderbal	15.81	54.83	881	43.4
19	Kishtwar	6.44	76.64	817	46.2
20	Reasi	8.58	71.17	802	48.8
21	Samba	16.81	79.06	802	43.25
22	Ramban	4.16	75.10	733	45.8
	Mean	19.54	70.06	773.13	48.94
	Standard deviation	20.45	9.55	113.12	18.21
	Coefficient of variation	104.65 %	13.63 %	14.63 %	37.20 %

Sources: Census of India, J&K Series, 2011

The table 17.6 shows the association of urbanization with different socio-economic variables. Positive relationship is seen between urbanization and different socio-economic determinants except sex ratio. %age of non-agricultural workers shows perfect positive correlation i.e. (r =.88) with the urbanization.

Table 17.6: Correlation Analyses of the Determinants of Urban Population

S/No.	*Variables*	*Correlation .R. Value*
1	Literacy	+0.48
2	Non-Agricultural Workers	+0.88
3	Sex Ratio	-0.24
4	Density of Towns	+0.15
5	Population distribution	+0.58

Table 17.7 shows the regression analysis of different socio-economic variables on the growth of urbanization taking urban population as a dependent variable. In the study, it has been seen that 1 unit change in the %age of non-agricultural workers increases the urban population by 1.09 %, followed by literacy (0.93 %).

Table 17.7: Regression Analysis of socio-economic variables and urbanization

Independent variables	*Intercept (a)*	*Slope (b)*
Literacy	-31.02	0.93
Non-agricultural workers	-33.56	1.09
Sex Ratio	132.36	-0.12
Population Distribution	-0.77	2.74

Conclusion

The present study appraised the spatio-temporal analysis of urban expansion in the three distinctive regions i.e. Jammu, Kashmir, and Ladakh (JKL) taking into account different socio-economic determinants. Regional difference in the socio-cultural and economic perspective has a significant impact on the growth of urbanization in the study region. The data retrieved from census of India from 1981-2011 depicts 6 % growth in the urban expansion from last three decades in the study area and is expected to increase in future at the faster rate. With the abrogation of article 370 on 5th August 2019, special status which earlier restricts the outsiders to settle in the region, might prove to be the content boon for the outsiders to settle in the region especially, in the three well established nodal regions that will lead to urban explosion to these saturated urban centres in the coming years. High concentration of urban population were recorded in Kashmir division i.e. 58 per cent with favorable geographical conditions people tend settle in the Kashmir valley, while as least share of urban population (1.5 %) were recorded in the Ladakh division which is predominately having hostile geographical conditions which tends people to migrate to other favorable areas. Jammu Kashmir together constitutes 98 % of the total urban population in the study region. With improved socio-economic conditions especially, in rural-urban fringes, region witnessed emergence of 42 new towns from 1981-2011 with 100 towns in the present context evolved due to creation of 8 new districts in 2007. Kashmir division with 58 % of the total urban population settled in 47 towns (2011 census) witnessed nearly 50% increase in the number of towns since 1981. Jammu division witnessed 36 % increase in number of towns from 1981-2011 and Ladakh region with limited geographical witnessed no growth in the number of towns during the last three decades. District wise urban population is unevenly distributed and high concentration of urban population resides in three nodal regions (Srinagar, Jammu, and Leh). High concentration of urban population having population >1 lac are distributed in two towns i.e. Srinagar and Jammu categorized (Class I), while as other classes contribute least urban population. The uneven distribution of urban population at inter-district level can be asserted to the thrust and administrative approach towards few selective districts (Srinagar, Jammu) which is gaining the political nepotism contributes 98.6 % and 50 % of the urban population respectively with 58.9 % urban agglomeration from these two districts while as remaining 42 % of the urban population is distributed in 20 districts. With such diversification in the distribution of the urban population and prevalent economic and service activities resembling them to be primate city. The engines of economic development are conspicuous by their absence in the rest of the districts in the state. Towns such as Anantnag, Baramulla, Sopore, Kathua and Udhampur have been witnessed to The size of population for towns in the state shows that only Srinagar and Jammu were the class I towns having population more than one lakh. The study concluded that towns in Class II such as Baramulla, Anantnag, Sopore, Udhampur and Kathua have the potential to thrive in the coming years as these towns are fully enriched with potential resources that can utilized in growth generating activities. Overall, slow rate of urbanization in the state as compared to national average during the last three decades in the region can be linked to low level of inter-sectorial diversification, weak trade linkages, political instability, traditional stage of development of agro-pastoral and horticulture resources and rudimentary low level of technology for harnessing and utilizing natural resources have contributed to the low level of urbanization in the state of Jammu and Kashmir.

In order to promote the urban growth population at least developing districts of the region and to retard the population explosion towards nodal region, government must take initiative to uplift the developmental infrastructure and standard of living in these deprived districts. Improving connectivity and accessibility can strength the direct trade link of these small urban areas with big urban centres that will boost their economic profitability and will curtail the migration flow towards two urban centres i.e. Srinagar and Jammu.

Reference

1. Baghat. R. B. (1992). Components of Urban Growth in India with Reference to Haryana. Finding from Recent Censuses Nagarlok; 25: 10-14.
2. Brockerhoff. (1999). Urban Growth in Developed Countries; a Review Projections and Prediction, Population and Development Review; 1999; 25:757-778.

3. Davis, K. (1965). The Urbanisation of the Human Population .Scientific American; 213: 41-53.
4. Hussain M (2000). Systematic Geography of Jammu and Kashmir, Rawat publications; 239-247. IX.
5. Kundu A. (2009). Exclusionary Urbanisation in Asia: A Macro Overview, Economic & Political Weekly; XLIV: 48-58.
6. Kundu A. (2011). Trends and Processes of Urbanization in India, IIED and UNFPA, Urbanization and Emerging population issues; -6.
7. Mohan, Rakesh, and Pant. (1982), Morphology of urbanisation in India: Some results from 1981 census, Economic and Political Weekly;
8. Moonis, Raza. (1981). Urbanization and National Development. In M. Honio (Ed.);Urbanization and Regional Development. Marazen, Asia Nagoya.
9. Nissar A. Kuchay, Bhat M S, Nuzhat S. 2015. Population growth, urban expansion and housing scenario in Srinagar city, J&K, India. Journal of Geography and Regional planning; 9(1), 1-11. DOI: 10.5897/JGRP2015.0506.
10. Peeyush G, Swati G. (2014). Urban Expansion and Its Impact on Green Spaces of Dehradun City, Uttarakhand, India, 3(4). Doi. https://doi.org/10.3126/ije.v3i4.11731.
11. Prakesh C. T, Abhinav T, Bhagwati J. 2018. Urban growth in Himalaya: undemanding the process and options for sustainable development. Journal of Urban and Regional Studies on Contemporary India 4(2): 15–27.
12. Sidiqque. (1988). Urbanization in Jammu and Kashmir- A Regional Analysis, in Geography of Jammu and Kashmir, Eds. Majid Hussain and Others,Arina Publishers; 215-239.
13. United Nations 1996 and 2010. World Urbanisation Prospects (revision figures for different years), UN Population Division, New York.
14. Zutshi. (1986). Population Distribution in Jammu and Kashmir, Ed. Geography of Jammu and Kashmir, Arana Publishing House, New Delhi.

Urban Environment and Spatial Science

Dr Mohd Akhter Ali, Dr. Kabir Mohan Sethy, Dr Muzafar Wani and M.Kamraju

Ane Books Pvt. Ltd. 2021, , ISBN : 978-93-90658-28-2, P.P. : 218 – 217

18

A Study on Educational Status of Muslim Community in Telangana Region

Dr. Mohd Hussamuddin

Office Superintendent

University college of Education

Osmania University

Hyderabad-Telangana

Introduction

In a society where religion and knowledge in general and science in particular do not go hand in hand, it seems necessary to briefly describe the position of Islam vis-à-vis knowledge, Islam, in theory as well as in practice, has always promoted knowledge. Distinctive mark of human beings over the angels is knowledge.

Educate a man, you educate a person. Educate a woman and you educate a family. Educate a family and you educate the Ummah.

Send our children to the public or private school for secular education; and for their religious education, send them to the: Sunday schools and summer programs. This is what we are doing at this stage of our settlement in this continent. But this short-term solution is not a complete solution, it's still suffers from the problem of separating religion from science; religion from real life issues. If the parents do not implement what is taught to the students at the Sunday schools, then there is the danger that the student might suffer from the double standard syndrome: behave as a Muslim in madrasah, masjid and majlis but. behave as a "regular" with others.

Corresponding Author: Dr. Mohd Hussamuddin

Creation of full time Islamic schools, this will provide the Muslim students with a morally Islamic atmosphere turning the peer pressure in favour of Islam rather than against Islam. Secondly, a full time Islamic school would integrate the secular sciences with religious sciences will became not only a servant of man but also a means of serving Allah, *subhanahu wa ta'ala*.

At the present stage of our settlement, on this continent, we cannot think of the same solution for the advanced level or education as we presented about the basic level of education. Maybe, our future generations may explore the means and ways of establishing an Islamic university which our students can study the so-called 'non-religious' sciences not as anti-religious but as part of their 'religious' outlook. At the moment, however, our efforts should be concentrated on bridging the gap between the *'ulama* and the scientists on the intellectual and mental levels. This may be done in two ways:

The Qur'an says.

"Are those who have knowledge equal to those who do not have knowledge?!"(39:9).

The Prophet of Islam (peace be upon him and his progeny) has also emphasized the importance of seeking knowledge in different ways:

(*a*) Time: "Seek knowledge from the cradle to the grave."

(*b*) Place: "Seek knowledge even if it is far as China."

(*c*) Gender: "Seeking of knowledge is a duty of every Muslim"

(*d*) Source: "Wisdom is the lost property of the believer, he should take it even if finds it in the mouth of a *mushrik*."

The Prophet did not only preach about importance of knowledge, he also gave examples of promoting knowledge. The level of education for every 1,000 persons in every age group is lower for Muslims when compared to Hindus both in the rural and urban areas, particularly among women. This is an important reason for the high fertility rates among them.

Higher Educational Attainment and Muslims

To attain higher education one has to go through the long process which start from the primary school enrolment, with in this process only a minority reach to the higher education and rest of the majority get eliminated, Indeed it is accepted that, the higher education is one of the important means of social mobility and human development. The development of a community is depended upon the educational attainment that a community make, which start from the literacy level to higher educational attainment. There is a scarcity of studies of the higher educational attainment separately for Muslims but Sachar Commission has made an assertion which is more or less the reality. Muslims in India perform very weak in all the human development indexes compared to their other counter parts, they rank considerably lower than national averages and in higher education indices they are even below the Scheduled Cast and Scheduled Tribes. 59 per cent of Muslims are literate when 65 per cent is the national average, and just above the scheduled casts and scheduled tribes. But there is a trend of declining the literacy growth of the Indian Muslims after the 2004,- and same time the growth rate of the literacy rate among the Muslims are 5.3 when this is 8.7 per cent for the scheduled cast, when it come to elementary, secondary enrolments the story is not different. Higher educational attainment of the Muslims is very less as the all other educational indicators.

Educational Development of Minorities

"Education is the single most important instrument for social and economic transformation. A well educated population, adequately equipped with knowledge and skill is not only essential to support economic growth, but is also a precondition for growth to be inclusive since it is the educated and skilled person who can stand to benefit most from the employment opportunities which growth will provide." (Para 10.1 of the Approach to the XIIth Five Year Plan). The Ministry of Human Resource Development has focused on an inclusive agenda, with a vision of realizing India's human resource potential to its fullest, with equity and excellence.

"All minorities...shall have the right to establish and administer education institutions of their own" is the mandate, as per Article 30(1) of the Constitution. Government is committed to address the existing backwardness in education of minorities, especially the Muslims, constituting the major chunk of the minorities. Therefore, the Prime Minister's New 15 Point Programme, inter-alia, aims to enhance opportunities for education of minorities ensuring an equitable share.

According to 'Sachar Committee Report' "one-fourth of Muslim children in the age group of 6-14 years have either never attended school or are drop-outs. For children above the age of 17 years, the educational attainment of Muslims at matriculation is 17%, as against national average at 26%. Only 50% of Muslims who complete middle school are likely to complete secondary education, compared to 62% at national level". The Report has also drawn attention to the low levels of educational attainment among Muslim women, Muslims in rural areas as well as in technical and higher education. The High Level Committee under the Chairmanship of Justice Rajinder Sachar has also made a number of recommendations for improvement of the educational status of the Muslim communities Further, the High Level Committee under the Chairmanship of Shri Mohd. A.A. Fatmi, the then Minister of State in the Ministry of HRD has also formulated a plan of action on the findings of the report of the Justice Sachar Committee.

Ministry of Human Resource Development has also constituted a National Monitoring Committee on Minorities' Education (NMCME) under the Chairmanship of Hon'ble Minister of Human Resource Development. A Standing Committee under the chairmanship of Shri Siraj Hussain, IAS, Additional Secretary, Government of India and former Vice-Chancellor, Jamia Hamdard has also been constituted to address issues relating to educational empowerment of minorities. The objective of the Standing Committee and its Sub-Committees are, as under:-

To monitor the minority related schemes/programmes being implemented by the Ministry of Human Resource Development; to suggest modifications, if required, in the schemes of the Ministry of Human Resource Development with a view to cater to the specific needs and requirements of the minority community.

The government will also allot model schools and colleges in minority-concentrated districts, the HRD ministry said. It has approved 277 model schools (special secondary schools in the line of central schools) in Muslim-dominated localities. In addition to these efforts, the minority affairs ministry plans to roll out coaching centres to train Muslim youths in job readiness and help them prepare for examinations to top engineering and management schools.

Reasons for Backwardness of Muslims

This fact of educational and economic backwardness of the Muslims has been conclusively established in several reports and surveys. The Gopal Singh Report, the Reports of 43rd Round and the 55th Round of the National Sample Survey and the Programme for Action under the New Education Policy of 1986 clearly show that the Muslim minority is educationally most backward segment of the nation.

Backwardness is circular in nature. If a community is educationally backward, it also becomes economically backward and the economic backwardness leads to social backwardness which in turn reinforces educational backwardness. And so this circular motion goes on throwing the community in poverty. In the world today, educational progress aims at establishment of a knowledge society which creates what may be called knowledge economy where the human 'brain' is the capital Muslim backwardness in education keeps them away from knowledge economy and further pushes them in the of poverty.

The first National policy on education was presented by the Kothari commission in 1966. After twenty years, late Rajiv Gandhi promulgated the National Policy on education in 1986, which contained one full chapter on educating the minorities. During the last eighteen years, the country and the world have witnessed revolutionary change both in content and methodology of education, and these call for a new National Policy on Education.

The educational requirements in general, the status with regards to the minorities and judicial pronouncements on these rights have hanged the position considerably. Further, India is a signatory to GATS which will be effective from 2005. It will be giving foreign educational organizations access in the country and create a new environment in our educational system and will call for several measures for readjustment. The new Commission on national education policy should also have a panel on minority education also to suggest measures for educational uplift of the backward segments of national minorities. The founding fathers of the Republic were mindful of the particular problems of the different segments of our society and included Article 30 of the Constitution to help the Muslim minority to catch up with the national standards. Unfortunately what was given by the Constitution was in practice, taken away by a biased and unsympathetic bureaucracy and later day politicians. The six-year-period of Sangh Combine rule was marked by discriminatory treatment in which education was also made a vehicle of their political ambitions. Condemning the Madrasas and not allowing opening of institutions of contemporary learning was leading the Muslim to become "hewers of wood and drawers of water."

The Madrasas should play a vital role in Jan Shiksha Abhiyan. In fact, they have enhanced literacy figures among the Muslims considerably. There are above thirty thousand Madrasas in the country – the largest non-governmental effort by an impoverished community in the field of education in history. Most of these Madrasas which cater to poor and destitute children also provide, besides meals, books and clothing, and expenditure on home travel. Since a large number of these Madrasas go only up to middle and secondary level, there is a strong case of roping them in Jan Shiksha Abhiyan and with the introduction of few more subjects, establish their equivalence with the institutions of mainstream education. The states of Bihar, Bengal and Uttar Pradesh has Madarsa Boards, which has registered a number of Madrasas. These Boards should register the remaining Madrasas and other states should follow their example. In view of the service being rendered by these Madrasas in educating the most uneducated community, it is imperative that these should get public financial support. The management of the Madrasas should be encouraged and guided by these Boards to examine a fresh their curricula and syllabi and introduce new subjects of contemporary nature, social and natural sciences to raise a generation of well-informed citizens.

Muslims of Telangana: A Ground Report

With the creation of Telangana, the polarization between Hindus and Muslims has become sharper. The new aspirations of the Muslims for socio-economic benefits and political representations are being viewed by the dominant community as aggressive re-assertion by the Muslims, who were otherwise dormant and subdued in the integrated state of Telangana.

Muslims constitute 12.5% in Telangana according 2001 census (Rao: 2014). However, the question that has gained prominence with the formation of Telangana is whether or not their social, political and economic position would improve, or will it further decline? Several other questions need to be looked into as well. What is the perception of Muslims about Telangana and their own future in this new state? Did they actively participate in the ten year long struggle for separate Telangana, or were they indifferent or even opposed to it? If so, which were the sections among the Muslims that opposed the statehood and why? Is Telangana prone to communal polarization or has it in course of this movement become more secular and identifies with its composite culture that is often referred to as the *Ganga-Jamuni tehjeeb*? Does the idea of *samajika Telangana* subsume the significance that needs to be accorded to this section of the population, or has it neglected the question of Muslims, ignored the possibility of communal polarization in course of its mobilization and thereby, willy-nilly, contributed to the age-old anxiety among the Hindu population that continues to suffer with the perception of Muslim `dominance` during the Nizam rule?

To address some of these questions, a survey was carried out by the author with the assistance of a Hyderabad-based research institute, Peoples Pulse, in March 2014 in three districts of Telangana that included Mahbubnagar, Nalgonda and Warangal.

The Government Schemes for the Development of Muslims

Education

To study report of previous Committees which have gone into the issues of minority education and welfare and suggest ways and means to implement the recommendations/conclusions of those Committees;

To advise the Committee on setting up a monitoring mechanism for minority related schemes/programmes being run by the Ministry of HRD and

Any other issues relating to minority education which the Committee may want to bring to the notice of the Government and NMCME.

Ministry of HRD has taken several significant initiatives, as detailed below, during XIth Five Year Plan and the momentum of which are being continued/accelerated during the XIIth Five **Year Plan**:

Scheme for Providing Quality Education in Madrasas (SPQEM)

Scheme for Infrastructure Development of Private Aided/Unaided Minority Institutions (IDMI)

Sarva Shiksha Abhiyan (SSA)

Kasturba Gandhi Balika Vidyalayas (KGBVs)

Extension of Mid-Day-Meals (MDM) Scheme to Madarsas/Maqtabs

'Saakshar Bharat'

Jan Shikshan Sansathan (JSS)

Rashtriya Madhyamik Shiksha Abhiyan (RMSA)

Strengthening of the National Council for Promotion of Urdu Language (NCPUL)

Establishment of the National Commission for Minority Educational Institutions (NCMEI)

List of Minority Concentration Districts

Sub-Mission on Polytechniques under the coordinated Action for skill development

Girls Hostel Scheme

Setting up model schools

The Human Resource Development (HRD) ministry on Monday said the two schemes will focus on improving education and employability of Muslim youths in minority-concentrated districts. India has nearly 110 so-called minority-concentrated districts, areas where Muslims account for at least 20% of the total population. One of the schemes will focus on improving the education and skills of Muslim girls, and the other will focus on socio-economic upliftment of all Muslims above 15 years.

Conclusion

The three crucial dimensions of social exclusion of Muslims are backwardness, marginalization and discrimination. More troublesome is the relationship between ethnic violence and socio-economic achievements. That a very high share of Muslim workers are engaged in self-employment activities, particularly in urban areas--street vending, small trades and related enterprises--ensures that the community is far more exposed to disruptions and damages caused by urban conflict and violence. The fragility of Muslim participation in the economy and the low level of asset accumulation further intensify their vulnerability to displacements caused by situations of continual communal strife, argues the paper.

Reference

1. Ahmed, Firoz Bhakth. Women Rights : Indian Express, News Daily, Chennai.2003
2. Ahmad,Sohail A Comparative study of Hindu and Muslim Women", Institute of Objectives studies, New Delhi(1996).
3. A study of Telangana Region, A.P. Ph.D. Thesis submitted to Department of Political Science , OU 1990.
4. Basant and Sen, Who Participates in Higher Education in India? Rethinking the Role of Affirmative Action," *Economic and Political Weekly*, Vol xlv no.39. 2010.
5. Chaturvedi, Archana. Encyclopedia of Muslim women", in Z.M.Khan Institute of Objective Studies, New Delhi.2003.
6. Desai and Kulkarni. Unequal Playing Field: Socio-religious Inequalities in Educational Attainment" in Basant R and Shariff, A (eds.) (2010),*Hand book of Muslims in India: Empirical and Policy Perspectives,* Oxford University Press. Chapter 12: 271-288. 2010
7. Engineer,Asghar Ali Equal Opportunity Comission—Is It Desirable,Muslim minority continuity and change, Gyan publishing house, New Delhi.ISBN;978-81-212-1013.3 2008.
8. Firoz ,Nikhat. Status of Women in Islam : Alternatives to legislative reforms, Journal of Social change, June, Vol.20, No.2, New Delhi.1990
9. Gudavarthy, Ajay ."Small states, big problems", *The Hindu*, 13 March,2014.
10. Hasan, Zoya and Menon, Ritu. 2005, *Educating Muslim Girls: A Comparison of* Five Cities,NewDelhi: Kali Unlimited, 2005.
11. Imadi, Abdul Khader"Nobles of Hyderabd" –Ph.D Thesis Department of Sociology, OU, 1978.
12. Jahangir, K.N A study on Muslims in West Bengal, Socio-economic and Political status, Minerva Associates (Publications) Pvt Ltd., Calcutta.1991
13. Krishna Kumar, Asha. The changing demographic pattern of the Muslims population ought to be studied in the context of their poor socio- economic conditions. Frontline, India's National Magazine, Volume 21—Issue, 20 Sept, 25—Oct 8, 2004)
14. Lehari,Chandralekha Socio-Demographic profile of Muslim, Study of Bhopal city, Rawat Publications, New Delhi. 1997.
15. Mehdi Hussain, Syed. A case study of Hyderabad in Asgar Ali Engineer, Status of Muslim Women, Economic and Political Weekly.1994.

16. Pande, Rekha A case from Hyderabad", *Journal of Indian Education*, Vol. XXXII, No.1. 2006.
17. Quasim, Syed. The Study on Education Background of Shia Muslims", NCERT, New Delhi (2003), *Indian Educational Abstract*, Vol. III.1993
18. Rahman, Zainab. Status of Women in Islam, Muslim women in India since Independence, edited by Haseena Hashia (ed), Institute of Objective Studies, New Delhi.1998.
19. Rao, CH Hanumantha (2014): "The New Telangana State: A Perspective for Inclusive and Sustainable Development",*Economic and Political Weekly*, 1 March, 2014.
20. Tripathy,S.N. The Rajinder Sachar Committee, appointed by the Prime Minister of India as a high level committee for preparation of a Report on the Social, Economic and Educational Status of the Muslim Community of India, Abhijeet publications, New Delhi—ISBN 978—93—81136—53—9-2012
21. Unni Informality and Gender in the Labour Market for Muslims: Has Education been a Route Out of Poverty", in Basant R and Shariff, A (eds.) (2010), *Handbook of Muslims in India: Empirical and Policy Perspectives,* Oxford University press.chapter9: 221-234. 2010.
22. Zainab Studies on Bohra Families of Udaipur Quoted by Asgar Ali Engineer, Status of Muslim Women, Economic and Political Weekly.1994.